D1002004

PROGRAMMING
LANGUAGE THEORY
AND ITS
IMPLEMENTATION

Prentice Hall International
Series in Computer Science

C. A. R. Hoare, Series Editor

BACKHOUSE, R.C., *Program Construction and Verification*
BACKHOUSE, R.C., *Syntax of Programming Languages: Theory and practice*
DE BAKKER, J.W., *Mathematical Theory of Program Correctness*
BIRD, R., AND WADLER, P., *Introduction to Functional Programming*
BJÖRNER, D., AND JONES, C.B., *Formal Specification and Software Development*
BORNAT, R., *Programming from First Principles*
BUSTARD, D., ELDER, J., AND WELSH, J., *Concurrent Program Structures*
CLARK, K.L., AND MCCABE, F.G., *micro-Prolog: Programming in logic*
CROOKES, D., *Introduction to Programming in Prolog*
DROMEY, R.G., *How to Solve it by Computer*
DUNCAN, F., *Microprocessor Programming and Software Development*
ELDER, J., *Construction of Data Processing Software*
GOLDSCHLAGER, L., AND LISTER, A., *Computer Science: A modern introduction (2nd edn)*
GORDON, M.J.C., *Programming Language Theory and its Implementation*
HAYES, I. (ED.), *Specification Case Studies*
HEHNER, E.C.R., *The Logic of Programming*
HENDERSON, P., *Functional Programming: Application and implementation*
HOARE, C.A.R., *Communicating Sequential Processes*
HOARE, C.A.R., AND SHEPHERDSON, J.C. (EDS), *Mathematical Logic and Programming Languages*
HUGHES, J.G., *Database Technology: A software engineering approach*
INMOS LTD, *occam Programming Manual*
INMOS LTD, *occam 2 Reference Manual*
JACKSON, M.A., *System Development*
JOHNSTON, H., *Learning to Program*
JONES, C.B., *Systematic Software Development using VDM*
JONES, G., *Programming in occam*
JOSEPH, M., PRASAD, V. R., AND NATARAJAN, N., *A Multiprocessor Operating System*
LEW, A., *Computer Science: A mathematical introduction*
MACCALLUM, I., *Pascal for the Apple*
MACCALLUM, I., *UCSD Pascal for the IBM PC*
MEYER, B., *Object-oriented Software Construction*
PEYTON JONES, S.L., *The Implementation of Functional Programming Languages*
POMBERGER, G., *Software Engineering and Modula-2*
REYNOLDS, J.C., *The Craft of Programming*
RYDEHEARD, D.E., AND BURSTALL, R. M., *Computational Category Theory*
SLOMAN, M., AND KRAMER, J., *Distributed Systems and Computer Networks*
TENNENT, R.D., *Principles of Programming Languages*
WATT, D.A., WICHMANN, B.A., AND FINDLAY, W., *ADA: Language and methodology*
WELSH, J., AND ELDER, J., *Introduction to Modula-2*
WELSH, J., AND ELDER, J., *Introduction to Pascal (3rd edn)*
WELSH, J., ELDER, J., AND BUSTARD, D., *Sequential Program Structures*
WELSH, J., AND HAY, A., *A Model Implementation of Standard Pascal*
WELSH, J., AND MCKEAG, M., *Structured System Programming*
WIKSTRÖM, Å., *Functional Programming using Standard ML*

PROGRAMMING LANGUAGE THEORY AND ITS IMPLEMENTATION

Applicative and imperative paradigms

Michael J.C. Gordon

Computer Laboratory,
University of Cambridge
and
SRI International

PRENTICE HALL

NEW YORK   LONDON   TORONTO   SYDNEY   TOKYO

First published 1988 by
Prentice Hall International (UK) Ltd,
66 Wood Lane End, Hemel Hempstead,
Hertfordshire, HP2 4RG
A division of
Simon & Schuster International Group

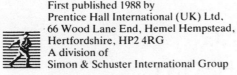

© 1988 Michael J.C. Gordon

All rights reserved. No part of this publication may be
reproduced, stored in a retrieval system, or transmitted, in any
form, or by any means, electronic, mechanical, photocopying,
recording or otherwise, without the prior permission, in
writing, from the publisher.
For permission within the United States of America contact
Prentice Hall Inc., Englewood Cliffs, NJ 07632.

Printed and bound in Great Britain by
A. Wheaton & Co. Ltd, Exeter.

Library of Congress Cataloging-in-Publication Data
Gordon, Michael J.C., 1948–
    Programming language theory and its
    implementation.

    (Prentice-Hall international series
    in computer science)
    Bibliography: p.
    Includes index.
    1. Programming languages (Electronic
    computers)
I. Title   II. Series.
QA76.7.G673   1988   005.13   88-9791
ISBN 0-13-730417-X

British Library Cataloguing in Publication Data
Gordon, Michael J.C., *1948–*
    Programming language theory and its
    implementation. –(Prentice Hall International
    series in computer science).
    1. Computer systems. Programming
    languages. Theories
    I. Title
    005.13'01
    ISBN 0-13-730417-X
    ISBN 0-13-730409-9 Pbk

---

1 2 3 4 5   92 91 90 89 88

ISBN 0-13-730417-X
ISBN 0-13-730409-9 PBK

To Avra

Contents

Preface

Formal methods are becoming an increasingly important part of the design of computer systems. This book provides elementary introductions to two of the mathematical theories upon which these methods are based:

(i) Floyd-Hoare logic, a formal system for proving the correctness of imperative programs.

(ii) The λ-calculus and combinators, the mathematical theory underlying functional programming.

The book is organised so that (i) and (ii) can be studied independently. The two theories are illustrated with working programs written in LISP, to which an introduction is provided. It is hoped that the programs will both clarify the theoretical material and show how it can be applied in practice. They also provide a starting point for student programming projects in some interesting and rapidly expanding areas of non-numerical computation.

Floyd-Hoare logic is a theory of reasoning about programs that are written in conventional *imperative* programming languages like Fortran, Algol, Pascal, Ada, Modula-2 etc. Imperative programming consists in writing commands that modify the state of a machine. Floyd-Hoare logic can be used to establish the correctness of programs already written, or (better) as the foundation for rigorous software development methodologies in which programs are constructed in parallel with their verifications (an example of such a methodology is VDM [37]). Furthermore, thinking about the logical properties of programs provides a useful perspective, even if one is not going to verify them in detail. Floyd-Hoare logic has influenced the design of several programming languages, notably Euclid [46]. It is also the basis for *axiomatic semantics*, in which the meaning of a programming language is specified by requiring that all programs written in it satisfy the rules and axioms of a formal logic. Since Hoare's first paper [32] was published, there have been many reformulations of his ideas, e.g. by Dijkstra [16]. We do not describe these developments here, partly because Hoare's original formulation is still the simplest and (in my opinion) the best to learn first, and partly because it is the basis for commercial program verifiers (e.g. Gypsy [20]). The principles underlying such verifiers are described in Chapter 3 and the implementation of an example system is presented in Chapter 11. Good introductions to the recent developments in verification theory are the books by Gries [26] and Backhouse [3].

The λ-calculus is a theory of *higher-order* functions, i.e. functions that take functions as arguments or return functions as results. It has inspired the design of *functional* programming languages including LISP [53], ML [55], Miranda [70] and Ponder [17]. These languages provide notations for defining functions that are based directly on the λ-calculus; they differ in the 'mathematical purity' of the other features provided. Closely related to the λ-calculus is the theory of combinators. This provides an elegant 'machine code' into which functional languages can be compiled and which is simple to interpret by firmware or hardware. It is straightforward to prove the correctness of the algorithm for compiling functional programs to combinators (see Section 8.2); proving the correctness of compiling algorithms for imperative languages is usually extremely difficult [13,54,62].

Although functional programs execute more slowly than imperative ones on current computers, it is possible that this situation will be reversed in the future. Functional languages are well suited to exploit the multiprocessor architectures that are beginning to emerge from research laboratories.

Both the λ-calculus and the theory of combinators were originally developed as foundations for mathematics before digital computers were invented. They languished as obscure branches of mathematical logic until rediscovered by computer scientists. It is remarkable that a theory developed by logicians has inspired the design of both the hardware and software for a new generation of computers. There is an important lesson here for people who advocate reducing support for 'pure' research: the pure research of today defines the applied research of tomorrow.

If one is forced to use an imperative language (as most programmers are), then Floyd-Hoare logic provides a tool for establishing program correctness. However, many people feel that imperative programs are intrinsically difficult to reason about and that functional programming is a better basis for formal correctness analysis [6]. One reason for this is that functions are well-understood mathematical objects and thus do not call for a special logic; ordinary mathematics suffices. However, this view is not universally held; an eloquent case for the mathematical simplicity of imperative programming can be found in recent work by Dijkstra [16], Hehner [27] and Hoare [34]. Furthermore, the functions arising in functional programming are often unlike traditional mathematical functions, and special logics, e.g. LCF [25,60], have had to be devised for reasoning about them.

My own view is that both imperative and functional programming have their place, but that it is likely that functional languages will gradually replace imperative ones for general purpose use. This is already beginning to happen; for example, ML replaced Pascal in 1987 as the first language that computer science students are taught at Cambridge University. There is growing evidence that

(i) programmers can solve problems more quickly if they use a functional language, and

(ii) the resulting solutions are more likely to be correct.

Because of (ii), and the relative ease of verifying the correctness of compilers for functional languages, functional programming is likely to have importance in safety-critical applications.

Parts I and II of this book provide an introduction to the theory underlying both imperative and functional programming. Part III contains some working programs which illustrate the material described in the first two parts. Floyd-Hoare logic is illustrated by an implementation of a complete program verifier. This consists of a verification condition generator and a simple theorem prover. The λ-calculus and combinators are illustrated by a toolkit for experimenting with the interpretation and compilation of functional programs. The example systems in Part III are implemented in LISP and are short enough that the reader can easily type them in and run them. A tutorial on the subset of LISP used is given in Chapter 9.

This book has evolved from the lecture notes for two undergraduate courses at Cambridge University which I have taught for the last few years. It should be possible to cover all the material in about thirty hours. There are no mathematical prerequisites besides school algebra. Familiarity with simple imperative programming (e.g. a first course in Pascal) would be useful, but is not essential.

I am indebted to the various students and colleagues at Cambridge who have provided me with feedback on the courses mentioned above, and to Graham Birtwistle of the University of Calgary and Elsa Gunter of the University of Pennsylvania, who pointed out errors in the notes and gave much advice and help on revising them into book form. In addition, Graham Birtwistle provided detailed and penetrating comments on the final draft of the manuscript, as did Jan van Eijck of SRI International, Mike Fourman of Brunel University and Avra Cohn of Cambridge University. These four people discovered various errors and made many helpful suggestions. Martin Hyland of Cambridge University explained to me a number of subtle points concerning the relationship between the λ-calculus and the theory of combinators.

The preparation of camera-ready copy was completed with the support of a Royal Society/SERC Industrial Fellowship at the Cambridge Computer Science Research Center of SRI International. The typesetting was done using LaTeX [41]. I am grateful to the versatile Elsa Gunter who, whilst simultaneously working as a researcher in the Cambridge Computer Laboratory and writing up her Ph.D. on group theory, was also employed by me to typeset this book. I would also like to thank Prentice Hall's copy editors for helping to counteract excesses of informality in my writing style.

Finally, this book would not exist without the encouragement and patience of Helen Martin, Prentice Hall's Acquisitions Editor, and Tony Hoare, the Series Editor.

M.J.C.G.
SRI International
Cambridge, England
April 8, 1988

Part I

Proving Programs Correct

Chapter 1

Program Specification

A simple programming language containing assignments, conditionals, blocks, WHILE-commands and FOR-commands is introduced. This language is then used to illustrate Hoare's notation for specifying the partial correctness of programs. Hoare's notation uses predicate calculus to express conditions on the values of program variables. A fragment of predicate calculus is introduced and illustrated with examples.

1.1 Introduction

In order to prove mathematically the correctness of a program one must first specify what it means for it to be correct. In this chapter a notation for specifying the desired behaviour of *imperative* programs is described. This notation is due to C.A.R. Hoare.

Executing an imperative program has the effect of changing the *state*, i.e. the values of program variables[1]. To use such a program, one first establishes an initial state by setting the values of some variables to values of interest. One then executes the program. This transforms the initial state into a final one. One then inspects (using print commands etc.) the values of variables in the final state to get the desired results. For example, to compute the result of dividing y into x one might load x and y into program variables X and Y, respectively. One might then execute a suitable program (see Example 7 in Section 1.4) to transform the initial state into a final state in which the variables QUOT and REM hold the quotient and remainder, respectively.

The programming language used in this book is described in the next section.

---

[1] For languages more complex than those described in this book, the state may consist of other things besides the values of variables [23].

1.2   A little programming language

Programs are built out of *commands* like assignments, conditionals etc. The terms 'program' and 'command' are really synonymous; the former will only be used for commands representing complete algorithms. Here the term 'statement' is used for conditions on program variables that occur in correctness specifications (see Section 1.3). There is a potential for confusion here because some writers use this word for commands (as in 'for-statement' [33]).

We now describe the *syntax* (i.e. form) and *semantics* (i.e. meaning) of the various commands in our little programming language. The following conventions are used:

1. The symbols V, V_1, ... , V_n stand for arbitrary variables. Examples of particular variables are X, REM, QUOT etc.

2. The symbols E, E_1, ... , E_n stand for arbitrary expressions (or terms). These are things like X + 1, $\sqrt{2}$ etc. which denote values (usually numbers).

3. The symbols S, S_1, ... , S_n stand for arbitrary statements. These are conditions like X < Y, $X^2 = 1$ etc. which are either true or false.

4. The symbols C, C_1, ... , C_n stand for arbitrary commands of our programming language; these are described in the rest of this section.

Terms and statements are described in more detail in Section 1.5.

1.2.1   Assignments

Syntax: $V := E$

Semantics: The state is changed by assigning the value of the term E to the variable V.

Example: X:=X+1

This adds one to the value of the variable X.

1.2.2   Sequences

Syntax: $C_1; \; \cdots \; ;C_n$

Semantics: The commands $C_1, \cdots, C_n$ are executed in that order.

Example: R:=X; X:=Y; Y:=R

The values of X and Y are swapped using R as a temporary variable. This command has the *side effect* of changing the value of the variable R to the old value of the variable X.

1.2.3 Blocks

Syntax: BEGIN VAR V_1; $\cdots$ VAR V_n; C END

Semantics: The command C is executed, and then the values of $V_1, \cdots, V_n$ are restored to the values they had before the block was entered. The initial values of $V_1, \cdots, V_n$ inside the block are unspecified.

Example: BEGIN VAR R; R:=X; X:=Y; Y:=R END

The values of X and Y are swapped using R as a temporary variable. This command does *not* have a side effect on the variable R.

1.2.4 One-armed conditionals

Syntax: IF S THEN C

Semantics: If the statement S is true in the current state, then C is executed. If S is false, then nothing is done.

Example: IF $\neg$(X=0) THEN R:= Y DIV X

If the value X is not zero, then R is assigned the result of dividing the value of Y by the value of X.

1.2.5 Two-armed conditionals

Syntax: IF S THEN C_1 ELSE C_2

Semantics: If the statement S is true in the current state, then C_1 is executed. If S is false, then C_2 is executed.

Example: IF X<Y THEN MAX:=Y ELSE MAX:=X

The value of the variable MAX it set to the maximum of the values of X and Y.

1.2.6   WHILE-commands

Syntax: WHILE S DO C

Semantics: If the statement S is true in the current state, then C is executed and the WHILE-command is then repeated. If S is false, then nothing is done. Thus C is repeatedly executed until the value of S becomes true. If S never becomes true, then the execution of the command never terminates.

Example: WHILE ¬(X=0) DO X:= X-2

   If the value of X is non-zero, then its value is decreased by 2 and then process is repeated. This WHILE-command will terminate (with X having value 0) if the value of X is an even non-negative number. In all other states it will not terminate.

1.2.7   FOR-commands

Syntax: FOR $V:=E_1$ UNTIL E_2 DO C

Semantics: If the values of terms E_1 and E_2 are positive numbers e_1 and e_2 respectively, and if $e_1 \leq e_2$, then C is executed $(e_2-e_1)+1$ times with the variable V taking on the sequence of values e_1, e_1+1, $\ldots$, e_2 in succession. For any other values, the FOR-command has no effect. A more precise description of this semantics is given in Section 2.1.11.

Example: FOR N:=1 UNTIL M DO X:=X+N

   If the value of the variable M is m and $m \geq 1$, then the command X:=X+N is repeatedly executed with N taking the sequence of values $1, \ldots , m$. If $m < 1$ then the FOR-command does nothing.

1.2.8   Summary of syntax

The syntax of our little language can be summarized with the following specification in BNF notation[2]

---

[2] BNF stands for Backus-Naur form; it is a well-known notation for specifying syntax.

<command>
    ::=   *<variable>*:=*<term>*
       | *<command>*; ... ;*<command>*
       | `BEGIN VAR` *<variable>*; ... `VAR` *<variable>*; *<command>* `END`
       | `IF` *<statement>* `THEN` *<command>*
       | `IF` *<statement>* `THEN` *<command>* `ELSE` *<command>*
       | `WHILE` *<statement>* `DO` *<command>*
       | `FOR` *<variable>*:=*<term>* `UNTIL` *<term>* `DO` *<command>*

Note that:

- *Variables*, *terms* and *statements* are as described in Section 1.5.

- Only declarations of the form '`VAR` *<variable>*' are needed. The types of variables need not be declared (unlike in Pascal).

- Sequences C_1; ... C_n are valid commands; they are equivalent to `BEGIN` C_1; ... C_n `END` (i.e. blocks without any local variables).

- The BNF syntax is ambiguous: it does not specify, for example, whether `IF` S_1 `THEN IF` S_2 `THEN` C_1 `ELSE` C_2 means

      `IF` S_1 `THEN (IF` S_2 `THEN` C_1 `ELSE` C_2`)`

  or

      `IF` S_1 `THEN (IF` S_2 `THEN` C_1`) ELSE` C_2

We will clarify, whenever necessary, using brackets.

1.3   Hoare's notation

In a seminal paper [32] C.A.R. Hoare introduced the following notation for specifying what a program does[3]:

$$\{P\}\ C\ \{Q\}$$

where:

- C is a program from the programming language whose programs are being specified (the language in Section 1.2 in our case).

---

[3] Actually, Hoare's original notation was $P\ \{C\}\ Q$ not $\{P\}\ C\ \{Q\}$, but the latter form is now more widely used.

- P and Q are conditions on the program variables used in C.

Conditions on program variables will be written using standard mathematical notations together with *logical operators* like $\land$ ('and'), $\lor$ ('or'), $\neg$ ('not') and $\Rightarrow$ ('implies'). These are described further in Section 1.5.

We say $\{P\}\ C\ \{Q\}$ is true, if whenever C is executed in a state satisfying P and if the execution of C terminates, then the state in which C's execution terminates satisfies Q.

Example: $\{X = 1\}$ X:=X+1 $\{X = 2\}$. Here P is the condition that the value of X is 1, Q is the condition that the value of X is 2 and C is the assignment command X:=X+1 (i.e. 'X becomes X+1'). $\{X = 1\}$ X:=X+1 $\{X = 2\}$ is clearly true. □

An expression $\{P\}\ C\ \{Q\}$ is called a *partial correctness specification*; P is called its *precondition* and Q its *postcondition*.

These specifications are 'partial' because for $\{P\}\ C\ \{Q\}$ to be true it is *not* necessary for the execution of C to terminate when started in a state satisfying P. It is only required that *if* the execution terminates, *then* Q holds.

A stronger kind of specification is a *total correctness specification*. There is no standard notation for such specifications. We shall use $[P]\ C\ [Q]$.

A total correctness specification $[P]\ C\ [Q]$ is true if and only if the following conditions apply:

(i) Whenever C is executed in a state satisfying P, then the execution of C terminates.

(ii) After termination Q holds.

The relationship between partial and total correctness can be informally expressed by the equation:

$$\text{Total correctness} = \text{Termination} + \text{Partial correctness.}$$

Total correctness is what we are ultimately interested in, but it is usually easier to prove it by establishing partial correctness and termination separately.

Termination is often straightforward to establish, but there are some well-known examples where it is not. For example[4], no one knows whether the program below terminates for all values if X:

```
WHILE X>1 DO
    IF ODD(X) THEN X := (3×X)+1 ELSE X := X DIV 2
```

---

[4] This example is taken from Exercise 2 on page 17 of Reynolds's book [63].

(The expression X DIV 2 evaluates to the result of rounding down X/2 to a whole number.)

Exercise 1
Write a specification which is true if and only if the program above terminates. □

In Part I of this book Floyd-Hoare logic is described; this only deals with partial correctness. Theories of total correctness can be found in the texts by Dijkstra [16] and Gries [26].

1.4   Some examples

The examples below illustrate various aspects of partial correctness specification.

In Examples 5, 6 and 7 below, T (for 'true') is the condition that is always true. In Examples 3, 4 and 7, $\wedge$ is the logical operator 'and', i.e. if P_1 and P_2 are conditions, then $P_1 \wedge P_2$ is the condition that is true whenever both P_1 and P_2 hold.

1. $\{X = 1\}$ Y:=X $\{Y = 1\}$

This says that if the command Y:=X is executed in a state satisfying the condition $X = 1$ (i.e. a state in which the value of X is 1), then, if the execution terminates (which it does), then the condition $Y = 1$ will hold. Clearly this specification is true.

2. $\{X = 1\}$ Y:=X $\{Y = 2\}$

This says that if the execution of Y:=X terminates when started in a state satisfying $X = 1$, then $Y = 2$ will hold. This is clearly false.

3. $\{X=x \wedge Y=y\}$ BEGIN R:=X; X:=Y; Y:=R END $\{X=y \wedge Y=x\}$

This says that if the execution of BEGIN R:=X; X:=Y; Y:=R END terminates (which it does), then the values of X and Y are exchanged. The variables x and y, which don't occur in the command and are used to name the initial values of program variables X and Y, are called *auxiliary* variables (or *ghost* variables).

4. $\{X=x \wedge Y=y\}$ BEGIN X:=Y; Y:=X END $\{X=y \wedge Y=x\}$

This says that BEGIN X:=Y; Y:=X END exchanges the values of X and Y. This is not true.

5. $\{T\}$ C $\{Q\}$

This says that whenever C halts, Q holds.

6. $\{P\}\ C\ \{\text{T}\}$

This specification is true for every condition P and every command C (because T is always true).

7. $\{\text{T}\}$

```
  BEGIN
    R:=X;
    Q:=0;
    WHILE Y≤R DO
        BEGIN R:=R-Y; Q:=Q+1 END
  END
```
C

$\{\text{R} < \text{Y} \wedge \ \text{X} = \text{R} + (\text{Y} \times \text{Q})\}$

This is $\{\text{T}\}\ C\ \{\text{R} < \text{Y}\ \wedge\ \text{X} = \text{R} + (\text{Y} \times \text{Q})\}$ where C is the command indicated by the braces above. The specification is true if whenever the execution of C halts, then Q is quotient and R is the remainder resulting from dividing Y into X. It is true (even if X is initially negative!)

In this example a program variable Q is used. This should not be confused with the Q used in 5 above. The program variable Q (notice the font) ranges over numbers, whereas the postcondition Q (notice the font) ranges over statements. In general, we use typewriter font for particular program variables and *italic font* for variables ranging over statements. Although this subtle use of fonts might appear confusing at first, once you get the hang of things the difference between the two kinds of 'Q' will be clear (indeed you should be able to disambiguate things from context without even having to look at the font).

Exercise 2

Let C be as in Example 7 above. Find a condition P such that:

$$[P]\ C\ [\text{R} < \text{Y} \wedge \text{X} = \text{R} + (\text{Y} \times \text{Q})]$$

is true. □

Exercise 3

When is $[\text{T}]\ C\ [\text{T}]$ true? □

Exercise 4

Write a partial correctness specification which is true if and only if the command C has the effect of multiplying the values of X and Y and storing the result in X. □

Exercise 5

Write a specification which is true if the execution of C always halts when execution is started in a state satisfying P. □

1.5   Terms and statements

The notation used here for expressing pre- and postconditions is based on a language called *first-order logic* invented by logicians around the turn of this century. For simplicity, only a fragment of this language will be used.

Things like:

$$T, \quad F, \quad X = 1, \quad R < Y, \quad X = R+(Y \times Q)$$

are examples of *atomic statements.* Statements are either true or false. The statement T is always true and the statement F is always false. The statement X = 1 is true if the value of X is equal to 1. The statement R < Y is true if the value of R is less than the value of Y. The statement X = R+(Y×Q) is true if the value of X is equal to the sum of the value of R with the product of Y and Q.

Statements are built out of *terms* like:

$$X, \quad 1, \quad R, \quad Y, \quad R+(Y \times Q), \quad Y \times Q$$

Terms denote *values* such as numbers and strings, unlike statements which are either true or false. Some terms, like 1 and $4 + 5$, denote a fixed value, whilst other terms contain *variables* like X, Y, Z etc. whose value can vary. We will use conventional mathematical notation for terms, as illustrated by the examples below:

$$X, \quad Y, \quad Z,$$

$$1, \quad 2, \quad 325,$$

$$-X, \quad -(X+1), \quad (X \times Y)+Z,$$

$$\sqrt{(1+X^2)}, \quad X!, \quad \sin(X), \quad rem(X,Y)$$

T and F are atomic statements that are always true and false respectively. Other atomic statements are built from terms using *predicates.* Here are some more examples:

$$ODD(X), \quad PRIME(3), \quad X = 1, \quad (X+1)^2 \geq X^2$$

ODD and PRIME are examples of predicates and = and $\geq$ are examples of *infixed* predicates. The expressions X, 1, 3, X+1, $(X+1)^2$, X^2 are examples of terms.

Compound statements are built up from atomic statements using the following logical operators:

$$\neg \quad \text{(not)}$$
$$\wedge \quad \text{(and)}$$
$$\vee \quad \text{(or)}$$
$$\Rightarrow \quad \text{(implies)}$$
$$\Leftrightarrow \quad \text{(if and only if)}$$

The single arrow $\rightarrow$ is commonly used for implication instead of $\Rightarrow$. We use $\Rightarrow$ to avoid possible confusion with the the use of $\rightarrow$ for λ-conversion in Part II.

Suppose P and Q are statements, then:

- $\neg P$ is true if P is false, and false if P is true.

- $P \wedge Q$ is true whenever both P and Q are true.

- $P \vee Q$ is true if either P or Q (or both) are true.

- $P \Rightarrow Q$ is true if whenever P is true, then Q is true also. By convention we regard $P \Rightarrow Q$ as being true if P is false. In fact, it is common to regard $P \Rightarrow Q$ as equivalent to $\neg P \vee Q$; however, some philosophers called intuitionists disagree with this treatment of implication.

- $P \Leftrightarrow Q$ is true if P and Q are either both true or both false. In fact $P \Leftrightarrow Q$ is equivalent to $(P \Rightarrow Q) \wedge (Q \Rightarrow P)$.

Examples of statements built using the connectives are:

ODD(X) $\vee$ EVEN(X)   X is odd or even.

$\neg$(PRIME(X) $\Rightarrow$ ODD(X))   It is not the case that if X is prime, then X is odd.

$X \leq Y \Rightarrow X \leq Y^2$ If X is less than or equal to Y, then X is less than or equal to Y^2.

To reduce the need for brackets it is assumed that $\neg$ is more binding than $\wedge$ and $\vee$, which in turn are more binding than $\Rightarrow$ and $\Leftrightarrow$. For example:

$\neg P \wedge Q$	is equivalent to	$(\neg P) \wedge Q$
$P \wedge Q \Rightarrow R$	is equivalent to	$(P \wedge Q) \Rightarrow R$
$P \wedge Q \Leftrightarrow \neg R \vee S$	is equivalent to	$(P \wedge Q) \Leftrightarrow ((\neg R) \vee S)$

Chapter 2

Floyd-Hoare Logic

The idea of formal proof is discussed. Floyd-Hoare logic is then introduced as a method for reasoning formally about programs.

In the last chapter three kinds of expressions that could be true or false were introduced:

(i) Partial correctness specifications $\{P\}\ C\ \{Q\}$.

(ii) Total correctness specifications $[P]\ C\ [Q]$.

(iii) Statements of mathematics (e.g. $(X+1)^2 = X^2 + 2 \times X + 1$).

It is assumed that the reader knows how to prove simple mathematical statements like the one in (iii) above. Here, for example, is a proof of this fact.

1.	$(X+1)^2$	$= (X+1) \times (X+1)$	Definition of $()^2$.
2.	$(X+1) \times (X+1)$	$= (X+1) \times X + (X+1) \times 1$	Left distributive law of $\times$ over $+$.
3.	$(X+1)^2$	$= (X+1) \times X + (X+1) \times 1$	Substituting line 2 into line 1.
4.	$(X+1) \times 1$	$= X+1$	Identity law for 1.
5.	$(X+1) \times X$	$= X \times X + 1 \times X$	Right distributive law of $\times$ over $+$.
6.	$(X+1)^2$	$= X \times X + 1 \times X + X + 1$	Substituting lines 4 and 5 into line 3.
7.	$1 \times X$	$= X$	Identity law for 1.
8.	$(X+1)^2$	$= X \times X + X + X + 1$	Substituting line 7 into line 6.
9.	$X \times X$	$= X^2$	Definition of $()^2$.
10.	$X + X$	$= 2 \times X$	2=1+1, distributive law.
11.	$(X+1)^2$	$= X^2 + 2 \times X + 1$	Substituting lines 9 and 10 into line 8.

This proof consists of a sequence of lines, each of which is an instance of an *axiom* (like the definition of $()^2$) or follows from previous lines by a

13

rule of inference (like the substitution of equals for equals). The statement occurring on the last line of a proof is the statement *proved* by it (thus $(X + 1)^2 = X^2 + 2 \times X + 1$ is proved by the proof above).

To construct formal proofs of partial correctness specifications axioms and rules of inference are needed. This is what Floyd-Hoare logic provides. The formulation of the deductive system is due to Hoare [32], but some of the underlying ideas originated with Floyd [18].

A proof in Floyd-Hoare logic is a sequence of lines, each of which is either an *axiom* of the logic or follows from earlier lines by a *rule of inference* of the logic.

The reason for constructing formal proofs is to try to ensure that only sound methods of deduction are used. With sound axioms and rules of inference, one can be confident that the conclusions are true. On the other hand, if any axioms or rules of inference are unsound then it may be possible to deduce false conclusions; for example[1]

1.	$\sqrt{-1 \times -1}$	$= \sqrt{-1 \times -1}$	Reflexivity of =.
2.	$\sqrt{-1 \times -1}$	$= (\sqrt{-1}) \times (\sqrt{-1})$	Distributive law of $\sqrt{}$ over $\times$.
3.	$\sqrt{-1 \times -1}$	$= (\sqrt{-1})^2$	Definition of $()^2$.
4.	$\sqrt{-1 \times -1}$	$= -1$	definition of $\sqrt{}$.
5.	$\sqrt{1}$	$= -1$	As $-1 \times -1 = 1$.
6.	1	$= -1$	As $\sqrt{1} = 1$.

A formal proof makes explicit what axioms and rules of inference are used to arrive at a conclusion. It is quite easy to come up with plausible rules for reasoning about programs that are actually unsound (some examples for FOR-commands can be found in Section 2.1.11). Proofs of correctness of computer programs are often very intricate and formal methods are needed to ensure that they are valid. It is thus important to make fully explicit the reasoning principles being used, so that their soundness can be analysed.

Exercise 6
Find the flaw in the 'proof' of $1 = -1$ above. □

For some applications, correctness is especially important. Examples include life-critical systems such as nuclear reactor controllers, car breaking systems, fly-by-wire aircraft and software controlled medical equipment. At the time of writing, there is a legal action in progress resulting from the death of several people due to radiation overdoses by a cancer treatment machine that had a software bug [38]. Formal proof of correctness provides a way of establishing the absence of bugs when exhaustive testing is impossible (as it almost always is).

---

[1] This example was shown to me by Sylva Cohn.

___

The Floyd-Hoare deductive system for reasoning about programs will be explained and illustrated, but the mathematical analysis of the soundness and completeness of the system is beyond the scope of this book (however, there is a brief discussion of what is involved in Section 2.2).

2.1   Axioms and rules of Floyd-Hoare logic

As discussed at the beginning of this chapter, a *formal proof* of a statement is a sequence of lines ending with the statement and such that each line is either an instance of an axiom or follows from previous lines by a rule of inference. If S is a statement (of either ordinary mathematics or Floyd-Hoare logic) then we write $\vdash S$ to mean that S has a proof. The statements that have proofs are called *theorems*. As discussed earlier, in this book only the axioms and rules of inference for Floyd-Hoare logic are described; we will thus simply assert $\vdash S$ if S is a theorem of mathematics without giving any formal justification. Of course, to achieve complete rigour such assertions must be proved, but for details of this the reader will have to consult a book (such as [10,47,49]) on formal logic.

The axioms of Floyd-Hoare logic are specified below by *schemas* which can be *instantiated* to get particular partial correctness specifications. The inference rules of Floyd-Hoare logic will be specified with a notation of the form:

$$\frac{\vdash S_1, \ldots, \vdash S_n}{\vdash S}$$

This means the *conclusion* $\vdash S$ may be deduced from the *hypotheses* $\vdash S_1, \ldots, \vdash S_n$. The hypotheses can either all be theorems of Floyd-Hoare logic (as in the sequencing rule below), or a mixture of theorems of Floyd-Hoare logic and theorems of mathematics (as in the rule of preconditioning strengthening described in Section 2.1.2).

2.1.1   The assignment axiom

The assignment axiom represents the fact that the value of a variable V *after* executing an assignment command $V := E$ equals the value of the expression E in the state *before* executing it. To formalize this, observe that if a statement P is to be true *after* the assignment, then the statement obtained by substituting E for V in P must be true *before* executing it.

In order to say this formally, define $P[E/V]$ to mean the result of replacing all occurrences of V in P by E. Read $P[E/V]$ as 'P with E for

V'. For example,

$$(\text{X}+1 > \text{X})[\text{Y}+\text{Z}/\text{X}] \;=\; ((\text{Y}+\text{Z})+1 > \text{Y}+\text{Z})$$

The way to remember this notation is to remember the 'cancellation law'

$$V[E/V] \;=\; E$$

which is analogous to the cancellation property of fractions

$$v \times (e/v) \;=\; e$$

The assignment axiom

$$\vdash \{P[E/V]\}\; V := E\; \{P\}$$

Where V is any variable, E is any expression, P is any statement and the notation $P[E/V]$ denotes the result of substituting the term E for all occurrences of the variable V in the statement P.

Instances of the assignment axiom are:

1. $\vdash \{\text{Y} = 2\}\; \text{X} := 2\; \{\text{Y} = \text{X}\}$

2. $\vdash \{\text{X} + 1 = \text{n} + 1\}\; \text{X} := \text{X} + 1\; \{\text{X} = \text{n} + 1\}$

3. $\vdash \{E = E\}\; \text{X} := E\; \{\text{X} = E\}$

Many people feel the assignment axiom is 'backwards' from what they would expect. Two common erroneous intuitions are that it should be as follows:

(i) $\vdash \{P\}\; V := E\; \{P[V/E]\}$.

Where the notation $P[V/E]$ denotes the result of substituting V for E in P.

This has the clearly false consequence that $\vdash \{\text{x=0}\}\; \text{x}:=1\; \{\text{x=0}\}$, since the $(\text{x=0})[\text{x}/1]$ is equal to (x=0) as 1 doesn't occur in (x=0).

(ii) $\vdash \{P\}\; V := E\; \{P[E/V]\}$.

This has the clearly false consequence $\vdash \{\text{x=0}\}\; \text{x}:=1\; \{1=0\}$ which follows by taking P to be X=0, V to be X and E to be 1.

The fact that it is easy to have wrong intuitions about the assignment axiom shows that it is important to have rigorous means of establishing the validity of axioms and rules. We will not go into this topic here aside from remarking that it is possible to give a *formal semantics* of our little programming language and then to *prove* that the axioms and rules of inference of Floyd-Hoare logic are sound. Of course, this process will only increase our confidence in the axioms and rules to the extent that we believe the correctness of the formal semantics. The simple assignment axiom above is not valid for 'real' programming languages. For example, work by G. Ligler [44] shows that it can fail to hold in six different ways for the language Algol 60.

One way that our little programming language differs from real languages is that the evaluation of expressions on the right of assignment commands cannot 'side effect' the state. The validity of the assignment axiom depends on this property. To see this, suppose that our language were extended so that it contained the 'block expression'

$$\texttt{BEGIN Y:=1; 2 END}$$

This expression, E say, has value 2, but its evaluation also 'side effects' the variable Y by storing 1 in it. If the assignment axiom applied to expressions like E, then it could be used to deduce:

$$\vdash \{\texttt{Y=0}\} \ \texttt{X:=BEGIN Y:=1; 2 END} \ \{\texttt{Y=0}\}$$

(since $(\texttt{Y=0})[E/X] = (\texttt{Y=0})$ as X does not occur in $(\texttt{Y=0})$). This is clearly false, as after the assignment Y will have the value 1.

2.1.2   Precondition strengthening

The next rule of Floyd-Hoare logic enables the preconditions of (i) and (ii) on page 16 to be simplified. Recall that

$$\frac{\vdash S_1, \ \ldots, \ \vdash S_n}{\vdash S}$$

means that $\vdash S$ can be deduced from $\vdash S_1, \ldots, \vdash S_n$.

Using this notation, the rule of precondition strengthening is

---

Precondition strengthening

$$\frac{\vdash P \Rightarrow P', \qquad \vdash \{P'\} \, C \, \{Q\}}{\vdash \{P\} \, C \, \{Q\}}$$

Examples

1. From the arithmetic fact ⊢ X+1=n+1 ⟹ X=n, and 2 on page 16 it follows by precondition strengthening that

$$\vdash \{X = n\}\ X := X + 1\ \{X = n + 1\}.$$

The variable n is an example of an *auxiliary* (or *ghost*) variable. As described earlier (see page 9), auxiliary variables are variables occurring in a partial correctness specification $\{P\}\ C\ \{Q\}$ which do not occur in the command C. Such variables are used to relate values in the state before and after C is executed. For example, the specification above says that if the value of X is n, then after executing the assignment X:=X+1 its value will be n+1.

2. From the logical truth ⊢ T ⟹ ($E=E$), and 3 on page 16 one can deduce[2]:

$$\vdash \{T\}\ X := E\ \{X = E\}$$

□

2.1.3   Postcondition weakening

Just as the previous rule allows the precondition of a partial correctness specification to be strengthened, the following one allows us to weaken the postcondition.

Postcondition weakening

$$\frac{\vdash \{P\}\ C\ \{Q'\}, \qquad \vdash Q' \Rightarrow Q}{\vdash \{P\}\ C\ \{Q\}}$$

Example: Here is a little formal proof.

1. ⊢ {R=X ∧ 0=0} Q:=0 {R=X ∧ Q=0}   By the assignment axiom.
2. ⊢ R=X ⟹ R=X ∧ 0=0   By pure logic.
3. ⊢ {R=X} Q:=0 {R=X ∧ Q=0}   By precondition strengthening.
4. ⊢ R=X ∧ Q=0 ⟹ R=X+(Y × Q)   By laws of arithmetic.
5. ⊢ {R=X} Q:=0 {R=X+(Y × Q)}   By postcondition weakening.

□

---

[2] If it is not obvious that ⊢ T ⟹ ($E=E$) is a logical truth, then you should read an elementary introduction to formal logic, e.g. [10,19,47,49].

The rules precondition strengthening and postcondition weakening are sometimes called the *rules of consequence*.

2.1.4   Specification conjunction and disjunction

The following two rules provide a method of combining different specifications about the same command.

Specification conjunction

$$\frac{\vdash \{P_1\}\ C\ \{Q_1\}, \qquad \vdash \{P_2\}\ C\ \{Q_2\}}{\vdash \{P_1 \wedge P_2\}\ C\ \{Q_1 \wedge Q_2\}}$$

Specification disjunction

$$\frac{\vdash \{P_1\}\ C\ \{Q_1\}, \qquad \vdash \{P_2\}\ C\ \{Q_2\}}{\vdash \{P_1 \vee P_2\}\ C\ \{Q_1 \vee Q_2\}}$$

These rules are useful for splitting a proof into independent bits. For example, they enable $\vdash \{P\}$ C $\{Q_1 \wedge Q_2\}$ to be proved by proving separately that both $\vdash \{P\}$ C $\{Q_1\}$ and $\vdash \{P\}$ C $\{Q_2\}$.

The rest of the rules allow the deduction of properties of compound commands from properties of their components.

2.1.5   The sequencing rule

The next rule enables a partial correctness specification for a sequence $C_1 ; C_2$ to be derived from specifications for C_1 and C_2.

The sequencing rule

$$\frac{\vdash \{P\}\ C_1\ \{Q\}, \qquad \vdash \{Q\}\ C_2\ \{R\}}{\vdash \{P\}\ C_1 ; C_2\ \{R\}}$$

Example: By the assignment axiom:

(i) ⊢ {X=x∧Y=y} R:=X {R=x∧Y=y}

(ii) ⊢ {R=x∧Y=y} X:=Y {R=x∧X=y}

(iii) ⊢ {R=x∧X=y} Y:=R {Y=x∧X=y}

Hence by (i), (ii) and the sequencing rule

(iv) ⊢ {X=x∧Y=y} R:=X; X:=Y {R=x∧X=y}

Hence by (iv) and (iii) and the sequencing rule

(v) ⊢ {X=x∧Y=y} R:=X; X:=Y; Y:=R {Y=x∧X=y}

□

2.1.6   The derived sequencing rule

The following rule is derivable from the sequencing and consequence rules.

The derived sequencing rule

$$
\begin{array}{ll}
 & \vdash P \Rightarrow P_1 \\
\vdash \{P_1\}\, C_1\, \{Q_1\} & \vdash Q_1 \Rightarrow P_2 \\
\vdash \{P_2\}\, C_2\, \{Q_2\} & \vdash Q_2 \Rightarrow P_3 \\
\quad\vdots & \quad\vdots \\
\vdash \{P_n\}\, C_n\, \{Q_n\} & \vdash Q_n \Rightarrow Q \\
\hline
\multicolumn{2}{c}{\vdash \{P\}\, C_1;\ \ldots\ ;\, C_n\, \{Q\}}
\end{array}
$$

The derived sequencing rule enables (v) in the previous example to be deduced directly from (i), (ii) and (iii) in one step.

2.1.7   The block rule

The block rule is like the sequencing rule, but it also takes care of local variables.

The block rule

$$\frac{\vdash \{P\}\ C\ \{Q\}}{\vdash \{P\}\ \texttt{BEGIN VAR}\ V_1;\ \ldots;\ \texttt{VAR}\ V_n;\ C\ \texttt{END}\ \{Q\}}$$

where none of the variables $V_1, \ldots, V_n$ occur in P or Q.

The syntactic condition that none of the variables $V_1, \ldots, V_n$ occur in P or Q is an example of a *side condition*. It is a syntactic condition that must hold whenever the rule is used. Without this condition the rule is invalid; this is illustrated in the example below.

Note that the block rule is regarded as including the case when there are no local variables (the '$n = 0$' case).

Example: From $\vdash \{\texttt{X=x} \wedge \texttt{Y=y}\}\ \texttt{R:=X; X:=Y; Y:=R}\ \{\texttt{Y=x} \wedge \texttt{X=y}\}$ (see page 20) it follows by the block rule that

$\vdash \{\texttt{X=x} \wedge \texttt{Y=y}\}\ \texttt{BEGIN VAR R; R:=X; X:=Y; Y:=R END}\ \{\texttt{Y=x} \wedge \texttt{X=y}\}$

since R does not occur in $\texttt{X=x} \wedge \texttt{Y=y}$ or $\texttt{X=y} \wedge \texttt{Y=x}$. Notice that from

$\vdash \{\texttt{X=x} \wedge \texttt{Y=y}\}\ \texttt{R:=X; X:=Y}\ \{\texttt{R=x} \wedge \texttt{X=y}\}$

one *cannot* deduce

$\vdash \{\texttt{X=x} \wedge \texttt{Y=y}\}\ \texttt{BEGIN VAR R; R:=X; X:=Y END}\ \{\texttt{R=x} \wedge \texttt{X=y}\}$

since R occurs in $\{\texttt{R=x} \wedge \texttt{X=y}\}$. This is as required, because assignments to local variables of blocks should not be felt outside the block body. Notice, however, that it is possible to deduce:

$\vdash \{\texttt{X=x} \wedge \texttt{Y=y}\}\ \texttt{BEGIN R:=X; X:=Y END}\ \{\texttt{R=x} \wedge \texttt{X=y}\}.$

This is correct because R is no longer a local variable. $\square$

The following exercise addresses the question of whether one can show that changes to local variables inside a block are invisible outside it.

Exercise 7

Consider the specification

$$\{\texttt{X=x}\}\ \texttt{BEGIN VAR X; X:=1 END}\ \{\texttt{X=x}\}$$

Can this be deduced from the rules given so far?

(i) If so, give a proof of it.

(ii) If not, explain why not and suggest additional rules and/or axioms to enable it to be deduced.

$\square$

2.1.8   The derived block rule

From the derived sequencing rule and the block rule the following rule for blocks can be derived.

The derived block rule

$$\vdash P \Rightarrow P_1$$
$$\vdash \{P_1\}\ C_1\ \{Q_1\} \quad \vdash Q_1 \Rightarrow P_2$$
$$\vdash \{P_2\}\ C_2\ \{Q_2\} \quad \vdash Q_2 \Rightarrow P_3$$
$$\vdots \qquad\qquad \vdots$$
$$\frac{\vdash \{P_n\}\ C_n\ \{Q_n\} \quad \vdash Q_n \Rightarrow Q}{\vdash \{P\}\ \text{BEGIN VAR } V_1;\ \ldots\ \text{VAR } V_n; C_1;\ \ldots\ ;\ C_n\ \{Q\}}$$

where none of the variables $V_1, \ldots, V_n$ occur in P or Q.

Using this rule, it can be deduced *in one step* from (i), (ii) and (iii) on page 20 that:

$$\vdash \{X=x \wedge Y=y\}\ \text{BEGIN VAR R; R:=X; X:=Y; Y:=R END}\ \{Y=x \wedge X=y\}$$

Exercise 8
Show $\vdash \{X=x \wedge Y=y\}$ X:=X+Y; Y:=X-Y; X:=X-Y $\{Y=x \wedge X=y\}$
□

Exercise 9
Show $\vdash \{X=R+(Y \times Q)\}$ BEGIN R:=R-Y; Q:=Q+1 END $\{X=R+(Y \times Q)\}$
□

2.1.9   The conditional rules

There are two kinds of conditional commands: one-armed conditionals and two-armed conditionals. There are thus two rules for conditionals.

The conditional rules

$$\frac{\vdash \{P \wedge S\}\, C\, \{Q\}, \qquad \vdash P \wedge \neg S \Rightarrow Q}{\vdash \{P\}\ \text{IF}\ S\ \text{THEN}\ C\ \{Q\}}$$

$$\frac{\vdash \{P \wedge S\}\, C_1\, \{Q\}, \qquad \vdash \{P \wedge \neg S\}\, C_2\, \{Q\}}{\vdash \{P\}\ \text{IF}\ S\ \text{THEN}\ C_1\ \text{ELSE}\ C_2\ \{Q\}}$$

Example: Suppose we are given that

(i) $\vdash$ X$\geq$Y $\Rightarrow$ max(X,Y)=X

(ii) $\vdash$ Y$\geq$X $\Rightarrow$ max(X,Y)=Y

Then by the conditional rules (and others) it follows that

$\vdash$ {T} IF X$\geq$Y THEN MAX:=X ELSE MAX:=Y {MAX=max(X,Y)}

$\square$

Exercise 10
Give a detailed formal proof that the specification in the previous example follows from hypotheses (i) and (ii). $\square$

Exercise 11
Devise an axiom and/or rule of inference for a command SKIP that has no effect. Show that if IF S THEN C is regarded as an abbreviation for IF S THEN C ELSE SKIP, then the rule for one-armed conditionals is derivable from the rule for two-armed conditionals and your axiom/rule for SWAP. $\square$

Exercise 12
Suppose we add to our little programming language commands of the form:

CASE E OF BEGIN C_1; ... ; C_n END

These are evaluated as follows:

(i) First E is evaluated to get a value x.

(ii) If x is not a number between 1 and n, then the CASE-command has no effect.

(iii) If $x = i$ where $1 \leq i \leq n$, then command C_i is executed.

Why is the following rule for CASE-commands wrong?

$$\frac{\vdash \{P \wedge E = 1\}\ C_1\ \{Q\},\ \ \ldots\ ,\ \vdash \{P \wedge E = n\}\ C_n\ \{Q\}}{\vdash \{P\}\ \mathtt{CASE}\ E\ \mathtt{OF}\ \mathtt{BEGIN}\ C_1;\ \ldots\ ;\ C_n\ \mathtt{END}\ \{Q\}}$$

Hint: Consider the case when P is '$X = 0$', E is 'X', C_1 is '$Y:=0$' and Q is '$Y = 0$'.

□

Exercise 13
Devise a proof rule for the CASE-commands in the previous exercise and use it to show:

```
⊢ {1≤X∧X≤3}
  CASE X OF
    BEGIN
      Y:=X-1;
      Y:=X-2;
      Y:=X-3
    END
  {Y=0}
```

□

Exercise 14
Show that if $\vdash \{P \wedge S\}\ \mathtt{C_1}\ \{Q\}$ and $\vdash \{P \wedge \neg S\}\ \mathtt{C_2}\ \{Q\}$, then it is possible to deduce:

$$\vdash \{P\}\ \mathtt{IF\ S\ THEN\ C_1\ ELSE\ IF\ \neg S\ THEN\ C_2}\ \{Q\}.$$

□

2.1.10   The WHILE-rule

If $\vdash \{P \wedge S\}\ C\ \{P\}$, we say: P is an *invariant* of C whenever S holds. The WHILE-rule says that if P is an invariant of the body of a WHILE-command whenever the test condition holds, then P is an invariant of the whole WHILE-command. In other words, if executing C once preserves the truth of P, then executing C any number of times also preserves the truth of P.

The WHILE-rule also expresses the fact that after a WHILE-command has terminated, the test must be false (otherwise, it wouldn't have terminated).

The WHILE-rule

$$\frac{\vdash \{P \wedge S\} \, C \, \{P\}}{\vdash \{P\} \text{ WHILE } S \text{ DO } C \, \{P \wedge \neg S\}}$$

Example: By Exercise 9 on page 22

$\vdash \{$X=R+(Y×Q)$\}$ BEGIN R:=R-Y; Q:=Q+1 END $\{$X=R+(Y×Q)$\}$

Hence by precondition strengthening

$\vdash \{$X=R+(Y×Q)∧Y≤R$\}$ BEGIN R:=R-Y; Q:=Q+1 END $\{$X=R+(Y×Q)$\}$

Hence by the WHILE-rule (with P = 'X=R+(Y×Q)')

(i) $\vdash$ $\{$X=R+(Y×Q)$\}$
    WHILE Y≤R DO
        BEGIN R:=R-Y; Q:=Q+1 END
    $\{$X=R+(Y×Q)∧¬(Y≤R)$\}$

It is easy to deduce that

(ii) $\{$T$\}$ R:=X; Q:=0 $\{$X=R+(Y×Q)$\}$

Hence by (i) and (ii), the sequencing rule and postcondition weakening

$\vdash$ $\{$T$\}$
    R:=X;
    Q:=0;
    WHILE Y≤R DO
        BEGIN R:=R-Y; Q:=Q+1 END
    $\{$R<Y∧X=R+(Y×Q)$\}$

□

With the exception of the WHILE-rule, all the axioms and rules described so far are sound for total correctness as well as partial correctness. This is because the only commands in our little language that might not terminate are WHILE-commands. Consider now the following proof:

1. $\vdash$ $\{$T$\}$ X:=0 $\{$T$\}$ (assignment axiom)
2. $\vdash$ $\{$T ∧ T$\}$ X:=0 $\{$T$\}$ (precondition strengthening)
3. $\vdash$ $\{$T$\}$ WHILE T DO X:=0 $\{$T ∧ ¬T$\}$ (2 and the WHILE-rule)

If the `WHILE`-rule were true for total correctness, then the proof above would show that:

$$\vdash \; [\text{T}] \; \texttt{WHILE T DO X:=0} \; [\text{T} \land \neg \text{T}]$$

but this is clearly false since `WHILE T DO X:=0` does not terminate, and even if it did then $\text{T} \land \neg \text{T}$ could not hold in the resulting state.

Extending Floyd-Hoare logic to deal with termination is quite tricky. One approach can be found in Dijkstra [16].

2.1.11   The `FOR`-rule

It is quite hard to capture accurately the intended semantics of `FOR`-commands in Floyd-Hoare logic. Axioms and rules are given here that *appear* to be sound, but they are not necessarily complete (see Section 2.2). An early reference on the logic of `FOR`-commands is Hoare's 1972 paper [33]; a comprehensive treatment can be found in Reynolds [63].

The intention here in presenting the `FOR`-rule is to show that Floyd-Hoare logic can get very tricky. All the other axioms and rules were quite straightforward and may have given a false sense of simplicity: it is very difficult to give adequate rules for anything other than very simple programming constructs. This is an important incentive for using simple languages.

One problem with `FOR`-commands is that there are many subtly different versions of them. Thus before describing the `FOR`-rule, the intended semantics of `FOR`-commands must be described carefully. In this book, the semantics of

$$\texttt{FOR } V := E_1 \texttt{ UNTIL } E_2 \texttt{ DO } C$$

is as follows:

(i) The expressions E_1 and E_2 are evaluated once to get values e_1 and e_2, respectively.

(ii) If either e_1 or e_2 is not a number, or if $e_1 > e_2$, then nothing is done.

(iii) If $e_1 \leq e_2$ the `FOR`-command is equivalent to:

```
BEGIN VAR V ;
    V:=e₁; C; V:=e₁+1; C ; ... ; V:=e₂; C
END
```

i.e. C is executed $(e_2 - e_1) + 1$ times with V taking on the sequence of values $e_1, e_1 + 1, \ldots, e_2$ in succession. Note that this description is not rigorous: 'e_1' and 'e_2' have been used both as numbers and as expressions of our little language; the semantics of `FOR`-commands should be clear despite this.

FOR-rules in different languages can differ in subtle ways from the one here. For example, the expressions E_1 and E_2 could be evaluated at each iteration and the controlled variable V could be treated as global rather than local. Note that with the semantics presented here, FOR-commands cannot go into infinite loops (unless, of course, they contain non-terminating WHILE-commands).

To see how the FOR-rule works, suppose that

$$\vdash \{P\}\ C\ \{P[V+1/V]\}$$

Suppose also that C does not contain any assignments to the variable V. If this is the case, then it is intuitively clear (and can be rigorously proved) that

$$\vdash \{(V = v)\}\ C\ \{(V = v)\}$$

hence by specification conjunction

$$\vdash \{P \wedge (V = v)\}\ C\ \{P[V+1/V]\ \wedge (V = v)\}$$

Now consider a sequence $V:=v;\ C$. By Example 2 on page 18,

$$\vdash \{P[v/V]\}\ V:=v\ \{P \wedge (V = v)\}$$

Hence by the sequencing rule

$$\vdash \{P[V/v]\}\ V:=v;\ C\ \{P[V+1/V]\ \wedge (V = v)\}$$

Now it is a truth of logic alone that

$$\vdash\ P[V+1/V] \wedge (V = v)\ \Rightarrow\ P[v+1/V]$$

hence by postcondition weakening

$$\vdash \{P[v/V]\}\ V:=v;\ C\ \{P[v+1/V]\}$$

Taking v to be e_1, e_1+1, $\ldots$, e_2 and using the derived sequencing rule we can thus deduce

$$\{P[e_1/V]\}\ V:=e_1;\ C;\ V:=e_1+1;\ \ldots\ ;\ V:=e_2;\ C\ \{P[e_2/V\}$$

This suggests that a FOR-rule could be:

$$\frac{\vdash \{P\}\ C\ \{P[V+1/V]\}}{\vdash \{P[E_1/V]\}\ \text{FOR}\ V:=E_1\ \text{UNTIL}\ E_2\ \text{DO}\ C\ \{P[E_2+1/V]\}}$$

Unfortunately, this rule is unsound. To see this, first note that:

1. $\vdash$ $\{$Y+1=Y+1$\}$ X:=Y+1 $\{$X=Y+1$\}$ (assignment axiom)
2. $\vdash$ $\{$T$\}$ X:=Y+1 $\{$X= Y+1$\}$ (1 and precondition strengthening)
3. $\vdash$ X=Y $\Rightarrow$ T   (logic: 'anything implies true')
4. $\vdash$ $\{$X=Y$\}$ X:=Y+1 $\{$X=Y+1$\}$ (2 and precondition strengthening)

Thus if P is 'X=Y' then:

$$\vdash \{P\} \text{ X:=Y+1 } \{P[\text{Y+1}/\text{Y}]\}$$

and so by the FOR-rule above, if we take V to be Y, E_1 to be 3 and E_2 to be 1, then

$$\vdash \{ \underbrace{\text{X=3}}_{P[3/Y]} \} \text{ FOR Y:=3 UNTIL 1 DO X:=Y+1 } \{ \underbrace{\text{X=2}}_{P[1+1/Y]} \}$$

This is clearly false: it was specified that if the value of E_1 were greater than the value of E_2 then the FOR-command should have no effect, but in this example it changes the value of X from 3 to 2.

To solve this problem, the FOR-rule can be modified to

$$\frac{\vdash \{P\}\, C\, \{P[V+1/V]\}}{\vdash \{P[E_1/V] \wedge E_1 \leq E_2\}\ \text{FOR } V:=E_1 \text{ UNTIL } E_2 \text{ DO } C\ \{P[E_2+1/V]\}}$$

If this rule is used on the example above all that can be deduced is

$$\vdash \{\text{X=3} \wedge \underbrace{3 \leq 1}_{\text{never true!}} \}\ \text{FOR Y:=3 UNTIL 1 DO X:=Y+1 } \{\text{X=2}\}$$

This conclusion is harmless since it only asserts that X will be changed if the FOR-command is executed in an impossible starting state.

Unfortunately, there is still a bug in our FOR-rule. Suppose we take P to be 'Y=1', then it is straightforward to show that:

$$\vdash \{\underbrace{\text{Y=1}}_{P}\} \text{ Y:=Y-1 } \{ \underbrace{\text{Y+1=1}}_{P[\text{Y+1}/\text{Y}]} \}$$

so by our latest FOR-rule

$$\vdash \{ \underbrace{\text{1=1}}_{P[1/Y]} \wedge 1 \leq 1\}\ \text{FOR Y:=1 UNTIL 1 DO Y:=Y-1 } \{ \underbrace{\text{2=1}}_{P[1+1/Y]} \}$$

Whatever the command does, it doesn't lead to a state in which 2=1. The problem is that the body of the FOR-command modifies the controlled variable. It is not surprising that this causes problems, since it was explicitly assumed that the body didn't modify the controlled variable when we motivated the FOR-rule. It turns out that problems also arise if any variables in the expressions E_1 and E_2 (which specify the upper and lower bounds) are modified. For example, taking P to be Z=Y, then it is straightforward to show

$$\vdash \{\underbrace{\text{Z=Y}}_{P}\} \; \text{Z:=Z+1} \; \{ \underbrace{\text{Z=Y+1}}_{P[\text{Y+1/Y}]} \}$$

hence the rule allows us the following to be derived:

$$\vdash \{ \underbrace{\text{Z=1}}_{P[\text{1/Y}]} \; \wedge \; 1 \leq \text{Z}\} \; \text{FOR} \; \text{Y:=1} \; \text{UNTIL} \; \text{Z} \; \text{DO} \; \text{Z:=Z+1} \; \{ \underbrace{\text{Z=Z+1}}_{P[\text{Z+1/Y}]} \}$$

This is clearly wrong as one can never have Z=Z+1 (subtracting Z from both sides would give 0=1). One might think that this is not a problem because the FOR-command would never terminate. In some languages this might be the case, but the semantics of our language were carefully defined in such a way that FOR-commands always terminate (see the beginning of this section).

To rule out the problems that arise when the controlled variable or variables in the bounds expressions, are changed by the body, we simply impose a side condition on the rule that stipulates that the rule cannot be used in these situations. The final rule is thus:

The FOR-rule

$$\frac{\vdash \{P \wedge (E_1 \leq V) \wedge (V \leq E_2)\} \; C \; \{P[V\text{+1}/V]\}}{\vdash \{P[E_1/V] \wedge (E_1 \leq E_2)\} \; \text{FOR} \; V := E_1 \; \text{UNTIL} \; E_2 \; \text{DO} \; C \; \{P[E_2\text{+1}/V]\}}$$

where neither V, nor any variable occurring in E_1 or E_2, is assigned to in the command C.

This rule does not enable anything to be deduced about FOR-commands whose body assigns to variables in the bounds expressions. This precludes such assignments being used if commands are to be reasoned about. The strategy of only defining rules of inference for non-tricky uses of constructs helps ensure that programs are written in a perspicuous manner. It is possible to devise a rule that does cope with assignments to variables in bounds expressions, but it is not clear whether it is a good idea to have such a rule.

The FOR-axiom

To cover the case when $E_2 < E_1$, we need the FOR-axiom below.

The FOR-axiom

$\vdash \{P \wedge (E_2 < E_1)\} \text{ FOR } V := E_1 \text{ UNTIL } E_2 \text{ DO } C \{P\}$

This says that when E_2 is less than E_1 the FOR-command has no effect.

Example: By the assignment axiom and precondition strengthening

$\vdash \{\text{X} = ((\text{N}-1)\times\text{N}) \text{ DIV } 2\} \text{ X}:=\text{X}+\text{N} \{\text{X}=(\text{N}\times(\text{N}+1)) \text{ DIV } 2\}$

Strengthening the precondition of this again yields

$\vdash \{(\text{X}=((\text{N}-1\times\text{N}) \text{ DIV } 2)\wedge(1\leq\text{N})\wedge(\text{N}\leq\text{M}\} \text{ X}:=\text{X}+\text{N} \{\text{X}=(\text{N}\times(\text{N}+1)) \text{ DIV } 2\}$

Hence by the FOR-rule

$\vdash \{(\text{X}=((1-1)\times1) \text{ DIV } 2)\wedge(1\leq\text{M})\}$
     $\text{FOR N}:=1 \text{ UNTIL M DO X}:=\text{X}+\text{N}$
     $\{\text{X}=(\text{M}\times(\text{M}+1)) \text{ DIV } 2\}$

Hence

$\vdash \{(\text{X}=0)\wedge(1\leq\text{M}\} \text{ FOR N}:=1 \text{ UNTIL M DO X}:=\text{X}+\text{N} \{\text{X}=(\text{M}\times(\text{M}+1)) \text{ DIV } 2\}$
□

Note that if

(i) $\vdash \{P\} C \{P[V+1/V]\}$, or

(ii) $\vdash \{P \wedge (E_1 \leq V)\} C \{P[V+1/V]\}$, or

(iii) $\vdash \{P \wedge (V \leq E_2)\} C \{P[V+1/V]\}$

then by precondition strengthening one can infer

$\vdash \{P \wedge (E_1 \leq V) \wedge (V \leq E_2)\} C \{P[V+1/V]\}$

Exercise 15
Show that

```
⊢ {M≥1}
   BEGIN
     X:=0;
     FOR N:=1 UNTIL M DO X:=X+N
   END
   {X=(M×(M+1)) DIV 2}
```

□

2.1.12   Arrays

Floyd-Hoare logic can be extended to cope with arrays so that, for example, the correctness of inplace sorting programs can be verified. However, it is not as straightforward as one might expect to do this. The main problem is that the assignment axiom does not apply to array assignments of the form $A(E_1):=E_2$ (where A is an array variable and E_1 and E_2 are expressions).

One might think that the axiom in Section 2.1.1 could be generalized to

$$⊢ \ \{P[E_2/A(E_1)]\} \ A(E_1) := E_2 \ \{P\}$$

where '$P[E_2/A(E_1)]$' denotes the result of substituting E_2 for all occurrences of $A(E_1)$ throughout P. Alas, this does not work. Consider the following case:

$$P \ \equiv \text{`A(Y)=0'}, \qquad E_1 \ \equiv \text{`X'}, \qquad E_2 \ \equiv \text{`1'}$$

Since A(X) does not occur in P, it follows that $P[1/A(X)] = P$, and hence the generalized axiom yields

$$⊢ \ \{A(Y)=0\} \ A(X):=1 \ \{A(Y)=0\}$$

This specification is clearly false if X=Y. To avoid this, the array assignment axiom must take into account the possibility that changes to A(X) may also change A(Y), A(Z), ... (since X might equal Y, Z, ...).

We will not go into details of the Floyd-Hoare logic of arrays here, but a thorough treatment can be found in more advanced books (e.g. [63,1,26]).

2.2   Soundness and completeness

It is clear from the discussion of the FOR-rule in Section 2.1.11 that it is not always straightforward to devise correct rules of inference. As discussed at the beginning of Chapter 2, it is very important that the axioms and rules be sound. There are two approaches to ensure this:

(i) Define the language by the axioms and rules of the logic.

(ii) Prove that the logic fits the language.

Approach (i) is called *axiomatic semantics*. The idea is to *define* the semantics of the language by requiring that it make the axioms and rules of inference true. It is then up to implementers to ensure that the logic matches the language. One snag with this approach is that most existing languages have already been defined in some other way (usually by informal and ambiguous natural language statements). An example of a language defined axiomatically is Euclid [46]. The other snag with axiomatic semantics is that it is known to be impossible to devise complete Floyd-Hoare logics for certain constructs (this is discussed further below). It could be argued that this is not a snag at all but an advantage, because it forces programming languages to be made logically tractable. I have some sympathy for this latter view; it is clearly not the position taken by the designers of Ada.

Approach (ii) requires that the axioms and rules of the logic be proved valid. To do this, a mathematical model of states is constructed and then a function, **Meaning** say, is defined which takes an arbitrary command C to a function **Meaning** (C) from states to states. Thus **Meaning** (C) (s) denotes the state resulting from executing command C in state s. The specification $\{P\}C\{Q\}$ is then defined to be true if whenever P is true in a state s and **Meaning** (C) $(s) = s'$ then Q is true in state s'. It is then possible to attempt to prove rigorously that all the axioms are true and that the rules of inference lead from true premises to true conclusions. Actually carrying out this proof is likely to be quite tedious, especially if the programming language is at all complicated, and there are various technical details which require care (e.g. defining **Meaning** to correctly model non-termination). The precise formulation of such soundness proofs is beyond the scope of this book, but details can be found in the text by Loeckx and Sieber [45].

Even if we are sure that our logic is sound, how can we be sure that every true specification can be proved? It might be the case that for some particular P, Q and C the specification $\{P\}C\{Q\}$ was true, but the rules of our logic were too weak to prove it (see Exercise 7 on page 21 for an example). A logic is said to be *complete* if every true statement in it is provable.

There are various subtle technical problems in formulating precisely what it means for a Floyd-Hoare logic to be complete. For example, it is necessary to distinguish incompleteness arising due to incompleteness in the assertion language (e.g. arithmetic) from incompleteness due to inadequate axioms and rules for programming language constructs. The completeness of a Floyd-Hoare logic must thus be defined independently of that of its assertion language. Good introductions to this area can be found in Loeckx and Sieber [45] and Clarke's paper [11]. Clarke's paper also contains a discussion of his important results showing the impossibility of giving complete inference systems for certain combinations of programming language constructs. For example, he proves that it is impossible to give a sound and complete system for any language combining procedures as parameters of procedure calls, recursion, static scopes, global variables and internal procedures as parameters of procedure calls. These features are found in Algol 60, which thus cannot have a sound and complete Floyd-Hoare logic.

2.3   Some exercises

The exercises in this section have been taken from various sources, including Alagić and Arbib's book [1] and Cambridge University Tripos examinations.

Exercise 16
The exponentiation function exp satisfies:

$$exp(m, 0) = 1$$
$$exp(m, n+1) = m \times exp(m, n)$$

Devise a command C that uses repeated multiplication to achieve the following partial correctness specification:

$$\{X = x \ \wedge \ Y = y \ \wedge \ Y \geq 0\} \ C \ \{Z = exp(x, y) \ \wedge \ X = x \ \wedge \ Y = y\}$$

Prove that your command C meets this specification. $\square$

Exercise 17
Show that

```
⊢ {M≥0}
  BEGIN
    X:=0;
    FOR N:=1 UNTIL M DO X:=X+N
  END
  {X=(M×(M+1)) DIV 2}
```

$\square$

Exercise 18

Deduce:

```
⊢ {S = (x×y)-(X×Y)}
    WHILE ¬ODD(X) DO
      BEGIN Y:=2×Y; X:=X DIV 2 END
    {S = (x×y)-(X×Y) ∧ ODD(X)}
```

□

Exercise 19

Deduce:

```
⊢ {S = (x×y)-(X×Y)}
    WHILE ¬(X=0) DO
      BEGIN
        WHILE ¬ODD(X) DO
          BEGIN Y:=2×Y; X:=X DIV 2 END;
        S:=S+Y;
        X:=X-1
      END
    {S = x×y}
```

□

Exercise 20

Deduce:

```
⊢ {X=x ∧ Y=y}
    BEGIN
      S:=0;
      WHILE ¬(X=0) DO
        BEGIN
          WHILE ¬ODD(X) DO
            BEGIN Y:=2×Y; X:=X DIV 2 END;
          S:=S+Y;
          X:=X-1
        END
    END
    {S = x×y}
```

□

Exercise 21
Prove the following invariant property.

$$\vdash \{S = (x-X)\times y\}$$
```
    BEGIN
      VAR R;
      R:=0;
      WHILE ¬(R=Y) DO
        BEGIN S:=S+1; R:=R+1 END;
        X:=X-1
    END
```
$$\{S = (x-X)\times y\}$$

Hint: Show that $S = (x-X)\times y + R$ is an invariant for $S:=S+1$; $R:=R+1$. $\square$

Exercise 22
Deduce:

$$\vdash \{X=x \wedge Y=y\}$$
```
    BEGIN
      S:=0;
      WHILE ¬(X=0) DO
        BEGIN
          VAR R;
          R:=0;
          WHILE ¬(R=Y) DO
            BEGIN S:=S+1; R:=R+1 END;
          X:=X-1
        END
    END
```
$$\{S = x\times y\}$$

$\square$

Exercise 23
Using $(P\times X^N=x^n) \wedge \neg(X=0) \wedge (N>0)$ as an invariant, deduce:

```
⊢ {X=x ∧ N=n}
  BEGIN
    P:=1;
    IF ¬(X=0)
      THEN
        WHILE ¬(N=0) DO
          BEGIN
            IF ODD(N) THEN P:=P×X;
            N:=N DIV 2;
            X:=X×X
          END
      ELSE P:=0
  END
  {P = xⁿ}
```

□

Exercise 24
Prove that the command

```
BEGIN
  Z:=0;
  WHILE ¬(X=0) DO
    BEGIN
      IF ODD(X) THEN Z:=Z+Y;
      Y:=Y×2;
      X:=X DIV 2
    END
END
```

computes the product of the initial values of X and Y and leaves the result in Z. □

Exercise 25
Prove that the command

```
BEGIN
  Z:=1;
  WHILE N>0 DO
    BEGIN
      IF ODD(N) THEN Z:=Z×X;
      N:=N DIV 2;
      X:=X×X
    END
END
```

assigns x^n to Z, where x and n are the initial values of X and N respectively and we assume $n \geq 0$. □

Exercise 26
Devise a proof rule for a command

>   REPEAT *command* UNTIL *statement*

The meaning of REPEAT C UNTIL S is that C is executed and then S is tested; if the result is true, then nothing more is done, otherwise the whole REPEAT command is repeated. Thus REPEAT C UNTIL S is equivalent to C; WHILE S DO C. □

Exercise 27
Use your REPEAT rule to deduce:

>   ⊢ {S = C+R ∧ R<Y}
>   REPEAT
>   S:=S+1; R:=R+1
>   UNTIL R=Y
>   {S = C+Y}

□

Exercise 28
Use your REPEAT rule to deduce:

>   ⊢ {X=x ∧ Y=y}
>   BEGIN
>   S:=0;
>   REPEAT
>   R:=0;
>   REPEAT
>   S:=S+1; R:=R+1
>   UNTIL R=Y;
>   X:=X-1
>   UNTIL X=0
>   END
>   {S = x×y}

□

Exercise 29
Assume gcd(X,Y) satisfies:

>   ⊢ (X>Y) ⇒ gcd(X,Y)=gcd(X-Y,Y)
>   ⊢ gcd(X,Y)=gcd(Y,X)
>   ⊢ gcd(X,X)=X

Prove:

```
⊢ {(A>0) ∧ (B>0) ∧ (gcd(A,B)=gcd(X,Y))}
  WHILE A>B DO A:=A-B;
  WHILE B>A DO B:=B-A
  {(0<B) ∧ (B≤A) ∧ (gcd(A,B)=gcd(X,Y))}
```

Hence, or otherwise, use your rule for REPEAT commands to prove:

```
⊢ {A=a ∧ B=b}
  REPEAT
    WHILE A>B DO A:=A-B;
    WHILE B>A DO B:=B-A
  UNTIL A=B
  {A=B ∧ A=gcd(a,b)}
```

☐

Exercise 30
Prove:

```
⊢ {N≥1}
  BEGIN
    PROD=0;
    FOR X:=1 UNTIL N DO PROD := PROD+M
  END
  {PROD = M×N}
```

☐

Exercise 31
Prove:

```
⊢ {X>0 ∧ Y>0}
  BEGIN
    S:=0;
    FOR I:=1 UNTIL X DO
      FOR J:=I UNTIL Y DO
        S:=S+1
  END
  {S = X×Y}
```

☐

Chapter 3

Mechanizing Program Verification

The architecture of a simple program verifier is described. Its operation is justified with respect to the rules of Floyd-Hoare logic.

After doing only a few exercises, the following two things will be painfully clear:

(i) Proofs are typically long and boring (even if the program being verified is quite simple).

(ii) There are lots of fiddly little details to get right, many of which are trivial (e.g. proving $\vdash$ (R=X $\wedge$ Q=0) $\Rightarrow$ (X = R + Y×Q)).

Many attempts have been made (and are still being made) to automate proof of correctness by designing systems to do the boring and tricky bits of generating formal proofs in Floyd-Hoare logic. Unfortunately logicians have shown that it is impossible in principle to design a decision procedure to decide automatically the truth or falsehood of an arbitrary mathematical statement [58]. However, this does not mean that one cannot have procedures that will prove many useful theorems. The non-existence of a general decision procedure merely shows that one cannot hope to prove *everything* automatically. In practice, it is quite possible to build a system that will mechanize many of the boring and routine aspects of verification. This chapter describes one commonly taken approach to doing this.

Although it is impossible to decide automatically the truth or falsity of arbitrary statements, it *is* possible to check whether an arbitrary formal proof is valid. This consists in checking that the results occurring on each line of the proof are indeed either axioms or consequences of previous lines. Since proofs of correctness of programs are typically very long and boring, they often contain mistakes when generated manually. It is thus useful to check proofs mechanically, even if they can only be generated with human assistance.

3.1 Overview

In the previous chapter it was shown how to prove $\{P\}C\{Q\}$ by proving properties of the components of C and then putting these together (with the appropriate proof rule) to get the desired property of C itself. For example, to prove $\vdash \{P\}C_1;C_2\{Q\}$ first prove $\vdash \{P\}C_1\{R\}$ and $\vdash \{R\}C_2\{Q\}$ (for suitable R), and then deduce $\vdash \{P\}C_1;C_2\{Q\}$ by the sequencing rule.

This process is called *forward proof* because one moves forward from axioms via rules to conclusions. In practice, it is more natural to work backwards: starting from the goal of showing $\{P\}C\{Q\}$ one generates subgoals, subsubgoals etc. until the problem is solved. For example, suppose one wants to show:

$$\{X=x \land Y=y\} \ R:=X; \ X:=Y; \ Y:=R \ \{Y=x \land X=y\}$$

then by the assignment axiom and sequencing rule it is sufficient to show the subgoal

$$\{X=x \land Y=y\} \ R:=X; \ X:=Y \ \{R=x \land X=y\}$$

(because $\vdash \ \{R=x \land X=y\} \ Y:=R \ \{Y=x \land X=y\}$). By a similar argument this subgoal can be reduced to

$$\{X=x \land Y=y\} \ R:=X \ \{R=x \land Y=y\}$$

which clearly follows from the assignment axiom.

This chapter describes how such a *goal oriented* method of proof can be formalized; in Chapter 11 a complete LISP program verifier is given to illustrate how it can be mechanized.

The verification system described here can be viewed as a proof checker that also provides some help with generating proofs. The following diagram gives an overview of the system.

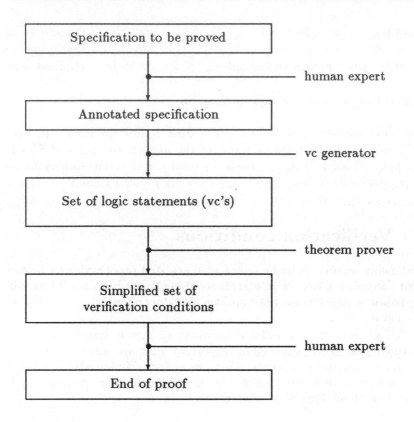

The system takes as input a partial correctness specification annotated with mathematical statements describing relationships between variables. From the annotated specification the system generates a set of purely mathematical statements, called *verification conditions* (or vc's). In Section 3.5 it is shown that if these verification conditions are provable, then the original specification can be deduced from the axioms and rules of Floyd-Hoare logic.

The verification conditions are passed to a *theorem prover* program which attempts to prove them automatically; if it fails, advice is sought from the user. We will concentrate on those aspects pertaining to Floyd-Hoare logic and say very little about theorem proving here. Chapter 10 contains the description of a very simple theorem prover based on rewriting and implemented in LISP. It is powerful enough to do most of the examples discussed in this chapter automatically.

The aim of much current research is to build systems which reduce the role of the slow and expensive human expert to a minimum. This can be achieved by:

- reducing the number and complexity of the annotations required, and

- increasing the power of the theorem prover.

The next section explains how verification conditions work. In Section 3.5 their use is justified in terms of the axioms and rules of Floyd-Hoare logic. Besides being the basis for mechanical verification systems, verification conditions are a useful way of doing proofs by hand.

3.2   Verification conditions

The following sections describe how a goal oriented proof style can be formalized. To prove a goal $\{P\}C\{Q\}$, three things must be done. These will be explained in detail later, but here is a quick overview:

(i) The program C is *annotated* by inserting into it statements (often called *assertions*) expressing conditions that are meant to hold at various intermediate points. This step is tricky and needs intelligence and a good understanding of how the program works. Automating it is a problem of artificial intelligence.

(ii) A set of logic statements called *verification conditions* (vc's for short) is then generated from the annotated specification. This process is purely mechanical and easily done by a program.

(iii) The verification conditions are proved. Automating this is also a problem of artificial intelligence.

It will be shown that if one can prove all the verification conditions generated from $\{P\}C\{Q\}$ (where C is suitably annotated), then $\vdash \{P\}C\{Q\}$.

Since verification conditions are just mathematical statements, one can think of step 2 above as the 'compilation', or translation, of a verification problem into a conventional mathematical problem.

The following example will give a preliminary feel for the use of verification conditions.

Suppose the goal is to prove (see the example on page 25)

```
{T}
BEGIN
  R:=X;
  Q:=0;
  WHILE Y≤R DO
      BEGIN R:=R-Y;  Q:=Q+1 END
END
{X = R+Y×Q  ∧  R<Y}
```

This first step (1 above) is to insert annotations. A suitable annotated specification is:

```
{T}
BEGIN
  R:=X;
  Q:=0; {R=X ∧ Q=0} ←—P₁
  WHILE Y≤R DO {X = R+Y×Q} ←—P₂
      BEGIN R:=R-Y;  Q:=Q+1 END
END
{X = R+Y×Q  ∧  R<Y}
```

The annotations P_1 and P_2 state conditions which are intended to hold *whenever* control reaches them. Control only reaches the point at which P_1 is placed once, but it reaches P_2 each time the WHILE body is executed and whenever this happens P_2 (i.e. X=R+Y×Q) holds, even though the values of R and Q vary. P_2 is an *invariant* of the WHILE-command.

The second step (2 above), which has yet to be explained, will generate the following four verification conditions:

(i) T ⇒ (X=X ∧ 0=0)

(ii) (R=X ∧ Q=0) ⇒ (X = R+(Y×Q))

(iii) (X = R+(Y×Q)) ∧ Y≤R) ⇒ (X = (R-Y)+(Y×(Q+1)))

(iv) (X = R+(Y×Q)) ∧ ¬(Y≤R) ⇒   (X = R+(Y×Q) ∧ R<Y)

Notice that these are statements of arithmetic; the constructs of our programming language have been 'compiled away'.

The third step (3 above) consists in proving these four verification conditions. They are all easy and are proved automatically by the theorem prover described in Chapter 11 (see page 212). The steps are now explained in detail.

3.3   Annotation

An annotated command is a command with statements (called *assertions*) embedded within it. A command is said to be properly annotated if statements have been inserted at the following places:

(i) Before each command C_i (where $i > 1$) in a sequence $C_1; C_2; \ldots ; C_n$ which is *not* an assignment command,

(ii) After the word DO in WHILE and FOR commands.

Intuitively, the inserted assertions should express the conditions one expects to hold *whenever* control reaches the point at which the assertion occurs.

A properly annotated specification is a specification $\{P\}C\{Q\}$ where C is a properly annotated command.

Example: To be properly annotated, assertions should be at points ① and ② of the specification below:

```
{X=n}
BEGIN
    Y:=1;  ←—①
    WHILE X≠0 DO  ←—②
        BEGIN Y:=Y×X; X:=X-1 END
END
{X=0 ∧ Y=n!}
```

Suitable statements would be:

at ①: $\{Y = 1 \wedge X = n\}$
at ②: $\{Y \times X! = n!\}$

□

The verification conditions generated from an annotated specification $\{P\}C\{Q\}$ are described by considering the various possibilities for C in turn. This process is justified in Section 3.5 by showing that $\vdash \{P\}C\{Q\}$ if all the verification conditions can be proved.

3.4   Verification condition generation

In this section a procedure is described for generating verification conditions for an annotated partial correctness specification $\{P\}C\{Q\}$. This procedure is *recursive* on C.

Assignment commands

The single verification condition generated by

$$\{P\}\ V := E\ \{Q\}$$

is

$$P \ \Rightarrow\ Q[E/V]$$

Example: The verification condition for

$$\{X=0\}\ X := X+1\ \{X=1\}$$

is

$$X=0\ \Rightarrow\ (X+1)=1$$

(which is clearly true). □

One-armed conditional

The verification conditions generated by

$$\{P\}\ \text{IF}\ S\ \text{THEN}\ C\ \{Q\}$$

are

(i) $(P \wedge \neg S)\ \Rightarrow\ Q$

(ii) the verifications generated by

$$\{P \wedge S\}\ C\ \{Q\}$$

Example: The verification conditions for

$$\{T\}\ \text{IF}\ X<0\ \text{THEN}\ X := -X\ \{X \geq 0\}$$

are $T \wedge \neg(X<0) \ \Rightarrow\ X \geq 0$ together with the verification conditions for $\{T \wedge (X<0)\}\ X := -X\ \{X \geq 0\}$, i.e. $T \wedge (X<0) \ \Rightarrow\ -X \geq 0$. The two vc's are thus:

(i) $T \wedge \neg(X>0)\ \Rightarrow\ X \geq 0$

(ii) $T \wedge (X<0) \Rightarrow -X \geq 0$

These are equivalent to $X \geq 0 \Rightarrow X \geq 0$ and $X<0 \Rightarrow -X \geq 0$, respectively, which are both clearly true. $\square$

Two-armed conditional

The verification conditions generated from

$$\{P\} \text{ IF } S \text{ THEN } C_1 \text{ ELSE } C_2 \{Q\}$$

are

(i) the verification conditions generated by

$$\{P \wedge S\} C_1 \{Q\}$$

(ii) the verifications generated by

$$\{P \wedge \neg S\} C_2 \{Q\}$$

Exercise 32
What are the verification conditions for the following specification?

$$\{T\} \text{ IF } X \geq Y \text{ THEN } MAX:=X \text{ ELSE } MAX:=Y \ \{MAX=max(X,Y)\}$$

Do they follow from the assumptions about max(X,Y) given in the example on page 23? $\square$

If $C_1; \ldots ; C_n$ is properly annotated, then (see page 44) it must be of one of the two forms:

1. $C_1; \ldots ; C_{n-1}; \{R\}C_n$, or

2. $C_1; \ldots ; C_{n-1}; V := E$.

where, in both cases, $C_1; \ldots ; C_{n-1}$ is a properly annotated command.

Sequences

1. The verification conditions generated by

$$\{P\}\ C_1;\ \ldots;C_{n-1};\ \{R\}\ C_n\ \{Q\}$$

(where C_n is not an assignment) are:

(a) the verification conditions generated by

$$\{P\}\ C_1;\ \ldots;C_{n-1}\ \{R\}$$

(b) the verifications generated by

$$\{R\}\ C_n\ \{Q\}$$

2. The verification conditions generated by

$$\{P\}\ C_1;\ \ldots;C_{n-1};I:=E\ \{Q\}$$

are the verification conditions generated by

$$\{P\}\ C_1;\ \ldots;C_{n-1}\ \{Q[E/V]\}$$

Example: The verification conditions generated from

$$\{\texttt{X=x} \land \texttt{Y=y}\}\ \texttt{R:=X;\ X:=Y;\ Y:=R}\ \{\texttt{X=y} \land \texttt{Y=x}\}$$

are those generated by

$$\{\texttt{X=x} \land \texttt{Y=y}\}\ \texttt{R:=X;\ X:=Y}\ \{\texttt{(X=y} \land \texttt{Y=x)[R/Y]}\}$$

which, after doing the substitution, simplifies to

$$\{\texttt{X=x} \land \texttt{Y=y}\}\ \texttt{R:=X;\ X:=Y}\ \{\texttt{X=y} \land \texttt{R=x}\}$$

The verification conditions generated by this are those generated by

$$\{\texttt{X=x} \land \texttt{Y=y}\}\ \texttt{R:=X}\ \{\texttt{(X=y} \land \texttt{R=x)[Y/X]}\}$$

which, after doing the substitution, simplifies to

$$\{\texttt{X=x} \land \texttt{Y=y}\}\ \texttt{R:=X}\ \{\texttt{Y=y} \land \texttt{R=x}\}.$$

The only verification condition generated by this is

$$X=x \ \wedge \ Y=y \ \Rightarrow \ (Y=y \ \wedge \ R=x) [X/R]$$

which, after doing the substitution, simplifies to

$$X=x \ \wedge \ Y=y \ \Rightarrow \ Y=y \ \wedge \ X=x$$

which is obviously true. $\square$

The procedure for generating verification conditions from blocks involves checking the syntactic condition that the local variables of the block do not occur in the precondition or postcondition. The need for this is clear from the side condition in the block rule (see page 20); this will be explained in more detail when the procedure for generating verification conditions is justified in Section 3.5.

Blocks

The verification conditions generated by

$$\{P\} \ \text{BEGIN VAR} \ V_1; \ldots \ ; \text{VAR} \ V_n; C \ \text{END} \ \{Q\}$$

are

(i) the verification conditions generated by $\{P\}C\{Q\}$, and

(ii) the syntactic condition that none of $V_1, \ldots, V_n$ occur in either P or Q.

Example: The verification conditions for

$$\{X=x \ \wedge \ Y=y\} \ \text{BEGIN VAR R; R:=X; X:=Y; Y:=R END} \ \{X=y \ \wedge \ Y=x\}$$

are those generated by $\{X=x \ \wedge \ Y=y\}$ R:=X; X:=Y; Y:=R $\{X=y \ \wedge \ Y=x\}$ (since R does not occur in $\{X=x \ \wedge \ Y=y\}$ or $\{X=y \ \wedge \ Y=x\}$). See the previous example for the verification conditions generated by this. $\square$

Exercise 33
What are the verification conditions for the following specification?

$$\{X = R+(Y \times Q)\} \ \text{BEGIN R:=R-Y; Q:=Q+1 END} \ \{X = R+(Y \times Q)\}$$

$\square$

Exercise 34
What are the verification conditions for the following specification?

$$\{X=x\} \text{ BEGIN VAR X; X:=1 END } \{X=x\}$$

Relate your answer to this exercise to your answer to Exercise 7 on page 21.
□

A correctly annotated specification of a WHILE-command has the form

$$\{P\} \text{ WHILE } S \text{ DO } \{R\} \ C \ \{Q\}$$

Following the usage on page 24, the annotation R is called an invariant.

WHILE-commands

The verification conditions generated from

$$\{P\} \text{ WHILE } S \text{ DO } \{R\} \ C \ \{Q\}$$

are

(i) $P \Rightarrow R$

(ii) $R \wedge \neg S \Rightarrow Q$

(iii) the verification conditions generated by $\{R \wedge S\} \ C\{R\}$.

Example: The verification conditions for

$$\{R=X \wedge Q=0\}$$
$$\text{WHILE } Y\leq R \text{ DO } \{X=R+Y\times Q\}$$
$$\quad \text{BEGIN R:=R-Y; Q=Q+1 END}$$
$$\{X = R+(Y\times Q) \wedge R<Y\}$$

are:

(i) $R=X \wedge Q=0 \Rightarrow (X = R+(Y\times Q))$

(ii) $X = R+Y\times Q \wedge \neg(Y\leq R) \Rightarrow (X = R+(Y\times Q) \wedge R<Y)$

together with the verification condition for

$$\{X = R+(Y\times Q) \wedge (Y\leq R)\}$$
$$\quad \text{BEGIN R:=R-Y; Q:=Q+1 END}$$
$$\{X=R+(Y\times Q)\}$$

which (see Exercise 33) consists of the single condition

(iii) $\mathtt{X = R+(Y{\times}Q) \land (Y{\leq}R) \Rightarrow X = (R-Y)+(Y{\times}(Q+1))}$

The WHILE-command specification is thus true if (i), (ii) and (iii) hold, i.e.

$$
\begin{array}{l}
\vdash \ \{\mathtt{R{=}X \land Q{=}0}\} \\
\quad \mathtt{WHILE\ Y{\leq}R\ DO} \\
\qquad \mathtt{BEGIN\ R{:=}R{-}Y;\ Q{:=}Q{+}1\ END} \\
\quad \{\mathtt{X = R+(Y{\times}Q) \land R{<}Y}\}
\end{array}
$$

if

$$\vdash \ \mathtt{R{=}X \land Q{=}0 \Rightarrow (X = R+(Y{\times}Q))}$$

and

$$\vdash \ \mathtt{X = R+(Y{\times}Q) \land \lnot(Y{\leq}R) \Rightarrow (X = R+(Y{\times}Q) \land R{<}Y)}$$

and

$$\vdash \ \mathtt{X = R+(Y{\times}Q) \land (Y{\leq}R) \Rightarrow X = (R-Y)+(Y{\times}(Q+1))}$$

□

Exercise 35
What are the verification conditions generated by the annotated program for computing n! (the factorial of n) given in the example on page 44? □

A correctly annotated specification of a FOR-command has the form

$$\{P\}\ \mathtt{FOR}\ V := E_1\ \mathtt{UNTIL}\ E_2\ \mathtt{DO}\ \{R\}\ C\ \{Q\}$$

FOR-commands

The verification conditions generated from

$$\{P\} \text{ FOR } V:=E_1 \text{ UNTIL } E_2 \text{ DO } \{R\}\ C\ \{Q\}$$

are

(i) $P \Rightarrow R[E_1/V]$

(ii) $R[E_2+1/V] \Rightarrow Q$

(iii) $P \wedge E_2 < E_1 \Rightarrow Q$

(iv) the verification conditions generated by

$$\{R \wedge E_1 \leq V \wedge V \leq E_2\}\ C\ \{R[V+1/V]\}$$

(v) the syntactic condition that neither V, nor any variable occurring in E_1 or E_2, is assigned to inside C.

Example: The verification conditions generated by

```
{X=0 ∧ 1≤M}
  FOR N:=1 UNTIL M DO {X=((N-1)×N) DIV 2} X:=X+N
{X = (M×(M+1)) DIV 2}
```

are

(i) $\text{X=0} \wedge \text{1≤M} \Rightarrow \text{X=((1-1)×1) DIV 2}$

(ii) $\text{X} = \text{((((M+1)-1)×(M+1)) DIV 2} \Rightarrow \text{X} = \text{(M×(M+1)) DIV 2}$

(iii) $\text{X=0} \wedge \text{1≤M} \wedge \text{M<1} \Rightarrow \text{X} = \text{(M×(M+1)) DIV 2}$

(iv) The verification condition generated by

```
{X = ((N-1)×N) DIV 2 ∧ 1≤N ∧ N≤M}
  X:=X+N
{X = (((N+1)-1)×(N+1)) DIV 2}
```

which, after some simplification, is

$$X = ((N-1) \times N) \text{ DIV } 2 \wedge 1 \leq N$$
$$\Rightarrow$$
$$N \leq M \Rightarrow X+N = (N \times (N+1)) \text{ DIV } 2$$

which is true since

$$\frac{(\texttt{N}-1)\times\texttt{N}}{2}+\texttt{N}=\frac{2\texttt{N}+(\texttt{N}-1)\times\texttt{N}}{2}$$

$$=\frac{2\texttt{N}+\texttt{N}^2-\texttt{N}}{2}$$

$$=\frac{\texttt{N}+\texttt{N}^2}{2}$$

$$=\frac{\texttt{N}\times(\texttt{N}+1)}{2}$$

(Exercise: justify this calculation in the light of the fact that

$$(x+y)\ \texttt{DIV}\ z \neq (x\ \texttt{DIV}\ z)+(y\ \texttt{DIV}\ z)$$

as is easily seen by taking x, y and z to be 3, 5 and 8, respectively.)

(v) Neither N or M is assigned to in X:=X+N

□

3.5   Justification of verification conditions

It will be shown in this section that an annotated specification $\{P\}C\{Q\}$ is provable in Floyd-Hoare logic (i.e. $\vdash \{P\}C\{Q\}$) if the verification conditions generated by it are provable. This shows that the verification conditions are *sufficient*, but not that they are necessary. In fact, the verification conditions are the weakest sufficient conditions, but we will neither make this more precise nor go into details here. An in-depth study of preconditions can be found in Dijkstra's book [16].

It is easy to show (see the exercise below) that the verification conditions are not necessary, i.e. that the verification conditions for $\{P\}C\{Q\}$ not being provable doesn't imply that $\vdash \{P\}C\{Q\}$ cannot be deduced.

Exercise 36
Show that

(i) The verification conditions from the annotated specification

   {T} WHILE F DO {F} X:=0 {T}

are not provable.

(ii) $\vdash$ $\{T\}$ `WHILE F DO X:=0` $\{T\}$

$\square$

The argument that the verification conditions are sufficient will be by *induction* on the structure of C. Such inductive arguments have two parts. First, it is shown that the result holds for assignment commands. Second, it is shown that when C is not an assignment command, then if the result holds for the constituent commands of C (this is called the *induction hypothesis*), then it holds also for C. The first of these parts is called the *basis* of the induction and the second is called the step. From the basis and the step it follows that the result holds for all commands.

Assignments

The only verification condition for $\{P\}V:=E\{Q\}$ is $P \Rightarrow Q[E/V]$. If this is provable, then as $\vdash$ $\{Q[E/V]\}V:=E\{Q\}$ (by the assignment axiom on page 16) it follows by precondition strengthening (page 17) that $\vdash$ $\{P\}V := E\{Q\}$.

One-armed conditionals

If the verification conditions for $\{P\}$ `IF` S `THEN` C $\{Q\}$ are provable, then $\vdash$ $P \wedge \neg S \Rightarrow Q$ and all the verification conditions for $\{P \wedge S\}$ C $\{Q\}$ are provable. Hence by the induction hypothesis $\vdash$ $\{P \wedge S\}$ C $\{Q\}$ and hence by the one-armed conditional rule (page 22) it follows that $\vdash$ $\{P\}$ `IF` S `THEN` C $\{Q\}$.

Two-armed conditionals

If the verification conditions for $\{P\}$ `IF` S `THEN` C_1 `ELSE` C_2 $\{Q\}$ are provable, then the verification conditions for both $\{P \wedge S\}$ C_1 $\{Q\}$ and $\{P \wedge \neg S\}$ C_2 $\{Q\}$ are provable. By the induction hypothesis we can assume that $\vdash$ $\{P \wedge S\}$ C_1 $\{Q\}$ and $\vdash$ $\{P \wedge \neg S\}$ C_2 $\{Q\}$. Hence by the two-armed conditional rule (page 22) $\vdash$ $\{P\}$ `IF` S `THEN` C_1 `ELSE` C_2 $\{Q\}$.

Sequences

There are two cases to consider:

(i) If the verification conditions for $\{P\}$ $C_1;\ldots;C_{n-1};\{R\}C_n$ $\{Q\}$ are provable, then the verification conditions for $\{P\}$ $C_1;\ldots;C_{n-1}$ $\{R\}$ and $\{R\}$ C_n $\{Q\}$ must both be provable and hence by induction we have $\vdash$ $\{P\}$ $C_1;\ldots;C_{n-1}$ $\{R\}$ and $\vdash$ $\{R\}$ C_n $\{Q\}$. Hence by the sequencing rule (page 19) $\vdash$ $\{P\}$ $C_1;\ldots;$ $C_{n-1};C_n$ $\{Q\}$.

(ii) If the verification conditions for $\{P\}\ C_1;\ \ldots;C_{n-1};V := E\ \{Q\}$ are provable, then it must be the case that the verification conditions for $\{P\}\ C_1;\ \ldots;C_{n-1}\ \{Q[E/V]\}$ are also provable and hence by induction we have $\vdash\ \{P\}\ C_1;\ \ldots;C_{n-1}\ \{Q[E/V]\}$. It then follows by the assignment axiom that $\vdash\ \{Q[E/I]\}\ V := E\ \{Q\}$, hence by the sequencing rule $\vdash\ \{P\}\ C_1;\ \ldots;C_{n-1};V := E\{Q\}$.

Blocks

If the verification conditions for $\{P\}\texttt{BEGIN VAR } V_1;\ \ldots;\texttt{VAR}\ \ V_n;C\ \texttt{END}\ \{Q\}$ are provable, then the verification conditions for $\{P\}\ C\ \{Q\}$ are provable and $V_1,\ \ldots,\ V_n$ do not occur in P or Q. By induction $\vdash \{P\}\ C\ \{Q\}$ hence by the block rule (page 20) $\vdash\ \{P\}\ \texttt{BEGIN VAR } V_1;\ \ldots;\texttt{VAR } V_n;C\ \texttt{END}\ \{Q\}$.

WHILE-commands

If the verification conditions for $\{P\}\ \texttt{WHILE } S\ \texttt{DO}\ \{R\}\ C\ \{Q\}$ are provable, then $\vdash\ P \Rightarrow R,\ \vdash\ (R \wedge \neg S)\ \Rightarrow\ Q$ and the verification conditions for $\{R \wedge S\}\ C\ \{R\}$ are provable. By induction $\vdash\ \{R \wedge S\}\ C\ \{R\}$, hence by the WHILE-rule (page 24) $\vdash\ \{R\}\ \texttt{WHILE } S\ \texttt{DO}\ C\ \{R \wedge \neg S\}$, hence by the consequence rules (see page 19) $\vdash\ \{P\}\ \texttt{WHILE } S\ \texttt{DO}\ C\ \{Q\}$.

FOR-commands

Finally, if the verification conditions for

$$\{P\}\ \texttt{FOR } V := E_1\ \texttt{UNTIL}\ E_2\ \texttt{DO}\ \{R\}\ C\ \{Q\}$$

are provable, then

(i) $\vdash\ P\ \Rightarrow\ R[E_1/V]$

(ii) $\vdash\ R[E_1/V]\ \Rightarrow\ Q$

(iii) $\vdash\ P \wedge E_2 < E_1\ \Rightarrow\ Q$

(iv) The verification conditions for

$$\{R \wedge\ E_1 \leq V \wedge\ V \leq E_2\}\ C\ \{R[V+1/V]\}$$

are provable.

(v) Neither V, nor any variable in E_1 or E_2, is assigned to in C.

By induction $\vdash \{R \wedge E_1 \leq V \wedge V \leq E_2\} \, C \, \{R[V + 1/V]\}$, hence by the FOR-rule

$\vdash \{R[E_1/V] \wedge E_1 \leq E_2\}$ FOR $V := E_1$ UNTIL E_2 DO $C \, \{R[E_2 + 1/V]\}$

hence by (i), (ii) and the consequence rules

(vi) $\vdash \{P \wedge E_1 \leq E_2\}$ FOR $V := E_1$ UNTIL E_2 DO $C \, \{Q\}$.

Now by the FOR-axiom (page 30)

$\vdash \{(P \wedge E_2 < E_1) \wedge E\}$ FOR $V := E_1$ UNTIL E_2 DO $C \, \{P \wedge E_2 < E_1\}$,

hence by the consequence rules and (iii)

$\vdash \{P \wedge E_2 < E_1\}$ FOR $V := E_1$ UNTIL E_2 DO $C \, \{Q\}$.

Combining this last specification with (vi) using specification disjunction (page 19) yields

$\vdash \{P \wedge E_2 < E_1) \vee (P \wedge E_1 \leq E_2)\}$ FOR $V := E_1$ UNTIL E_2 DO $C \, \{Q \vee Q\}$

Now $\vdash Q \vee Q \Rightarrow Q$ and

$\vdash (P \wedge E_2 < E_1) \vee (P \wedge E_1 \leq E_2) \Rightarrow P \wedge (E_2 < E_1 \vee E_1 \leq E_2)$

but $\vdash E_2 < E_1 \vee E_1 \leq E_2$, hence

$\vdash (P \wedge E_2 < E_1) \vee (P \wedge E_1 \leq E_2)$

and so one can conclude:

$\vdash \{P\}$ FOR $V := E_1$ UNTIL E_2 DO $C \, \{Q\}$

Thus the verification conditions for the FOR-command are sufficient.

Exercise 37
Annotate the specifications in Exercises 17 to 25 (they start on page 33) and then generate the corresponding verification conditions. □

Exercise 38
Devise verification conditions for commands of the form

REPEAT C UNTIL S

(See Exercise 26, page 37.) □

Exercise 39
Do Exercises 27–31 using verification conditions. □

Exercise 40
Show that if no variable occurring in P is assigned to in C, then $\vdash \{P\} \, C\{P\}$. *Hint:* Use induction on the structure of C, see page 52. □

Part II

The λ-calculus and Combinators

Chapter 4

Introduction to the λ-calculus

The λ-calculus notation for specifying functions is introduced. Various technical definitions are explained and motivated, including the rules of α-, β- and η-conversion.

The λ-calculus (or lambda-calculus) is a theory of functions that was originally developed by the logician Alonzo Church as a foundation for mathematics. This work was done in the 1930s, several years before digital computers were invented. A little earlier (in the 1920s) Moses Schönfinkel developed another theory of functions based on what are now called 'combinators'. In the 1930s, Haskell Curry rediscovered and extended Schönfinkel's theory and showed that it was equivalent to the λ-calculus. About this time Kleene showed that the λ-calculus was a universal computing system; it was one of the first such systems to be rigorously analysed. In the 1950s John McCarthy was inspired by the λ-calculus to invent the programming language LISP. In the early 1960s Peter Landin showed how the meaning of imperative programming languages could be specified by translating them into the λ-calculus. He also invented an influential prototype programming language called ISWIM [42]. This introduced the main notations of functional programming and influenced the design of both functional and imperative languages. Building on this work, Christopher Strachey laid the foundations for the important area of denotational semantics [23,67]. Technical questions concerning Strachey's work inspired the mathematical logician Dana Scott to invent the theory of domains, which is now one of the most important parts of theoretical computer science. During the 1970s Peter Henderson and Jim Morris took up Landin's work and wrote a number of influential papers arguing that functional programming had important advantages for software engineering [29,28]. At about the same time David Turner proposed that Schönfinkel and Curry's combinators could be used as the machine code of computers for executing functional programming languages. Such computers could exploit mathematical properties of the λ-calculus for the parallel evaluation of programs. During the 1980s several research groups took up Henderson's and Turner's ideas and started working on making functional programming practical by designing special architectures to support it, some of them with many processors.

We thus see that an obscure branch of mathematical logic underlies important developments in programming language theory, such as:

(i) The study of fundamental questions of computation.

(ii) The design of programming languages.

(iii) The semantics of programming languages.

(iv) The architecture of computers.

4.1   Syntax and semantics of the λ-calculus

The λ-calculus is a notation for defining functions. The expressions of the notation are called λ-*expressions* and each such expression denotes a function. It will be seen later how functions can be used to represent a wide variety of data and data-structures including numbers, pairs, lists etc. For example, it will be demonstrated how an arbitrary pair of numbers (x, y) can be represented as a λ-expression. As a notational convention, mnemonic names are assigned in **bold** or underlined to particular λ-expressions; for example 1 is the λ-expression (defined in Section 5.3) which is used to represent the number one.

There are just three kinds of λ-expressions:

(i) **Variables:** x, y, z etc. The functions denoted by variables are determined by what the variables are bound to in the *environment*. Binding is done by abstractions (see 3 below). We use V, V_1, V_2 etc. for arbitrary variables.

(ii) **Function applications** or **combinations:** if E_1 and E_2 are λ-expressions, then so is $(E_1\ E_2)$; it denotes the result of applying the function denoted by E_1 to the function denoted by E_2. E_1 is called the *rator* (from 'operator') and E_2 is called the *rand* (from 'operand'). For example, if $(\underline{m}, \underline{n})$ denotes a function representing the pair of numbers m and n (see Section 5.2) and **sum** denotes the addition function [1] λ-calculus (see Section 5.5), then the application $(\mathbf{sum}(\underline{m}, \underline{n}))$ denotes $\underline{m+n}$.

---

[1] Note that **sum** is a λ-expression, whereas + is a mathematical symbol in the 'metalanguage' (i.e. English) that we are using for talking about the λ-calculus.

(iii) **Abstractions:** if V is a variable and E is a λ-expression, then $\lambda V.\ E$ is an abstraction with *bound variable* V and *body E*. Such an abstraction denotes the function that takes an argument a and returns as result the function denoted by E in an environment in which the bound variable V denotes a. More specifically, the abstraction $\lambda V.\ E$ denotes a function which takes an argument E' and transforms it into the thing denoted by $E\,[E'/V]$ (the result of substituting E' for V in E, see Section 4.8). For example, $\lambda x.\ \mathrm{sum}(x, \underline{1})$ denotes the add-one function.

Using BNF, the syntax of λ-expressions is just:

$<$ λ-expression$>$ ::= $<$variable$>$
    | $(<$ λ-expression$> <$ λ-expression$>)$
    | $(\lambda <$variable$> . < $λ-expression$>)$

If V ranges over the syntax class $<$ variable $>$ and E, E_1, E_2, ... etc. range over the syntax class $<$ λ-expression $>$, then the BNF simplifies to:

$$E ::= V \mid (E_1\ E_2) \mid \lambda V.\ E$$

variables   applications   abstractions
(combinations)

The description of the meaning of λ-expressions just given above is vague and intuitive. It took about 40 years for logicians (Dana Scott, in fact [66]) to make it rigorous in a useful way. We shall not be going into details of this.

Example: $(\lambda x.\ x)$ denotes the 'identity function': $((\lambda x.\ x)\ E) = E.$ □

Example: $(\lambda x.\ (\lambda f.\ (f\ x)))$ denotes the function which when applied to E yields $(\lambda f.\ (f\ x))\,[E/x]$, i.e. $(\lambda f.\ (f\ E))$. This is the function which when applied to E' yields $(f\ E)\,[E'/f]$ i.e. $(E'\ E)$. Thus

$$((\lambda x.\ (\lambda f.\ (f\ x)))\ E) = (\lambda f.\ (f\ E))$$

and

$$((\lambda f.\ (f\ E))\ E') = (E'\ E)$$

□

Exercise 41
Describe the function denoted by $(\lambda x.\ (\lambda y.\ y))$. □

Example: Section 5.3 describes how numbers can be represented by λ-expressions. Assume that this has been done and that $\underline{0}$, $\underline{1}$, $\underline{2}$, ... are λ-expressions which represent 0, 1, 2, ..., respectively. Assume also that **add** is a λ-expression denoting a function satisfying:

$$((\text{add } \underline{m})\ \underline{n}) = \underline{m+n}.$$

Then $(\lambda x.\ ((\text{add } \underline{1})\ x))$ is a λ-expression denoting the function that transforms $\underline{n}$ to $\underline{1+n}$, and $(\lambda x.\ (\lambda y.\ ((\text{add } x)y)))$ is a λ-expression denoting the function that transforms $\underline{m}$ to the function which when applied to $\underline{n}$ yields $\underline{m+n}$, namely $\lambda y.\ ((\text{add } \underline{m})y))$. □

The relationship between the function **sum** in (ii) at the beginning of this section (page 60) and the function **add** in the previous example is explained in Section 5.5.

4.2   Notational conventions

The following conventions help minimize the number of brackets one has to write.

1. Function application associates to the left, i.e. $E_1\ E_2\ \cdots\ E_n$ means $((\ \cdots\ (E_1\ E_2)\ \cdots\ )\ E_n)$. For example:

$E_1\ E_2$	means	$(E_1\ E_2)$
$E_1\ E_2\ E_3$	means	$((E_1\ E_2)E_3)$
$E_1\ E_2\ E_3\ E_4$	means	$(((E_1\ E_2)E_3)E_4)$

2. $\lambda V.\ E_1\ E_2\ \ldots\ E_n$ means $(\lambda V.\ (E_1\ E_2\ \ldots\ E_n))$. Thus the scope of '$\lambda V$' extends as far to the right as possible.

3. $\lambda V_1\ \cdots\ V_n.\ E$ means $(\lambda V_1.\ (\ \cdots\ .\ (\lambda V_n.\ E)\ \cdots\ ))$. For example:

$\lambda x\ y.\ E$	means	$(\lambda x.\ (\lambda y.\ E))$
$\lambda x\ y\ z.\ E$	means	$(\lambda x.\ (\lambda y.\ (\lambda z.\ E)))$
$\lambda x\ y\ z\ w.\ E$	means	$(\lambda x.\ (\lambda y.\ (\lambda z.\ (\lambda w.\ E))))$

Example: $\lambda x\ y.\ \text{add } y\ x$ means $(\lambda x.\ (\lambda y.\ ((\text{add } y)\ x)))$. □

4.3   Free and bound variables

An occurrence of a variable V in a λ-expression is *free* if it is not within the scope of a 'λV', otherwise it is *bound*. For example

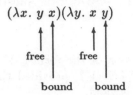

4.4   Conversion rules

In Chapter 5 it is explained how λ-expressions can be used to represent data objects like numbers, strings etc. For example, an arithmetic expression like $(2 + 3) \times 5$ can be represented as a λ-expression and its 'value' 25 can also be represented as a λ-expression. The process of 'simplifying' $(2+3) \times 5$ to 25 will be represented by a process called *conversion* (or *reduction*). The rules of λ-conversion described below are very general, yet when they are applied to λ-expressions representing arithmetic expressions they simulate arithmetical evaluation.

There are three kinds of λ-conversion called α-conversion, β-conversion and η-conversion (the original motivation for these names is not clear). In stating the conversion rules the notation $E[E'/V]$ is used to mean the result of substituting E' for each *free* occurrence of V in E. The substitution is called *valid* if and only if no free variable in E' becomes bound in $E[E'/V]$. Substitution is described in more detail in Section 4.8.

The rules of λ-conversion

- **α-conversion.**

    Any abstraction of the form $\lambda V.\ E$ can be converted to $\lambda V'.\ E[V'/V]$ provided the substitution of V' for V in E is valid.

- **β-conversion.**

    Any application of the form $(\lambda V.\ E_1)\ E_2$ can be converted to $E_1[E_2/V]$, provided the substitution of E_2 for V in E_1 is valid.

- **η-conversion.**

    Any abstraction of the form $\lambda V.\ (E\ V)$ in which V has no free occurrence in E can be reduced to E.

The following notation will be used:

- $E_1 \xrightarrow{\alpha} E_2$ means E_1 α-converts to E_2.

- $E_1 \xrightarrow{\beta} E_2$ means E_1 β-converts to E_2.

- $E_1 \xrightarrow{\eta} E_2$ means E_1 η-converts to E_2.

In Section 4.4.4 below this notation is extended.

The most important kind of conversion is β-conversion; it is the one that can be used to simulate arbitrary evaluation mechanisms. α-conversion is to do with the technical manipulation of bound variables and η-conversion expresses the fact that two functions that always give the same results on the same arguments are equal (see Section 4.7). The next three subsections give further explanation and examples of the three kinds of conversion (note that 'conversion' and 'reduction' are used below as synonyms).

4.4.1   α-conversion

A λ-expression (necessarily an abstraction) to which α-reduction can be applied is called an *α-redex*. The term 'redex' abbreviates 'reducible expression'. The rule of α-conversion just says that bound variables can be renamed provided no 'name-clashes' occur.

Examples

$$\lambda x.\ x \xrightarrow{\alpha} \lambda y.\ y$$

$$\lambda x.\ f\ x \xrightarrow{\alpha} \lambda y.\ f\ y$$

It is *not* the case that

$$\lambda x.\ \lambda y.\ \textbf{add}\ x\ y \xrightarrow{\alpha} \lambda y.\ \lambda y.\ \textbf{add}\ y\ y$$

because the substitution $(\lambda y.\ \textbf{add}\ x\ y)[y/x]$ is not valid since the y that replaces x becomes bound. $\Box$

4.4.2 β-conversion

A λ-expression (necessarily an application) to which β-reduction can be applied is called a β-*redex*. The rule of β-conversion is like the evaluation of a function call in a programming language: the body E_1 of the function $\lambda V.\ E_1$ is evaluated in an environment in which the 'formal parameter' V is bound to the 'actual parameter' E_2.

Examples

$$(\lambda x.\ f\ x)\ E \xrightarrow{\beta} f\ E$$

$$(\lambda x.\ (\lambda y.\ \textbf{add}\ x\ y))\ \underline{3} \xrightarrow{\beta} \lambda y.\ \textbf{add}\ \underline{3}\ y$$

$$(\lambda y.\ \textbf{add}\ \underline{3}\ y)\ \underline{4} \xrightarrow{\beta} \textbf{add}\ \underline{3}\ \underline{4}$$

It is *not* the case that

$$(\lambda x.\ (\lambda y.\ \textbf{add}\ x\ y))\ (\textbf{square}\ y) \xrightarrow{\beta} \lambda y.\ \textbf{add}\ (\textbf{square}\ y)\ y$$

because the substition $(\lambda y.\ \textbf{add}\ x\ y)[(\textbf{square}\ y)/x]$ is not valid, since y is free in $(\textbf{square}\ y)$ but becomes bound after substitution for x in $(\lambda y.\ \textbf{add}\ x\ y)$. $\Box$

It takes some practice to parse λ-expressions according to the conventions of Section 4.2 so as to identify the β-redexes. For example, consider the application:

$$(\lambda x.\ \lambda y.\ \textbf{add}\ x\ y)\ \underline{3}\ \underline{4}.$$

Putting in brackets according to the conventions expands this to:

$$(((\lambda x. \; (\lambda y. \; ((\textbf{add} \; x) \; y))) \; \underline{3}) \; \underline{4})$$

which has the form:

$$((\lambda x. \; E) \; \underline{3}) \; \underline{4}$$

where

$$E = \; (\lambda y. \; \textbf{add} \; x \; y)$$

$(\lambda x. \; E) \; \underline{3}$ is a β-redex and could be reduced to $E\,[\underline{3}/x]$.

4.4.3 η-conversion

A λ-expression (necessarily an abstraction) to which η-reduction can be applied is called an η-redex. The rule of η-conversion expresses the property that two functions are equal if they give the same results when applied to the same arguments. This property is called *extensionality* and is discussed further in Section 4.7. For example, η-conversion ensures that $\lambda x. \; (\textbf{sin} \; x)$ and $\textbf{sin}$ denote the same function. More generally, $\lambda V. \; (E \; V)$ denotes the function which when applied to an argument E' returns $(E \; V)\,[E'/V]$. If V does not occur free in E then $(E \; V)\,[E'/V] = (E \; E')$. Thus $\lambda V. \; E \; V$ and E both yield the same result, namely $E \; E'$, when applied to the same arguments and hence they denote the same function.

Examples

$$\lambda x. \; \textbf{add} \; x \; \xrightarrow[\eta]{} \; \textbf{add}$$

$$\lambda y. \; \textbf{add} \; x \; y \; \xrightarrow[\eta]{} \; \textbf{add} \; x$$

It is *not* the case that

$$\lambda x. \; \textbf{add} \; x \; x \; \xrightarrow[\eta]{} \; \textbf{add} \; x$$

because x is free in $\textbf{add} \; x$. □

4.4.4   Generalized conversions

The definitions of $\xrightarrow[\alpha]{}$, $\xrightarrow[\beta]{}$ and $\xrightarrow[\eta]{}$ can be generalized as follows:

- $E_1 \; \xrightarrow[\alpha]{} \; E_2$ if E_2 can be got from E_1 by α-converting any subterm.

- $E_1 \xrightarrow{\beta} E_2$ if E_2 can be got from E_1 by β-converting any subterm.

- $E_1 \xrightarrow{\eta} E_2$ if E_2 can be got from E_1 by η-converting any subterm.

Examples

$$((\lambda x.\ \lambda y.\ \text{add } x\ y)\ \underline{3})\ \underline{4} \xrightarrow{\beta} (\lambda y.\ \text{add } \underline{3}\ y)\ \underline{4}$$

$$(\lambda y.\ \text{add } \underline{3}\ y)\ \underline{4} \xrightarrow{\beta} \text{add } \underline{3}\ \underline{4}$$

□

The first of these is a β-conversion in the generalized sense because $(\lambda y.\ \text{add } \underline{3}\ y)\underline{4}$ is obtained from $((\lambda x.\ \lambda y.\ \text{add } x\ y)\underline{3})\underline{4}$ (which is not itself a β-redex) by reducing the subexpression $(\lambda x.\ \lambda y.\ \text{add } x\ y)\underline{3}$. We will sometimes write a sequence of conversions like the two above as:

$$((\lambda x.\ \lambda y.\ \text{add } x\ y)\ \underline{3})\ \underline{4} \xrightarrow{\beta} (\lambda y.\ \text{add } \underline{3}\ y)\ \underline{4} \xrightarrow{\beta} \text{add } \underline{3}\ \underline{4}$$

Exercise 42
Which of the three β-reductions below are generalized conversions (i.e. reductions of subexpressions) and which are conversions in the sense defined on page 63? □

(i) $(\lambda x.\ x)\ \underline{1} \xrightarrow{\beta} \underline{1}$

(ii) $(\lambda y.\ y)\ ((\lambda x.\ x)\ \underline{1}) \xrightarrow{\beta} (\lambda y.\ y)\underline{1} \xrightarrow{\beta} \underline{1}$

(iii) $(\lambda y.\ y)\ ((\lambda x.\ x)\ \underline{1}) \xrightarrow{\beta} (\lambda x.\ x)\ \underline{1} \xrightarrow{\beta} \underline{1}$

In reductions (ii) and (iii) in the exercise above one starts with the same λ-expression, but reduce redexes in different orders.

An important property of β-reductions is that no matter in which order one does them, one always ends up with equivalent results. If there are several disjoint redexes in an expression, one can reduce them in parallel. Note, however, that some reduction sequences may never terminate. This is discussed further in connection with the normalization theorem of Chapter 7. It is a current hot research topic in 'fifth-generation computing' to design processors which exploit parallel evaluation to speed up the execution of functional programs.

4.5   Equality of λ-expressions

The three conversion rules preserve the meaning of λ-expressions, i.e. if E_1 can be converted to E_2 then E_1 and E_2 denote the same function. This property of conversion should be intuitively clear. It is possible to give a mathematical definition of the function denoted by a λ-expression and then to prove that this function is unchanged by α-, β- or η-conversion. Doing this is surprisingly difficult [67] and is beyond the scope of this book.

We will simply *define* two λ-expressions to be equal if they can be transformed into each other by a sequence of (forwards or backwards) λ-conversions. It is important to be clear about the difference between *equality* and *identity*. Two λ-expressions are identical if they consist of *exactly* the same sequence of characters; they are equal if one can be converted to the other. For example, $\lambda x.\ x$ is equal to $\lambda y.\ y$, but not identical to it. The following notation is used:

- $E_1 \equiv E_2$ means E_1 and E_2 are identical.

- $E_1 = E_2$ means E_1 and E_2 are equal.

Equality ($=$) is defined in terms of identity ($\equiv$) and conversion ($\underset{\alpha}{\longrightarrow}$, $\underset{\beta}{\longrightarrow}$ and $\underset{\eta}{\longrightarrow}$) as follows.

Equality of λ-expressions

If E and E' are λ-expressions then $E = E'$ if $E \equiv E'$ or there exist expressions E_1, E_2, ..., E_n such that:

1. $E \equiv E_1$

2. $E' \equiv E_n$

3. For each i either

     (a) $E_i \underset{\alpha}{\longrightarrow} E_{i+1}$ or $E_i \underset{\beta}{\longrightarrow} E_{i+1}$ or $E_i \underset{\eta}{\longrightarrow} E_{i+1}$ or

     (b) $E_{i+1} \underset{\alpha}{\longrightarrow} E_i$ or $E_{i+1} \underset{\beta}{\longrightarrow} E_i$ or $E_{i+1} \underset{\eta}{\longrightarrow} E_i$.

Examples

$$(\lambda x.\ x)\ \underline{1}\ =\ \underline{1}$$

$$(\lambda x.\ x)\ ((\lambda y.\ y)\ \underline{1}) = \underline{1}$$

$$(\lambda x.\ \lambda y.\ \text{add}\ x\ y)\ \underline{3}\ \underline{4} = \text{add}\ \underline{3}\ \underline{4}$$

□

From the definition of = it follows that:

(i) For any E it is the case that $E = E$ (equality is *reflexive*).

(ii) If $E = E'$, then $E' = E$ (equality is *symmetric*).

(iii) If $E = E'$ and $E' = E''$, then $E = E''$ (equality is *transitive*).

If a relation is reflexive, symmetric and transitive then it is called an *equivalence relation*. Thus = is an equivalence relation.

Another important property of = is that if $E_1 = E_2$ and if E'_1 and E'_2 are two λ-expressions that only differ in that where one contains E_1 the other contains E_2, then $E'_1 = E'_2$. This property is called *Leibnitz's law*. It holds because the same sequence of reduction for getting from E_1 to E_2 can be used for getting from E'_1 to E'_2. For example, if $E_1 = E_2$, then by Leibnitz's law $\lambda V.\ E_1 = \lambda V.\ E_2$.

It is essential for the substitutions in the α- and β-reductions to be valid. The validity requirement disallows, for example, $\lambda x.\ (\lambda y.\ x)$ being α-reduced to $\lambda y.\ (\lambda y.\ y)$ (since y becomes bound after substitution for x in $\lambda y.\ x$). If this invalid substitution were permitted, then it would follow by the definition of = that:

$$\lambda x.\ \lambda y.\ x = \lambda y.\ \lambda y.\ y$$

But then since:

$$(\lambda x.\ (\lambda y\ .x))\ \underline{1}\ \underline{2} \xrightarrow{\beta} (\lambda y.\ \underline{1})\ \underline{2} \xrightarrow{\beta} \underline{1}$$

and

$$(\lambda y.\ (\lambda y.\ y))\ \underline{1}\ \underline{2} \xrightarrow{\beta} (\lambda y.\ y)\ \underline{2} \xrightarrow{\beta} \underline{2}$$

one would be forced to conclude that $\underline{1} = \underline{2}$. More generally by replacing $\underline{1}$ and $\underline{2}$ by any two expressions, it could be shown that any two expressions are equal!

Exercise 43
Find an example which shows that if substitutions in β-reductions are allowed to be invalid, then it follows that any two λ-expressions are equal.
□

Example: If V_1, V_2, ..., V_n are all distinct and none of them occur free in any of E_1, E_2,..., E_n, then

$$(\lambda V_1\ V_2 \cdots V_n.\ E)\ E_1\ E_2 \cdots E_n$$
$$=\quad ((\lambda V_1.\ (\lambda V_2 \cdots V_n.\ E))E_1)\ E_2 \cdots E_n$$
$$\underset{\beta}{\longrightarrow}\quad ((\lambda V_2 \cdots V_n.\ E)[E_1/V_1])\ E_2 \cdots E_n$$
$$=\quad (\lambda V_2 \ldots V_n.\ E[E_1/V_1])E_2 \cdots E_n$$
$$\vdots$$
$$=\quad E[E_1/V_1][E_2/V_2] \cdots [E_n/V_n]$$

□

Exercise 44
In the last example, where was the assumption used that V_1, V_2,..., V_n are all distinct and that none of them occur free in any of E_1, E_2,..., E_n? □

Exercise 45
Find an example to show that if $V_1 = V_2$, then even if V_2 is not free in E_1, it is not necessarily the case that:

$$(\lambda V_1 V_2.E)\ E_1\ E_2 = E[E_1/V_1][E_2/V_2]$$

□

Exercise 46
Find an example to show that if $V_1 \neq V_2$, but V_2 occurs free in E_1, then it is not necessarily the case that:

$$(\lambda V_1 V_2.\ E)\ E_1\ E_2 = E[E_1/V_1][E_2/V_2]$$

□

4.6   The $\longrightarrow$ relation

In the previous section $E_1 = E_2$ was defined to mean that E_2 could be obtained from E_1 by a sequence of forwards *or backwards* conversions. A special case of this is when E_2 is got from E_1 using only forwards conversions. This is written $E_1 \longrightarrow E_2$.

Definition of $\longrightarrow$

If E and E' are λ-expressions, then $E \longrightarrow E'$ if $E \equiv E'$ or there exist expressions $E_1, E_2, \ldots, E_n$ such that:

1. $E \equiv E_1$

2. $E' \equiv E_n$

3. For each i either $E_i \xrightarrow{\alpha} E_{i+1}$ or $E_i \xrightarrow{\beta} E_{i+1}$ or $E_i \xrightarrow{\eta} E_{i+1}$.

Notice that the definition of $\longrightarrow$ is just like the definition of $=$ on page 68 except that part (b) of 3 is missing.

Exercise 47
Find E, E' such that $E = E'$ but it is not the case that $E \longrightarrow E'$. $\square$

Exercise 48
[very hard!] Show that if $E_1 = E_2$, then there exists E such that $E_1 \longrightarrow E$ and $E_2 \longrightarrow E$. (This property is called the Church-Rosser theorem. Some of its consequences are discussed in Chapter 7.) $\square$

4.7 Extensionality

Suppose V does not occur free in E_1 or E_2 and

$$E_1 \ V = E_2 \ V$$

Then by Leibnitz's law (see page 69)

$$\lambda V. \ E_1 \ V = \lambda V. \ E_2 \ V$$

so by η-reduction applied to both sides

$$E_1 = E_2$$

It is often convenient to prove that two λ-expressions are equal using this property, i.e. to prove $E_1 = E_2$ by proving $E_1 \ V = E_2 \ V$ for some V not occuring free in E_1 or E_2. We will refer to such proofs as being *by extensionality*.

Exercise 49
Show that

$$(\lambda f\ g\ x.\ f\ x\ (g\ x))\ (\lambda x\ y.\ x)\ (\lambda x\ y.\ x)\ =\ \lambda x.\ x$$

□

4.8   Substitution

At the beginning of Section 4.4 $E[E'/V]$ was defined to mean the result of substituting E' for each *free* occurrence of V in E. The substitution was said to be valid if no free variable in E' became bound in $E[E'/I]$. In the definitions of α- and β-conversion, it was stipulated that the substitutions involved must be valid. Thus, for example, it was only the case that

$$(\lambda V.\ E_1)\ E_2 \xrightarrow[\beta]{} E_1[E_2/V]$$

as long as the substitution$E_1[E_2/V]$ was valid.

It is very convenient to extend the meaning of $E[E'/V]$ so that we don't have to worry about validity. This is achieved by the definition below which has the property that for *all* expressions E, E_1 and E_2 and *all* variables V and V':

$$(\lambda V.\ E_1)\ E_2 \longrightarrow E_1[E_2/V] \quad \text{and} \quad \lambda V.\ E \longrightarrow \lambda V'.\ E[V'/V]$$

To ensure this property holds, $E[E'/V]$ is defined recursively on the structure of E as follows:

E	$E[E'/V]$
V	E'
V' (where $V \neq V'$)	V'
$E_1 \, E_2$	$E_1[E'/V] \; E_2[E'/V]$
$\lambda V. \, E_1$	$\lambda V. \, E_1$
$\lambda V'. \, E_1$ (where $V \neq V'$ and V' is not free in E')	$\lambda V'. \, E_1[E'/V]$
$\lambda V'. \, E_1$ (where $V \neq V'$ and V' is free in E')	$\lambda V''. \, E_1[V''/V'][E'/V]$ where V'' is a variable not free in E' or E_1

This particular definition of $E[E'/V]$ is based on (but not identical to) the one in Appendix C of [4]. A LISP implementation of it is given in Chapter 12 on page 228.

To illustrate how this works consider $(\lambda y. \, y \, x)[y/x]$. Since y is free in $y \, x$ we must use the last case of the table above. Since z does not occur in $y \, x$ or y,

$$(\lambda y. \, y \, x)[y/x] \equiv \lambda z. \, (y \, x)[z/y][y/x] \equiv \lambda z. \, (z \, x)[y/x] \equiv \lambda z. \, z \, y$$

In the last line of the table above, the particular choice of V'' is not specified. Any variable not occurring in E' or E_1 will do. In Chapter 12 an implementation of substitution in LISP is given.

A good discussion of substitution can be found in the book by Hindley and Seldin [31] where various technical properties are stated and proved. The following exercise is taken from that book.

Exercise 50
Use the table above to work out

  (i) $(\lambda y. \, x \, (\lambda x. \, x))[(\lambda y. \, y \, x)/x]$.

  (ii) $(y \, (\lambda z. \, x \, z))[(\lambda y. \, z \, y)/x]$.

□

It is straightforward, but rather tedious, to prove from the definition of $E[E'/V]$ just given that indeed

$$(\lambda V.\ E_1)\ E_2 \longrightarrow E_1[E_2/V] \quad \text{and} \quad \lambda V.\ E \longrightarrow \lambda V'.\ E[V'/V]$$

for all expressions E, E_1 and E_2 and all variables V and V'.

In Chapter 8 it will be shown how the theory of combinators can be used to decompose the complexities of substitution into simpler operations. Instead of combinators it is possible to use the so-called *nameless terms* of De Bruijn [8]. De Bruijn's idea is that variables can be thought of as 'pointers' to the λs that bind them. Instead of 'labelling' λs with names (i.e. bound variables) and then pointing to them via these names, one can point to the appropriate λ by giving the number of levels 'upwards' needed to reach it. For example, $\lambda x.\ \lambda y.\ x\ y$ would be represented by $\lambda\lambda 2\ 1$. As a more complicated example, consider the expression below in which we indicate the number of levels separating a variable from the λ that binds it.

$$\lambda x.\ \lambda y.\ x\ y\ (\lambda y.\ x\ y\ y)$$

In De Bruijn's notation this is $\lambda\lambda 2\ 1\ \lambda 3\ 1\ 1$.

A free variable in an expression is represented by a number bigger than the depth of λs above it; different free variables being assigned different numbers. For example,

$$\lambda x.\ (\lambda y.\ y\ x\ z)\ x\ y\ w$$

would be represented by

$$\lambda(\lambda 1\ 2\ 3)\ 1\ 2\ 4$$

Since there are only two λs above the occurrence of 3, this number must denote a free variable; similarly there is only one λ above the second occurrence of 2 and the occurrence of 4, so these too must be free variables. Note that 2 could not be used to represent w since this had already been used to represent the free y; we thus chose the first available number bigger than 2 (3 was already in use representing z).

Care must be taken to assign big enough numbers to free variables. For example, the first occurrence of z in $\lambda x.\ z\ (\lambda y.\ z)$ could be represented by 2, but the second occurrence requires 3; since they are the same variable we must use 3.

Example: With De Bruijn's scheme $\lambda x.\ x\ (\lambda y.\ x\ y\ y)$ would be represented by $\lambda 1(\lambda 2\ 1\ 1)$. □

Exercise 51
What λ-expression is represented by $\lambda 2(\lambda 2)$? □

Exercise 52
Describe an algorithm for computing the De Bruijn representation of the expression $E[E'/V]$ from the representations of E and E'. □

Chapter 5

Representing Things in the λ-calculus

The representation in the λ-calculus of various data objects (e.g. numbers), data-structures (e.g. pairs) and useful functions (e.g. addition) is described. Definition by recursion using the fixed-point operator Y is explained. It is shown that all the recursive functions can be represented by suitable λ-expressions.

The λ-calculus appears at first sight to be a very primitive language. However, it can be used to represent most of the objects and structures needed for modern programming. The idea is to code these objects and structures in such a way that they have the required properties. For example, to represent the truth values *true* and *false* and the Boolean function ¬ ('not'), λ-expressions **true**, **false** and **not** are devised with the properties that:

$$\textbf{not true} = \textbf{false}$$
$$\textbf{not false} = \textbf{true}$$

To represent the Boolean function ∧ ('and') a λ-expression **and** is devised such that:

$$\textbf{and true true} = \textbf{true}$$
$$\textbf{and true false} = \textbf{false}$$
$$\textbf{and false true} = \textbf{false}$$
$$\textbf{and false false} = \textbf{false}$$

and to represent ∨ ('or') an expression **or** such that:

$$\textbf{or true true} = \textbf{true}$$
$$\textbf{or true false} = \textbf{true}$$
$$\textbf{or false true} = \textbf{true}$$
$$\textbf{or false false} = \textbf{false}$$

The λ-expressions used to represent things may appear completely un-motivated at first. However, the definitions are chosen so that they work together in unison.

We will write

$$\text{LET} \sim = \lambda\text{-expression}$$

to introduce $\sim$ as a new notation. Usually $\sim$ will just be a name such as **true** or **and**. Such names are written in **bold** face, or underlined, to distinguish them from variables. Thus, for example, *true* is a variable but **true** is the λ-expression $\lambda x.\ \lambda y.\ x$ (see Section 5.1 below) and 2 is a number but $\underline{2}$ is the λ-expression $\lambda f\ x.\ f(f\ x)$ (see Section 5.3).

Sometimes $\sim$ will be a more complicated form like the conditional notation $(E \to E_1 \mid E_2)$.

5.1   Truth-values and the conditional

This section defines λ-expressions **true**, **false**, **not** and $(E \to E_1 \mid E_2)$ with the following properties:

$$\textbf{not true} = \textbf{false}$$
$$\textbf{not false} = \textbf{true}$$

$$(\textbf{true} \to E_1 \mid E_2) = E_1$$
$$(\textbf{false} \to E_1 \mid E_2) = E_2$$

The λ-expressions **true** and **false** represent the truth-values *true* and *false*, **not** represents the negation function $\neg$ and $(E \to E_1 \mid E_2)$ represents the conditional 'if E then E_1 else E_2'.

There are infinitely many different ways of representing the truth-values and negation that work; the ones used here are traditional and have been developed over the years by logicians.

LET true $= \lambda x.\ \lambda y.\ x$

LET false $= \lambda x.\ \lambda y.\ y$

LET not $= \lambda t.\ t$ **false true**

It is easy to use the rules of λ-conversion to show that these definitions have the desired properties. For example:

$$\textbf{not true} = (\lambda t.\ t\ \textbf{false true})\ \textbf{true}\ \text{(definition of \textbf{not})}$$

$$= \textbf{true false true} \qquad (\beta\text{-conversion})$$
$$= (\lambda x.\ \lambda y.\ x)\ \textbf{false true} \ (\text{definition of } \textbf{true})$$
$$= (\lambda y.\ \textbf{false})\ \textbf{true} \qquad (\beta\text{-conversion})$$
$$= \textbf{false} \qquad (\beta\text{-conversion})$$

Similarly **not false** = **true**.

Conditional expressions $(E \rightarrow E_1 \mid E_2)$ can be defined as follows:

LET $(E \rightarrow E_1 \mid E_2) = (E\ E_1\ E_2)$

This means that for any λ-expressions E, E_1 and E_2, $(E \rightarrow E_1 \mid E_2)$ stands for $(E\ E_1\ E_2)$.

The conditional notation behaves as it should:

$$(\textbf{true} \rightarrow E_1 \mid E_2) = \textbf{true}\ E_1\ E_2$$
$$= (\lambda x\ y.\ x)\ E_1\ E_2$$
$$= E_1$$

and

$$(\textbf{false} \rightarrow E_1 \mid E_2) = \textbf{false}\ E_1\ E_2$$
$$= (\lambda x\ y.\ y)\ E_1\ E_2$$
$$= E_2$$

Exercise 53

Let **and** be the λ-expression $\lambda x\ y.\ (x \rightarrow y \mid \textbf{false})$. Show that:

$$\textbf{and true true} = \textbf{true}$$
$$\textbf{and true false} = \textbf{false}$$
$$\textbf{and false true} = \textbf{false}$$
$$\textbf{and false false} = \textbf{false}$$

☐

Exercise 54

Devise a λ-expression **or** such that:

$$\textbf{or true true} = \textbf{true}$$
$$\textbf{or true false} = \textbf{true}$$
$$\textbf{or false true} = \textbf{true}$$
$$\textbf{or false false} = \textbf{false}$$

☐

5.2   Pairs and tuples

The following abbreviations represent pairs and n-tuples in the λ-calculus.

LET fst $= \lambda p.\ p$ true

LET snd $= \lambda p.\ p$ false

LET $(E_1, E_2) = \lambda f.\ f\ E_1\ E_2$

(E_1, E_2) is a λ-expression representing an ordered pair whose first component (i.e. E_1) is accessed with the function **fst** and whose second component (i.e. E_2) is accessed with **snd**. The following calculation shows how the various definitions co-operate together to give the right results.

$$
\begin{aligned}
\textbf{fst }(E_1, E_2) &= (\lambda p.\ p\ \textbf{true})\ (E_1, E_2) \\
&= (E_1, E_2)\ \textbf{true} \\
&= (\lambda f.\ f\ E_1\ E_2)\ \textbf{true} \\
&= \textbf{true}\ E_1\ E_2 \\
&= (\lambda x\ y.\ x)\ E_1\ E_2 \\
&= E_1
\end{aligned}
$$

Exercise 55
Show that $\textbf{snd}(E_1, E_2) = E_2$.
□

A pair is a data-structure with two components. The generalization to n components is called an *n-tuple* and is easily defined in terms of pairs.

LET $(E_1, E_2, \ldots, E_n) = (E_1, (E_2, (\cdots (E_{n-1}, E_n) \cdots)))$

$(E_1, \ldots, E_n)$ is an *n-tuple* with *components* $E_1, \ldots, E_n$ and *length* n. Pairs are 2-tuples. The abbreviations defined next provide a way of extracting the components of n-tuples.

LET $E \overset{n}{\downarrow} 1 = $ fst E

LET $E \overset{n}{\downarrow} 2 = $ fst(snd E)

$\vdots$

LET $E \overset{n}{\downarrow} i = $ fst(snd(snd($\cdots$(snd $\underbrace{E)\cdots)))}_{i-1 \text{ snds}}$ (if $i < n$)

$\vdots$

LET $E \overset{n}{\downarrow} n = \underbrace{\text{snd(snd}(\ldots(\text{snd }}_{n-1 \text{ snds}} E)\ldots)))$

It is easy to see that these definitions work, for example:

$$(E_1, E_2, \ldots, E_n) \overset{n}{\downarrow} 1 = (E_1, (E_2, (\ldots))) \overset{n}{\downarrow} 1$$
$$= \text{fst } (E_1, (E_2, (\ldots)))$$
$$= E_1$$

$$(E_1, E_2, \ldots, E_n) \overset{n}{\downarrow} 2 = (E_1, (E_2, (\ldots))) \overset{n}{\downarrow} 2$$
$$= \text{fst } (\text{snd } (E_1, (E_2, (\ldots))))$$
$$= \text{fst } (E_2, (\ldots))$$
$$= E_2$$

In general $(E_1, E_2, \ldots, E_n) \overset{n}{\downarrow} i = E_i$ for all i such that $1 \leq i \leq n$.

Convention

We will usually just write $E \downarrow i$ instead of $E \overset{n}{\downarrow} i$ when it is clear from the context what n should be. For example,

$$(E_1, \ldots, E_n) \downarrow i = E_i \quad (\text{where } 1 \leq i \leq n)$$

5.3   Numbers

There are many ways to represent numbers by λ-expressions, each with their own advantages and disadvantages [72,40]. The goal is to define for each number n a λ-expression $\underline{n}$ that represents it. We also want to define λ-expressions to represent the primitive arithmetical operations. For example, we will need λ-expressions **suc**, **pre**, **add** and **iszero** representing the successor function $(n \mapsto n + 1)$, the predecessor function $(n \mapsto n-1)$, addition and a test for zero, respectively. These λ-expressions will represent the numbers correctly if they have the following properties:

$$\text{suc } \underline{n} = \underline{n+1} \quad \text{(for all numbers } n)$$

$$\text{pre } \underline{n} = \underline{n-1} \quad \text{(for all numbers } n)$$

$$\text{add } \underline{m} \; \underline{n} = \underline{m+n} \quad \text{(for all numbers } m \text{ and } n)$$

$$\text{iszero } \underline{0} = \text{true}$$

$$\text{iszero } (\text{suc } \underline{n}) = \text{false}$$

The representation of numbers described here is the original one due to Church. In order to explain this it is convenient to define $f^n \; x$ to mean n applications of f to x. For example,

$$f^5 \; x \;=\; f(f(f(f(f \; x))))$$

By convention $f^0 \; x$ is defined to mean x. More generally:

$$\boxed{\begin{array}{l} \text{LET } E^0 \; E' \;=\; E' \\[2mm] \text{LET } E^n \; E' \;=\; \underbrace{E(E(\cdots(E \; E') \cdots))}_{n \; E\text{s}} \end{array}}$$

Note that $E^n(EE') \;=\; E^{n+1} \; E' \;=\; E(E^n \; E')$; we will use the fact later.

Example

$$f^4 x \;=\; f(f(f(f \; x))) \;=\; f(f^3 x) \;=\; f^3(f \; x)$$

□

Using the notation just introduced we can now define Church's numerals. Notice how the definition of the λ-expression $\underline{n}$ below encodes a unary representation of n.

$$\text{LET } \underline{0} = \lambda f\ x.\ x$$

$$\text{LET } \underline{1} = \lambda f\ x.\ f\ x$$

$$\text{LET } \underline{2} = \lambda f\ x.\ f(f\ x)$$

$$\vdots$$

$$\text{LET } \underline{n} = \lambda f\ x.\ f^n\ x$$

$$\vdots$$

The representations of **suc**, **add** and **iszero** are now magically pulled out of a hat. The best way to see how they work is to think of them as operating on unary representations of numbers. The exercises that follow should help.

$$\text{LET suc} = \lambda n\ f\ x.\ n\ f(f\ x)$$

$$\text{LET add} = \lambda m\ n\ f\ x.\ m\ f\ (n\ f\ x)$$

$$\text{LET iszero} = \lambda n.\ n\ (\lambda x.\ \text{false})\ \text{true}$$

Exercise 56
Show:

  (i) **suc** $\underline{0} = \underline{1}$

  (ii) **suc** $\underline{5} = \underline{6}$

  (iii) **iszero** $\underline{0} = $ **true**

  (iv) **iszero** $\underline{5} = $ **false**

  (v) **add** $\underline{0}\ \underline{1} = \underline{1}$

  (vi) **add** $\underline{2}\ \underline{3} = \underline{5}$

□

Exercise 57
Show for all numbers m and n:

  (i) **suc** $\underline{n} = \underline{n{+}1}$

  (ii) **iszero** (**suc** $\underline{n}$) $= $ **false**

  (iii) **add** $\underline{0}\ \underline{n} = \underline{n}$

(iv) **add** $\underline{m}$ $\underline{0}$ = $\underline{m}$

(v) **add** $\underline{m}$ $\underline{n}$ = $\underline{m+n}$

□

The predecesor function is harder to define than the other primitive functions. The idea is that the predecessor of $\underline{n}$ is defined by using $\lambda f\ x.\ f^n\ x$ (i.e. $\underline{n}$) to obtain a function that applies f only $n-1$ times. The trick is to 'throw away' the first application of f in f^n. To achieve this, we first define a function **prefn** that operates on pairs and has the property that:

(i) **prefn** f (**true**, x) = (**false**, x)

(ii) **prefn** f (**false**, x) = (**false**, $f\ x$)

From this it follows that:

(iii) (**prefn** f)^n (**false**, x) = (**false**, $f^n\ x$)

(iv) (**prefn** f)^n (**true**, x) = (**false**, $f^{n-1}\ x$)   (if $n > 0$)

Thus n applications of **prefn** to (**true**, x) result in $n-1$ applications of f to x. With this idea, the definition of the predecessor function **pre** is straightforward. Before giving it, here is the definition of **prefn**:

> **LET prefn** = $\lambda f\ p.$ (**false**, (**fst** $p \rightarrow$ **snd** $p\ |\ (f(\text{snd}\ p))))$

Exercise 58
Show **prefn** f (b, x) = (**false**, $(b \rightarrow x\ |\ f\ x))$ and hence:

(i) **prefn** f (**true**, x) = (**false**, x)

(ii) **prefn** f (**false**, x) = (**false**, $f\ x$)

(iii) (**prefn** f)^n (**false**, x) = (**false**, $f^n\ x$)

(iv) (**prefn** f)^n (**true**, x) = (**false**, $f^{n-1}\ x$)   (if $n > 0$)

□

The predecessor function **pre** can now be defined.

> **LET pre** = $\lambda n\ f\ x.$ **snd** $(n$ (**prefn** f) (**true**, $x))$

It follows that if $n > 0$

$$\begin{aligned}
\text{pre } \underline{n} \ f \ x &= \text{snd } (\underline{n} \ (\text{prefn } f) \ (\text{true}, x)) & \text{(definition of pre)} \\
&= \text{snd } ((\text{prefn } f)^n \ (\text{true}, x)) & \text{(definition of } \underline{n}) \\
&= \text{snd}(\text{false}, f^{n-1} \ x) & \text{(by (v) above)} \\
&= f^{n-1} \ x
\end{aligned}$$

hence by extensionality (Section 4.7 on page 71)

$$\begin{aligned}
\text{pre } \underline{n} &= \lambda f \ x. \ f^{n-1} \ x \\
&= \underline{n-1} & \text{(definition of } \underline{n-1})
\end{aligned}$$

Exercise 59
Using the results of the previous exercise (or otherwise) show that

(i) $\text{pre } (\text{suc } \underline{n}) = \underline{n}$

(ii) $\text{pre } \underline{0} = \underline{0}$

□

The numeral system in the next exercise is the one used in [4] and has some advantages over Church's (e.g. the predecessor function is easier to define).

Exercise 60

$$\text{LET } \widehat{\underline{0}} = \lambda x.x$$

$$\text{LET } \widehat{\underline{1}} = (\text{false}, \widehat{\underline{0}})$$

$$\text{LET } \widehat{\underline{2}} = (\text{false}, \widehat{\underline{1}})$$

$$\vdots$$

$$\text{LET } \widehat{\underline{n+1}} = (\text{false}, \widehat{\underline{n}})$$

$$\vdots$$

Devise λ-expressions $\widehat{\text{suc}}$, $\widehat{\text{iszero}}$, $\widehat{\text{pre}}$ such that for all n:

(i) $\widehat{\text{suc}} \ \widehat{\underline{n}} = \widehat{\underline{n+1}}$

(ii) $\widehat{\text{iszero}} \ \widehat{\underline{0}} = \text{true}$

(iii) $\widehat{\text{iszero}} \ (\widehat{\text{suc}} \ \widehat{\underline{n}}) = \text{false}$

(iv) $\widehat{\text{pre}} \ (\widehat{\text{suc}} \ \widehat{\underline{n}}) = \widehat{\underline{n}}$

□

5.4   Definition by recursion

To represent the multiplication function in the λ-calculus we would like to define a λ-expression, **mult** say, such that:

$$\text{mult } m \; n = \underbrace{\text{add } n \; (\text{add } n \; (\; \cdots \; (\text{add } n \; \underline{0}) \; \cdots \;))}_{m \text{ adds}}$$

This would be achieved if **mult** could be defined to satisfy the equation:

$$\text{mult } m \; n = (\text{iszero } m \rightarrow \underline{0} \mid \text{add } n \; (\text{mult } (\text{pre } m) \; n))$$

If this held then, for example,

$$\text{mult } \underline{2} \; \underline{3} = (\text{iszero } \underline{2} \rightarrow \underline{0} \mid \text{add } \underline{3} \; (\text{mult } (\text{pre } \underline{2}) \; \underline{3}))$$

(by the equation)

$$= \text{add } \underline{3} \; (\text{mult } \underline{1} \; \underline{3})$$

(by properties of **iszero**, the conditional and **pre**)

$$= \text{add } \underline{3} \; (\text{iszero } \underline{1} \rightarrow \underline{0} \mid \text{add } \underline{3} \; (\text{mult } (\text{pre } \underline{1}) \; \underline{3}))$$

(by the equation)

$$= \text{add } \underline{3} \; (\text{add } \underline{3} \; (\text{mult } \underline{0} \; \underline{3}))$$

(by properties of **iszero**, the conditional and **pre**)

$$= \text{add } \underline{3} \; (\text{add } \underline{3} \; (\text{iszero } \underline{0} \rightarrow \underline{0} \mid \text{add } \underline{3} \; (\text{mult } (\text{pre } \underline{0}) \; \underline{3})))$$

(by the equation)

$$= \text{add } \underline{3} \; (\text{add } \underline{3} \; \underline{0})$$

(by properties of **iszero** and the conditional)

The equation above suggests that **mult** be defined by:

$$\text{mult} = \lambda m \; n. \; (\text{iszero } m \rightarrow \underline{0} \mid \text{add } n \; (\text{mult } (\text{pre } m) \; n))$$

N.B.

Unfortunately, this cannot be used to define **mult** because, as indicated by the arrow, **mult** must already be defined for the λ-expression to the right of the equals to make sense.

Fortunately, there is a technique for constructing λ-expressions that satisfy arbitrary equations. When this technique is applied to the equation above it gives the desired definition of **mult**. First define a λ-expression **Y** that, for any expression E, has the following odd property:

$$\mathbf{Y} \; E = E \; (\mathbf{Y} \; E)$$

This says that $\mathbf{Y}\ E$ is unchanged when the function E is applied to it. In general, if $E\ E' = E'$ then E' is called a *fixed point* of E. A λ-expression **Fix** with the property that **Fix** $E = E(\mathbf{Fix}\ E)$ for any E is called a *fixed-point operator*. There are known to be infinitely many different fixed-point operators [57]; $\mathbf{Y}$ is the most famous one, and its definition is:

LET $\mathbf{Y} = \lambda f.\ (\lambda x.\ f(x\ x))\ (\lambda x.\ f(x\ x))$

It is straightforward to show that $\mathbf{Y}$ is indeed a fixed-point operator:

$$
\begin{aligned}
\mathbf{Y}\ E &= (\lambda f.\ (\lambda x.\ f(x\ x))\ (\lambda x.\ f(x\ x)))\ E && \text{(definition of } \mathbf{Y}\text{)} \\
&= (\lambda x.\ E(x\ x))\ (\lambda x.\ E(x\ x)) && (\beta\text{-conversion)} \\
&= E\ ((\lambda x.\ E(x\ x))\ (\lambda x.\ E(x\ x))) && (\beta\text{-conversion)} \\
&= E\ (\mathbf{Y}\ E) && \text{(the line before last)}
\end{aligned}
$$

This calculation shows that every λ-expression E has a fixed point (namely $\mathbf{Y}\ E$); this is sometimes referred to as the *first fixed-point theorem*. The second fixed-point theorem is introduced in Section 7.1.

Armed with $\mathbf{Y}$, we can now return to the problem of solving the equation for **mult**. Suppose **multfn** is defined by

LET $\mathbf{multfn} = \lambda f\ m\ n.\ (\mathbf{iszero}\ m \rightarrow \underline{0}\ |\ \mathbf{add}\ n\ (f\ (\mathbf{pre}\ m)\ n))$

$\qquad\qquad\qquad\qquad\quad\uparrow\qquad\qquad\qquad\qquad\qquad\qquad\uparrow$

and then define **mult** by:

LET $\mathbf{mult} = \mathbf{Y}\ \mathbf{multfn}$

Then:

$$
\begin{aligned}
\mathbf{mult}\ m\ n &= (\mathbf{Y}\ \mathbf{multfn})\ m\ n && \text{(definition of } \mathbf{mult}\text{)} \\
&= \mathbf{multfn}\ (\mathbf{Y}\ \mathbf{multfn})\ m\ n && \text{(fixed-point property of } \mathbf{Y}\text{)} \\
&= \mathbf{multfn}\ \mathbf{mult}\ m\ n && \text{(definition of } \mathbf{mult}\text{)} \\
&= (\lambda f\ m\ n.\ (\mathbf{iszero}\ m \rightarrow \underline{0}\ |\ \mathbf{add}\ n\ (f\ (\mathbf{pre}\ m)\ n)))\ \mathbf{mult}\ m\ n \\
& && \text{(definition of } \mathbf{multfn}\text{)} \\
&= (\mathbf{iszero}\ m \rightarrow \underline{0}\ |\ \mathbf{add}\ n\ (\mathbf{mult}\ (\mathbf{pre}\ m)\ n)) && (\beta\text{-conversion)}
\end{aligned}
$$

An equation of the form $f\ x_1\ \cdots\ x_n = E$ is called *recursive* if f occurs free in E. $\mathbf{Y}$ provides a general way of solving such equations. Start with an equation of the form:

$$\mathbf{f}\ x_1 \ldots x_n = \ \sim\!\mathbf{f}\!\sim$$

where $\frown$f$\frown$ is some λ-expression containing **f**. To obtain an **f** so that this equation holds define:

$$\text{LET } \mathbf{f} = \mathbf{Y} \ (\lambda f \ x_1 \ldots x_n. \frown f \frown)$$

The fact that the equation is satisfied can be shown as follows:

$$\mathbf{f} \ x_1 \ldots x_n = \mathbf{Y} \ (\lambda f \ x_1 \ldots x_n. \frown f \frown) \ x_1 \ldots x_n \qquad \text{(definition of } \mathbf{f})$$
$$= (\lambda f \ x_1 \ldots x_n. \frown f \frown) \ (\mathbf{Y} \ (\lambda f \ x_1 \ldots x_n. \frown f \frown)) \ x_1 \ldots x_n$$
$$\text{(fixed-point property)}$$
$$= (\lambda f \ x_1 \ldots x_n. \frown f \frown) \ \mathbf{f} \ x_1 \ldots x_n \qquad \text{(definition of } \mathbf{f})$$
$$= \frown \mathbf{f} \frown \qquad \text{(β-conversion)}$$

Exercise 61
Construct a λ-expression **eq** such that

$$\mathbf{eq} \ m \ n = (\mathbf{iszero} \ m \rightarrow \mathbf{iszero} \ n \ |$$
$$(\mathbf{iszero} \ n \rightarrow \mathbf{false} \ | \ \mathbf{eq} \ (\mathbf{pre} \ m) \ (\mathbf{pre} \ n)))$$

□

Exercise 62
Show that if $\mathbf{Y}_1$ is defined by:

$$\text{LET } \mathbf{Y}_1 = \mathbf{Y} \ (\lambda y \ f. \ f(y \ f))$$

then $\mathbf{Y}_1$ is a fixed-point operator, i.e. for any E:

$$\mathbf{Y}_1 \ E = E \ (\mathbf{Y}_1 \ E)$$

□

The fixed-point operator in the next exercise is due to Turing (Barendregt [4], page 132).

Exercise 63
Show that $(\lambda x \ y. \ y \ (x \ x \ y)) \ (\lambda x \ y. \ y \ (x \ x \ y))$ is a fixed-point operator. □

The next exercise also comes from Barendregt's book, where it is attributed to Klop.

Exercise 64
Show that $\mathbf{Y}_2$ is a fixed-point operator, where:

$$\text{LET } \pounds = \lambda abcdefghijklmnopqstuvwxyzr.$$
$$r(thisisafixedpointcombinator)$$
$$\text{LET } \mathbf{Y}_2 = \pounds$$

□

Exercise 65
Is it the case that $\mathbf{Y}\,f \longrightarrow f\,(\mathbf{Y}\,f)$? If so prove it; if not find a λ-expression $\widehat{\mathbf{Y}}$ such that $\widehat{\mathbf{Y}}\,f \longrightarrow f\,(\widehat{\mathbf{Y}}\,f)$. $\square$

In the pure λ-calculus as defined on page 60, λ-expressions could only be applied to a single argument; however, this argument could be a *tuple* (see page 80). Thus one can write:

$$E(E_1, \ldots, E_n)$$

which actually abbreviates:

$$E(E_1, (E_2, (\cdots (E_{n-1}, E_n) \cdots)))$$

For example, $E(E_1, E_2)$ abbreviates $E(\lambda f.\ f\ E_1\ E_2)$.

5.5   Functions with several arguments

In conventional mathematical usage, the application of an n-argument function f to arguments $x_1, \ldots, x_n$ would be written as $f(x_1, \ldots, x_n)$. There are two ways of representing such applications in the λ-calculus:

(i) as $(f\ x_1\ \ldots\ x_n)$, or

(ii) as the application of f to an n-tuple $(x_1, \ldots, x_n)$.

In case (i), f expects its arguments 'one at a time' and is said to be *curried* after a logician called Curry (the idea of currying was actually invented by Schönfinkel [65]). The functions **and**, **or** and **add** defined earlier were all curried. One advantage of curried functions is that they can be 'partially applied'; for example, **add** $\underline{1}$ is the result of partially applying **add** to $\underline{1}$ and denotes the function $n \mapsto n{+}1$.

Although it is often convenient to represent n-argument functions as curried, it is also useful to be able to represent them, as in case (ii) above, by λ-expressions expecting a single n-tuple argument. For example, instead of representing $+$ and $\times$ by λ-expressions **add** and **mult** such that

$$\mathbf{add}\ \underline{m}\ \underline{n} = \underline{m{+}n}$$
$$\mathbf{mult}\ \underline{m}\ \underline{n} = \underline{m{\times}n}$$

it might be more convenient to represent them by functions, **sum** and **prod** say, such that

$$\mathbf{sum}\ (\underline{m}, \underline{n}) = \underline{m{+}n}$$
$$\mathbf{prod}\ (\underline{m}, \underline{n}) = \underline{m{\times}n}$$

This is nearer to conventional mathematical usage and has applications that will be encountered later. One might say that **sum** and **prod** are *uncurried* versions of **add** and **mult** respectively.

Define:

$$\textbf{LET curry} = \lambda f \ x_1 \ x_2. \ f \ (x_1, x_2)$$

$$\textbf{LET uncurry} = \lambda f \ p. \ f \ (\textbf{fst } p) \ (\textbf{snd } p)$$

then defining

$$\begin{aligned} \textbf{sum} &= \quad \textbf{uncurry add} \\ \textbf{prod} &= \quad \textbf{uncurry mult} \end{aligned}$$

results in **sum** and **prod** having the desired properties; for example:

$$\begin{aligned} \textbf{sum} \ (\underline{m}, \underline{n}) \ &= \textbf{uncurry add} \ (\underline{m}, \underline{n}) \\ &= (\lambda f \ p. \ f \ (\textbf{fst } p) \ (\textbf{snd } p)) \textbf{add} \ (\underline{m}, \underline{n}) \\ &= \textbf{add} \ (\textbf{fst} \ (\underline{m}, \underline{n})) \ (\textbf{snd} \ (\underline{m}, \underline{n})) \\ &= \textbf{add} \ \underline{m} \ \underline{n} \\ &= \underline{m + n} \end{aligned}$$

Exercise 66
Show that for any E:

$$\begin{aligned} \textbf{curry} \ (\textbf{uncurry } E) &= E \\ \textbf{uncurry} \ (\textbf{curry } E) &= E \end{aligned}$$

hence show that:

$$\begin{aligned} \textbf{add} &= \textbf{curry sum} \\ \textbf{mult} &= \textbf{curry prod} \end{aligned}$$

□

We can define *n*-ary functions for currying and uncurrying. For $n > 0$ define:

$$\textbf{LET curry}_n = \lambda f \ x_1 \cdots x_n. \ f \ (x_1, \ldots, x_n)$$

$$\textbf{LET uncurry}_n = \lambda f \ p. \ f \ (p \overset{n}{\downarrow} 1) \ \cdots \ (p \overset{n}{\downarrow} n)$$

If E represents a function expecting an n-tuple argument, then $\mathbf{curry}_n\ E$ represents the curried function which takes its arguments one at a time. If E represents a curried function of n arguments, then $\mathbf{uncurry}_n\ E$ represents the uncurried version which expects a single n-tuple as argument.

Exercise 67
Show that:

(i) $\mathbf{curry}_n\ (\mathbf{uncurry}_n\ E) = E$

(ii) $\mathbf{uncurry}_n\ (\mathbf{curry}_n\ E) = E$

$\square$

Exercise 68
Devise λ-expressions E_1^n and E_2^n built out of **curry** and **uncurry** such that $\mathbf{curry}_n = E_1^n$ and $\mathbf{uncurry}_n = E_2^n$. $\square$

The following notation provides a convenient way to write λ-expressions which expect tuples as arguments.

Generalized λ-abstractions

$$\text{LET } \lambda(V_1, \ldots, V_n).\ E = \mathbf{uncurry}_n\ (\lambda V_1\ \ldots\ V_n.\ E)$$

Example: $\lambda(x, y).\ \mathbf{mult}\ x\ y$ abbreviates:

$$\mathbf{uncurry}_2\ (\lambda x\ y.\ \mathbf{mult}\ x\ y) = (\lambda f\ p.\ f\ (p \overset{2}{\downarrow} 1)\ (p \overset{2}{\downarrow} 2))\ (\lambda x\ y.\ \mathbf{mult}\ x\ y)$$
$$= (\lambda f\ p.\ f\ (\mathbf{fst}\ p)\ (\mathbf{snd}\ p))\ (\lambda x\ y.\ \mathbf{mult}\ x\ y)$$
$$= \lambda p.\ \mathbf{mult}\ (\mathbf{fst}\ p)(\mathbf{snd}\ p)$$

Thus:

$$(\lambda(x, y).\ \mathbf{mult}\ x\ y)\ (E_1, E_2) = (\lambda p.\ \mathbf{mult}\ (\mathbf{fst}\ p)\ (\mathbf{snd}\ p))\ (E_1, E_2)$$
$$= \mathbf{mult}\ (\mathbf{fst}(E_1, E_2))\ (\mathbf{snd}(E_1, E_2))$$
$$= \mathbf{mult}\ E_1\ E_2$$

$\square$

This example illustrates the rule of *generalized β-conversion* in the box below. This rule can be derived from ordinary β-conversion and the definitions of tuples and generalized λ-abstractions. The idea is that a tuple of arguments is passed to each argument position in the body of the generalized abstraction; then each individual argument can be extracted from the tuple without affecting the others.

Generalized β-conversion

$$(\lambda(V_1, \ldots, V_n).\ E)\ (E_1, \ldots, E_n) = E[E_1, \ldots, E_n/V_1, \ldots, V_n]$$

where $E[E_1, \ldots, E_n/V_1, \ldots, V_n]$ is the *simultaneous substitution* of $E_1, \ldots, E_n$ for $V_1, \ldots, V_n$ respectively and none of these variables occur free in any of $E_1, \ldots, E_n$.

It is convenient to extend the notation $\lambda V_1\ V_2 \ldots V_n.\ E$ described on page 62 so that each V_i can either be an identifier or a tuple of identifiers. The meaning of $\lambda V_1\ V_2 \ldots V_n.\ E$ is still $\lambda V_1.(\lambda V_2.(\cdots(\lambda V_n.\ E)\cdots))$, but now if V_i is a tuple of identifiers then the expression is a generalized abstraction.

Example: $\lambda f\ (x, y).\ f\ x\ y$ means $\lambda f.\ (\lambda(x, y).\ f\ x\ y)$ which in turn means $\lambda f.\ \textbf{uncurry}\ (\lambda x\ y.\ f\ x\ y)$ which equals $\lambda f.\ (\lambda p.\ f\ (\textbf{fst}\ p)\ (\textbf{snd}\ p))$. $\square$

Exercise 69
Show that if the only free variables in E are $x_1, \ldots, x_n$ and f, then if:

$$\mathbf{f} = \mathbf{Y}\ (\lambda f\ (x_1, \ldots, x_n).\ E)$$

then

$$\mathbf{f}\ (x_1, \ldots, x_n) = E[\mathbf{f}/f]$$

$\square$

Exercise 70
Define a λ-expression **div** with the property that:

$$\textbf{div}\ (\underline{m}, \underline{n}) = (\underline{q}, \underline{r})$$

where q and r are the quotient and remainder of dividing n into m. $\square$

5.6   Mutual recursion

To solve a set of mutually recursive equations like:

$$\mathbf{f}_1 = F_1\ \mathbf{f}_1 \cdots \mathbf{f}_n$$
$$\mathbf{f}_2 = F_2\ \mathbf{f}_1 \cdots \mathbf{f}_n$$
$$\vdots$$
$$\mathbf{f}_n = F_n\ \mathbf{f}_1 \cdots \mathbf{f}_n$$

we simply define for $1 \le i \le n$

$$\mathbf{f}_i = \mathbf{Y} \ (\lambda(f_1, \ldots f_n).\ (F_1 \ f_1 \cdots f_n, \ \ldots, F_n \ f_1 \cdots f_n)) \downarrow i$$

This works because if

$$\vec{\mathbf{f}} = \mathbf{Y} \ (\lambda(f_1, \ldots f_n).\ (F_1 \ f_1 \cdots f_n, \ \ldots, F_n \ f_1 \cdots f_n))$$

then $\mathbf{f}_i = \vec{\mathbf{f}} \downarrow i$ and hence:

$$
\begin{aligned}
\vec{\mathbf{f}} &= (\lambda(f_1, \ldots, f_n).\ (F_1 \ f_1 \cdots f_n, \ \ldots, F_n \ f_1 \cdots f_n))\vec{\mathbf{f}} \\
&= (F_1(\vec{\mathbf{f}} \downarrow 1) \cdots (\vec{\mathbf{f}} \downarrow n), \ \ldots, F_n(\vec{\mathbf{f}} \downarrow 1) \cdots (\vec{\mathbf{f}} \downarrow n)) \\
&= (F_1 \ \mathbf{f}_1 \cdots \mathbf{f}_n, \ \ldots, F_n \ \mathbf{f}_1 \cdots \mathbf{f}_n) \qquad\qquad \text{(since } \vec{\mathbf{f}} \downarrow i = \mathbf{f}_i).
\end{aligned}
$$

Hence:

$$\mathbf{f}_i = F_i \ \mathbf{f}_1 \cdots \mathbf{f}_n$$

5.7   Representing the recursive functions

The *recursive functions* form an important class of numerical functions. Shortly after Church invented the λ-calculus, Kleene proved that every recursive function could be represented in it [39]. This provided evidence for *Church's thesis*, the hypothesis that any intuitively computable function could be represented in the λ-calculus. It has been shown that many other models of computation define the same class of functions that can be defined in the λ-calculus [56].

In this section it is described what it means for an arithmetic function to be represented in the λ-calculus. Two classes of functions, the *primitive recursive* functions and the *recursive* functions, are defined and it is shown that all the functions in these classes can be represented in the λ-calculus.

In Section 5.3 it was explained how a number n is represented by the λ-expression $\underline{n}$. A λ-expression $\underline{f}$ is said to represent a mathematical function f if for all numbers $x_1, \ldots, x_n$:

$$\underline{f}(\underline{x_1}, \ldots, \underline{x_n}) = \underline{y} \quad \text{if} \quad f(x_1, \ldots, x_n) = y$$

5.7.1   The primitive recursive functions

A function is called *primitive recursive* if it can be constructed from 0 and the functions S and U_n^i (defined below) by a finite sequence of applications of the operations of substitution and primitive recursion (also defined below).

The successor function S and projection functions U_n^i (where n and i are numbers) are defined by:

(i) $S(x) = x + 1$

(ii) $U_n^i(x_1, x_2, \ldots, x_n) = x_i$

Substitution

Suppose g is a function of r arguments and $h_1, \ldots, h_r$ are r functions each of n arguments. We say f is defined from g and $h_1, \ldots, h_r$ by substitution if:

$$f(x_1, \ldots, x_n) = g(h_1(x_1, \ldots, x_n), \ldots, h_r(x_1, \ldots, x_n))$$

Primitive recursion

Suppose g is a function of $n-1$ arguments and h is a function of $n+1$ arguments. We say f is defined from g and h by primitive recursion if:

$$f(0, x_2, \ldots, x_n) = g(x_2, \ldots, x_n)$$
$$f(S(x_1), x_2, \ldots, x_n) = h(f(x_1, x_2, \ldots, x_n), x_1, x_2, \ldots, x_n)$$

g is called the *base function* and h is called the *step function*. It can proved that for any base and step function there always exists a unique function defined from them by primitive recursion. This result is called the primitive recursion theorem; proofs of it can be found in textbooks on mathematical logic (e.g. [64]).

Example: The addition function *sum* is primitive recursive because:

$$sum(0, x_2) = x_2$$
$$sum(S(x_1), x_2) = S(sum(x_1, x_2))$$

□

It is now shown that every primitive recursive function can be represented by λ-expressions.

It is obvious that the λ-expressions $\underline{0}$, suc, $\lambda p.\, p \overset{n}{\downarrow} i$ represent the initial functions 0, S and U_n^i respectively.

Suppose function g of r variables is represented by $\mathbf{g}$ and functions h_i ($1 \leq i \leq r$) of n variables are represented by $\mathbf{h}_i$. Then if a function f of n variables is defined by substitution by:

$$f(x_1, \ldots, x_n) = g(h_1(x_1, \ldots, x_n), \ldots, h_r(x_1, \ldots, x_n))$$

then f is represented by $\mathbf{f}$ where:

$$\mathbf{f} = \lambda(x_1, \ldots, x_n).\, \mathbf{g}(\mathbf{h}_1(x_1, \ldots, x_n), \ldots, \mathbf{h}_r(x_1, \ldots, x_n))$$

Suppose function f of n variables is defined inductively from a base function g of $n-1$ variables and an inductive step function h of $n+1$ variables. Then

$$f(0, x_2, \ldots, x_n) = g(x_2, \ldots, x_n)$$
$$f(S(x_1), x_2, \ldots, x_n) = h(f(x_1, x_2, \ldots, x_n), x_1, x_2, \ldots, x_n)$$

Thus if **g** represents g and **h** represents h then **f** will represent f if

$$\textbf{f}\,(x_1, x_2, \ldots, x_n) =$$
$$(\text{iszero } x_1 \rightarrow \textbf{g}(x_2, \ldots, x_n) \mid$$
$$\textbf{h}(\textbf{f}\,(\text{pre } x_1, x_2, \ldots, x_n), \text{pre } x_1, x_2, \ldots, x_n))$$

Using the fixed-point trick, an **f** can be constructed to satisfy this equation defining **f** to be[1]:

$$\textbf{Y}(\lambda f.\ \lambda(x_1, x_2, \ldots, x_n).$$
$$(\text{iszero } x_1 \rightarrow \textbf{g}(x_2, \ldots, x_n) \mid$$
$$\textbf{h}(f(\text{pre } x_1, x_2, \ldots, x_n), \text{pre } x_1, x_2, \ldots, x_n)))$$

Thus any primitive recursive function can be represented by a λ-expression.

5.7.2 The recursive functions

A function is called *recursive* if it can be constructed from 0, the successor function and the projection functions (see page 93) by a sequence of substitutions, primitive recursions and *minimizations*.

Minimization

Suppose g is a function of n arguments. We say f is defined from g by minimization if:

$$f(x_1, x_2, \ldots, x_n) = \text{'the smallest } y \text{ such that } g(y, x_2, \ldots, x_n) = x_1\text{'}$$

The notation MIN(f) is used to denote the minimization of f. Functions defined by minimization may be undefined for some arguments. For example, if *one* is the function that always returns 1, i.e. $one(x) = 1$ for every x, then MIN(one) is only defined for arguments with value 1. This is obvious because if $f(x) = \text{MIN}(one)(x)$, then:

$$f(x) = \text{'the smallest } y \text{ such that } one(y) = x\text{'}$$

---

[1] See Exercise 69 on page 92.

and clearly this is only defined if $x = 1$. Thus

$$\text{MIN}(one)(x) = \begin{cases} \underline{0} & \text{if } x = 1 \\ \text{undefined} & \text{otherwise} \end{cases}$$

To show that any recursive function can be represented in the λ-calculus it is necessary to show how to represent the minimization of an arbitrary function. Suppose g represents a function g of n variables and f is defined by:

$$f = \text{MIN}(g)$$

Then if a λ-expression **min** can be devised such that **min** $\underline{x}$ **f** $(\underline{x}_1, \ldots, \underline{x}_n)$ represents the least number y greater than x such that

$$f(y, x_2, \ldots, x_n) = x_1$$

then **g** will represent g where:

$$\mathbf{g} \;=\; \lambda(x_1, x_2, \ldots, x_n).\ \mathbf{min}\ \underline{0}\ \mathbf{f}\ (x_1, x_2, \ldots, x_n)$$

min will clearly have the desired property if:

$$\mathbf{min}\ x\ f\ (x_1, x_2, \ldots, x_n) =$$
$$(\text{eq}\ (f(x, x_2, \ldots, x_n))\ x_1) \to x \mid \mathbf{min}\ (\text{suc}\ x)\ f\ (x_1, x_2, \ldots, x_n))$$

where eq $\underline{m}\ \underline{n}$ is equal to **true** if $m = n$ and **false** otherwise (a suitable definition of **eq** occurs on page 88). Thus **min** can simply be defined to be:

$$\mathbf{Y}(\lambda m.$$
$$\lambda x\ f\ (x_1, x_2, \ldots, x_n).$$
$$(\text{eq}\ (f(x, x_2, \ldots, x_n))\ x_1\ \to x \mid m\ (\text{suc}\ x)\ f\ (x_1, x_2, \ldots, x_n)))$$

Thus any recursive function can be represented by a λ-expression.

Higher-order primitive recursion

There are functions which are recursive but not primitive recursive. An example given in Barendregt ([4], page 569) is the version of Ackermann's function, ψ, defined by:

$$\psi(0, n) = n{+}1$$
$$\psi(m{+}1, 0) = \psi(m, 1)$$
$$\psi(m{+}1, n{+}1) = \psi(m, \psi(m{+}1, n))$$

However, if one allows functions as arguments, then any recursive function can be defined by a primitive recursion. For example, if the higher-order function *rec* is defined by primitive recursion as follows:

$$rec(0, x_2, x_3) = x_2$$
$$rec(S(x_1), x_2, x_3) = x_3(rec(x_1, x_2, x_3))$$

then ψ can be defined by:

$$\psi(m, n) = rec\ (m,\ S,\ f \mapsto (x \mapsto rec(x, f(1), f)))\ (n)$$

where $x \mapsto \theta(x)$ denotes the function[2] that maps x to $\theta(x)$. Notice that the third argument of *rec* , viz. x_3, must be a function. In the definition of ψ we also took x_1 to be a function, viz. S.

Exercise 71
Show that the definition of ψ in terms of *rec* works, i.e. that with ψ defined as above:

$$\psi(0, n) = n+1$$
$$\psi(m+1, 0) = \psi(m, 1)$$
$$\psi(m+1, n+1) = \psi(m, \psi(m+1, n))$$

□

A function which takes another function as an argument, or returns another function as a result, is called *higher-order*. The example ψ shows that higher-order primitive recursion is more powerful than ordinary primitive recursion[3]. The use of operators like *rec* is one of the things that makes functional programming very powerful. The functions **map** and **lit** described in Section 6.5 illustrate this further.

5.7.3   The partial recursive functions

A partial function is one that is not defined for all arguments. For example, the function MIN(*one*) described above is partial. Another example is the division function, since division by 0 is not defined. Functions that are defined for all arguments are called *total*.

A partial function is called *partial recursive* if it can be constructed from 0, the successor function and the projection functions by a sequence of substitutions, primitive recursions and minimizations. Thus the recursive

---

[2] Note that $\lambda x.\ \theta(x)$ is an expression of the λ-calculus whereas $x \mapsto \theta(x)$ is a notation of informal mathematics.

[3] The kind of primitive recursion defined in Section 5.7.1 is *first-order* primitive recursion.

functions are just the partial recursive functions which happen to be total. It can be shown that every partial recursive function f can be represented by a λ-expression $\underline{f}$ in the sense that

(i) $\underline{f}(\underline{x_1}, \ldots, \underline{x_n}) = \underline{y}$ if $f(x_1, \ldots, x_n) = y$

(ii) If $f(x_1, \ldots, x_n)$ is undefined then $\underline{f}(\underline{x_1}, \ldots, \underline{x_n})$ has no normal form.

Note that despite (ii) above, it is not in general correct to regard expressions with no normal form as being 'undefined'; this subtle point is discussed further on page 120 (see also pages 41 and 42 of Barendregt [4]).

Exercise 72
Write down the λ-expression that represents $\text{MIN}(f)$, where $f(x) = 0$ for all x. □

5.8   Representing lists (LISP S-expressions)

The data-structures manipulated by LISP (see Chapter 9) are called symbolic expressions or *S-expressions*. The LISP primitives for operating on these include **car**, **cdr** and **cons**. A first approximation to representing S-expressions is to represent the formation of LISP's dotted-pairs (i.e. **cons**-cells) by the λ-calculus pairing defined in Section 5.2 (see page 80).

This appears to work at first, since by defining **car** = **fst** and **cdr** = **snd** then, since $(E_1, E_2, \ldots, E_n) = (E_1, (E_2, \ldots, E_n))$, it follows that

$$\textbf{car } (E_1, E_2, \ldots, E_n) = E_1$$
$$\textbf{cdr } (E_1, E_2, \ldots, E_n) = (E_2, \ldots, E_n)$$

as in LISP. The only thing that is missing is the empty list **nil**. Unfortunately, we cannot simply devise some λ-expression E to represent **nil** because there would be no way (see Exercise 87 on page 127) of defining a λ-expression **null** such that:

$$\textbf{null } E = \begin{cases} \textbf{true} & E = \textbf{nil} \\ \\ \textbf{false} & \text{otherwise} \end{cases}$$

In LISP implementations, machine words are marked to indicate whether they represent atoms (e.g. **nil**) or dotted pairs. One can adopt the same approach in the λ-calculus and represent a list by a pair (b, E) where b represents a boolean which indicates whether the list is empty or not. Then a **null** test can easily be represented by inspecting the first component:

$$\text{LET null} = \text{fst}$$

To avoid confusion between λ-expressions representing pairs and those representing S-expressions (defined below) we will use $[E_1; \cdots; E_n]$ to represent an S-expression list whose components are $E_1, \ldots, E_n$. This notation is similar to the M-expression syntax of LISP 1.5 [53].

The empty list, for which we will use the notation $[\ ]$, is represented by a pair of the form $(\textbf{true}, \frown)$. Thus ensuring that:

$$\text{null } [\ ] = \textbf{true}$$

It doesn't really matter what $\frown$ is, but we will use a special λ-expression called $\bot$ (pronounced 'bottom'). We can also use $\bot$ as the head (**car**) and tail (**cdr**) of the empty list. The λ-expression $\bot$ is supposed to represent an 'undefined function'. Intuitively, the result of applying such a function to *any* argument is also 'undefined', so it is natural to require for every E that:

$$\bot\, E = \bot$$

Using **Y** we can solve the equation $\bot\, x = \bot$.

$$\text{LET } \bot = \textbf{Y}\ (\lambda f\ x.\ f)$$

Now define

$$\text{LET } [\ ] = (\textbf{true}, \bot)$$

$$\text{LET } [E] = (\textbf{false}, (E, [\ ]))$$

$$\text{LET } [E_1; E_2] = (\textbf{false}, (E_1, [E_2]))$$

$$\vdots$$

$$\text{LET } [E_1; \cdots; E_n] = (\textbf{false}, (E_1, [E_2; \cdots; E_n]))$$

The primitive functions can then be defined by:

LET hd = $\lambda l.$ (null $l \to \perp$ | fst(snd l))

LET tl = $\lambda l.$ (null $l \to \perp$ | snd(snd l))

LET cons = $\lambda x\, l.$ (false, (x, l))

Exercise 73

Show that the following properties hold:

hd (cons $x\ l$) = x

tl (cons $x\ l$) = l

null (cons $x\ l$) = false

$[E_1; \cdots; E_n]$ = cons E_1 (cons E_2 ($\cdots$ (cons E_n [ ]) $\cdots$))

□

Example: A function for appending one list to another can be defined by constructing a λ-expression **append** such that:

append $x\ y$ = (null $x \to y$ | cons (hd x) (append(tl $x)y$))

i.e.

LET append = **Y** $(\lambda f\ x\ y.$ (null $x \to y$ | cons (hd x) (f (tl x) y))))

Then, for example,

append$[E_1; E_2][E_3; E_4]$
= (null$[E_1; E_2] \to [E_3; E_4]$ |
        cons (hd$[E_1; E_2]$) (append(tl$[E_1; E_2]$)$[E_3; E_4]$))
= cons E_1 (append$[E_2][E_3; E_4]$)
= cons E_1 (cons E_2 (append[ ]$[E_3; E_4]$))
= cons E_1 (cons $E_2[E_3; E_4]$)
= $[E_1; E_2; E_3; E_4]$)

In general:

$$\text{append}[E_1; \cdots; E_n][E_1'; \cdots; E_m'] = [E_1; \cdots; E_n; E_1'; \cdots; E_m']$$

□

Exercise 74
Define a λ-expression **reverse** such that:

$$\text{reverse}[E_1; E_2; \cdots; E_{n-1}; E_n] = [E_n; E_{n-1}; \cdots; E_2; E_1]$$

□

There is an important difference between the lists we have just represented in the λ-calculus and LISP lists: the former lists can be *infinite*. To see this consider the equation:

$$\text{from } n = \text{cons } n \text{ (from (suc } n))$$

Then

$$\text{from } \underline{0} = \text{cons } \underline{0} \text{ (from } \underline{1})$$
$$= \text{cons } \underline{0} \text{ (from } \underline{1})$$
$$= \text{cons } \underline{0} \text{ (cons } \underline{1} \text{ (from } \underline{2}))$$
$$= \text{cons } \underline{0} \text{ (cons } \underline{1} \text{ (cons } \underline{2} \text{ (from } \underline{3})))$$
$$\vdots$$
$$= [\underline{0}; \underline{1}; \underline{2}; \underline{3}; \cdots]$$

If one attempts to define **from** in LISP, then because the LISP evaluator does *call by value* (i.e. it always evaluates arguments before entering functions), expressions like hd (**from** $\underline{0}$) would generate non-terminating evaluations. However, from the definitions above it is straightforward to show that, for example,

$$\text{hd (from } \underline{0}) = \underline{0}$$

Languages with this behaviour (i.e. **from** works) are said to employ *lazy* or *normal order* evaluation. There is more on this topic in the next chapter (e.g. see the normalization theorem on page 121).

5.9   Extending the λ-calculus

Although it is possible to represent data-objects and data-structures with λ-expressions, it is often inefficient to do so. For example, most computers have hardware for arithmetic and it is reasonable to use this, rather than

λ-conversion, to compute with numbers. A mathematically clean way of 'interfacing' computation rules to the λ-calculus is via so called δ-*rules*. The idea is to add a new constant, c say, and then to specify an algorithm, called a δ-rule, for reducing applications c $E_1 \ldots E_n$. For example, one might add $+$ as a new constant together with the δ-rule:

$$+ \; \underline{m} \; \underline{n} \xrightarrow[\delta]{} \underline{m+n}$$

($E_1 \xrightarrow[\delta]{} E_2$ means E_2 results by applying a δ-rule to some subexpression of E_1).

When adding such constants and rules to the λ-calculus one must be careful not to destroy its nice properties, e.g. the Church-Rosser theorem (see page 118). For example, suppose the following rule were added:

$$+ \; E_1 \; E_2 \xrightarrow[\delta]{} \begin{cases} \underline{m+n} & \text{if } E_1 \equiv \underline{m} \text{ and } E_2 \equiv \underline{n} \\ \\ \bot & \text{otherwise} \end{cases}$$

Then

$$+ \; ((\lambda x.x)\underline{0}) \; \underline{0} \xrightarrow[\delta]{} \bot$$

because although $(\lambda x.x)\underline{0} = \underline{0}$, it is not the case that $(\lambda x.x)\underline{0} \equiv \underline{m}$ for any number m. It would also follow that

$$+ \; ((\lambda x.x)\underline{0}) \; \underline{0} \xrightarrow[\beta]{} + \; \underline{0} \; \underline{0} \xrightarrow[\delta]{} \underline{0}$$

This shows that $\underline{0} = \bot$ if the above rule for $+$ is added (and the definition of $=$ on page 68 is extended to include δ-reduction).

The following condition due to Mitschke (see Barendregt [4], page 401) guarantees that a δ-rule preserves the Church-Rosser theorem.

Suppose the following three things hold:

1. $R_1(E_1, \ldots, E_n)$, $R_2(E_1, \ldots, E_n)$, $\ldots$, $R_m(E_1, \ldots, E_n)$ are disjoint relations. This means that:

   (a) $R_i(E_1, \ldots, E_n)$ is either true or false.

   (b) For a given $E_1, \ldots, E_n$ at most one of $R_i(E_1, \ldots, E_n)$ is true.

2. The relations R_i are closed under λ-conversion. This means that if $R_i(E_1, \ldots, E_j, \ldots, E_n)$ is true and also if $E_j \longrightarrow E_j'$ then $R_i(E_1, \ldots, E_j', \ldots, E_n)$ is also true.

3. The relations R_i are closed under substitution. This means that if $R_i(E_1, \ldots, E_j, \ldots, E_n)$ is true, E is any expression and V is any variab'e then $R_i(E_1, \ldots, E_i[E/V], \ldots, E_n)$ is also true.

If 1, 2 and 3 hold, then adding a constant c together with the δ-reductions:

$$c\ E_1\ \ldots\ E_n\ \xrightarrow[\delta]{}\ E^1 \quad \text{If } R_1(E_1,\ldots,E_n) \text{ holds}$$

$$\vdots$$

$$c\ E_1\ \ldots\ E_n\ \xrightarrow[\delta]{}\ E^m \quad \text{If } R_m(E_1,\ldots,E_n) \text{ holds}$$

(where $E^1, \ldots, E^n$ are arbitrary λ-expressions) results in an extension of the λ-calculus for which the Church-Rosser theorem still holds.

Exercise 75
Devise δ-rules for arithmetic and show that they satisfy Mitschke's conditions. $\square$

Chapter 6

Functional Programs

Functional programming is briefly described and illustrated with some simple examples. A little functional programming language is defined. It is shown how it can be translated into the λ-calculus.

Functional programming languages all contain some subset equivalent to the λ-calculus. They differ in the particular notation used and in the 'impure' features provided. A feature is impure if it cannot be viewed as an abbreviation for some λ-calculus construct (and hence cannot be analysed using λ-calculus theory). For example, older functional languages like LISP contain imperative features such as assignment and *goto* commands.

In the rest of this chapter some typical functional programming notations are described; these descend from Landin's pioneering work in the 1960s [42]. It is shown that these notations are 'pure', i.e. that they can be viewed as abbreviations for λ-calculus constructs.

6.1 Functional notation

Let let $x = E_1$ in E_2 be written to mean $(\lambda x. E_2) E_1$. Then, for example, let $n = \underline{0}$ in suc n means $(\lambda n.\text{suc } n) \underline{0}$. By the rules of λ-conversion this reduces to $\underline{1}$.

Here is another example in which there is a let inside a let.

$$\text{let } m = \underline{0} \text{ in}$$
$$\text{let } n = \underline{1} \text{ in}$$
$$\text{add } m \; n$$

This means:

$$(\lambda m. \text{let } n = \underline{1} \text{ in add } m \; n) \underline{0}$$

105

By the rules of λ-conversion

$$(\lambda m. \text{ let } n = \underline{1} \text{ in add } m\ n)\ \underline{0} = (\lambda m.\ (\lambda n.\ \text{add } m\ n)\ \underline{1})\ \underline{0}$$
$$= \text{add } \underline{0}\ \underline{1}$$
$$= \underline{1}$$

One can think of $\text{let } x = E$ as a kind of *local declaration* of x with value E. The *scope* of the declaration is written after in.

The basic idea can be extended in various ways:

$$\text{let } (x_1, \ldots, x_n) = E_1 \text{ in } E_2$$

means:

$$(\lambda(x_1, \ldots, x_n).\ E_2)\ E_1$$

Example

$$\text{let}(x, y) = (\underline{2}, \underline{3}) \text{ in add } x\ y$$

means

$$(\lambda(x, y).\ \text{add } x\ y)\ (\underline{2}, \underline{3})$$

This is equal to $\underline{5}$ by λ-conversion. $\square$

The notation:

$$\text{let } x_1 = E_1 \text{ and } x_2 = E_2 \cdots \text{ and } x_n = E_n \text{ in } E$$

is defined to mean:

$$\text{let } (x_1, x_2, \ldots, x_n) = (E_1, E_2, \ldots, E_n) \text{ in } E$$

i.e.

$$(\lambda(x_1, x_2, \ldots, x_n).\ E)\ (E_1, E_2, \ldots, E_n)$$

Note that:

$$\text{let } x_1 = E_1 \text{ in}$$
$$\text{let } x_2 = E_2 \text{ in}$$
$$\vdots$$
$$\text{let } x_n = E_n \text{ in } E$$

is different from:

$$\text{let } x_1 = E_1$$
$$\text{and } x_2 = E_2$$
$$\vdots$$
$$\text{and } x_n = E_n \text{ in } E$$

In the former, the scope of each let $x_i = E_i$ is

$$\text{let } x_{i+1} = E_{i+1} \text{ in let } x_{i+2} = E_{i+2} \text{ in } \cdots \text{ let } x_n = E_n \text{ in } E$$

In the latter, the declarations let $x_i = E_i$ are done 'in parallel'. For example,

$$\text{let } x = \underline{1} \text{ in let } y = \text{suc } x \text{ in } y$$

is equal to $\underline{2}$, but

$$\text{let } x = \underline{1} \text{ and } y = \text{suc } x \text{ in } y$$

is equal to suc x, since the declaration let $x = \underline{1}$ isn't felt by the x in suc x.

In general:

$$\text{let } x_1 = E_1 \text{ in}$$
$$\text{let } x_2 = E_2 \text{ in}$$
$$\vdots$$
$$\text{let } x_n = E_n \text{ in } E$$

means $E[E_n/x_n] \cdots [E_2/x_2][E_1/x_1]$, whereas:

$$\text{let } x_1 = E_1$$
$$\text{and } x_2 = E_2$$
$$\vdots$$
$$\text{and } x_n = E_n \text{ in } E$$

means $E[E_1, E_2, \ldots, E_n/x_1, x_2, \ldots, x_n]$.

To make the definitions of functions look nicer, the notation:

$$\text{let } f \, x_1 \cdots x_n = E$$

is defined to mean:

$$\text{let } f = \lambda x_1 \cdots x_n . \, E$$

and

$$\text{let } f \, (x_1, \ldots, x_n) = E$$

is defined to mean:

$$\text{let } f = \lambda(x_1, \ldots, x_n). \, E$$

Example

$$\text{let suc } n = \lambda f \, x. \, n \, f \, (f \, x) \text{ in suc } \underline{0}$$

means
$$\text{let } suc = \lambda n. \ \lambda f \ x. \ n \ f \ (f \ x) \text{ in } suc \ \underline{0}$$

By λ-conversion it follows that:

$$(\lambda suc. \ suc \ \underline{0}) \ (\lambda n. \ \lambda f \ x. \ n \ f \ (f \ x)) \quad \begin{aligned} &= (\lambda n. \ \lambda f \ x. \ n \ f \ (f \ x)) \ \underline{0} \\ &= \lambda f \ x. \ \underline{0} \ f \ (f \ x) \\ &= \lambda f \ x. \ f \ x \\ &= \underline{1} \end{aligned}$$

See the description of **suc** on page 83 for more explanation. $\square$

Example

$$\text{let } sum \ (m, n) = \lambda f \ x. \ m \ (n \ f \ x) \text{ in } E$$

means:

$$\text{let } sum = \lambda (m, n). \ \lambda f \ x. \ m \ (n \ f \ x) \text{ in } E$$

which is:

$$(\lambda sum. \ E) \ (\lambda (m, n). \ \lambda f \ x. \ (n \ f \ x))$$

i.e.

$$E[(\lambda (m, n). \ \lambda f \ x. \ (n \ f \ x))/sum]$$

See the description of **sum** on page 90 for more explanation. $\square$

A common notation for recursive definition is:

$$\text{letrec } f = E$$

This is defined to mean:

$$\text{let } f = \mathbf{Y} \ (\lambda f. \ E)$$

For simultaneous recursive definitions, the notation

$$\text{letrec } f_1 = E_1 \text{ and } \cdots \text{ and } f_n = E_n$$

is defined to mean:

$$\text{let } (f_1, \ldots, f_n) = \mathbf{Y} \ (\lambda (f_1, \ldots, f_n). \ (E_1, \ldots E_n))$$

The function-defining notation described above can also be used with **letrec** as well as with **let**, thus:

$$\text{letrec } f \ x_1 \cdots x_n = E$$

means:
$$\texttt{letrec } f = \lambda x_1 \cdots x_n.\ E$$

and
$$\texttt{letrec } f\ (x_1 \cdots x_n) = E$$

means:
$$\texttt{letrec } f = \lambda(x_1, \ldots, x_n).\ E$$

Example: The declaration:

$$\texttt{letrec mult } m\ n = (\texttt{iszero } m \rightarrow \underline{0}\ |\ \texttt{add } n\ (\texttt{mult } (\texttt{pre } m)\ n))$$

is equivalent to:

$$\texttt{let mult} = \mathbf{Y}\ (\lambda mult\ m\ n.\ (\texttt{iszero } m \rightarrow \underline{0}\ |\ \texttt{add } n\ (mult\ (\texttt{pre } m)\ n)))$$

□

6.2 Combining declarations

So far declarations have just been things of the form $\texttt{let }B$ or $\texttt{letrec }B$. One can introduce some operators for combining such declarations. For example, suppose D_1 and D_2 are declarations, then:

1. $D_1 ; D_2$ is a declaration whose meaning is defined by;

$$(D_1 ; D_2)\ \texttt{in}\ E = D_1\ \texttt{in}\ (D_2\ \texttt{in}\ E)$$

2. $D_1\ \texttt{ins}\ D_2$ is a declaration in which the bindings in D_1 only apply to the expressions in D_2 (i.e. the scope of D_1 is D_2) and these bindings are not exported as bindings of the compound declaration $D_1\ \texttt{ins}\ D_2$. This is clarified by the examples below.

Examples

(i) $\texttt{let } x = \underline{1}; \texttt{let } y = x + \underline{1}$ is equivalent to $\texttt{let } x = \underline{1}$ and $y = \underline{2}$.

(ii) $\texttt{let } x = \underline{1}\ \texttt{ins}\ \texttt{let } y = x + \underline{1}$ is equivalent to $\texttt{let } y = \underline{2}$.

□

In general, if D_2 is equivalent to:

$$\texttt{let } X_1 = E_1\ \texttt{and}\ \cdots\ \texttt{and}\ X_n = E_n$$

then D_1 **ins** D_2 is equivalent to:

$$\text{let } X_1 = (D_1 \text{ in } E_1) \text{ and } \cdots \text{ and } X_n = (D_1 \text{ in } E_n)$$

If D_2 is equivalent to:

$$\text{letrec } X_1 = E_1 \text{ and } \cdots \text{ and } X_n = E_n$$

then D_1 **ins** D_2 is equivalent to:

$$\text{letrec } X_1 = (D_1 \text{ in } E_1) \text{ and } \cdots \text{ and } X_n = (D_1 \text{ in } E_n)$$

The name **ins** derives from 'inside'.

6.3   Predeclared definitions

The names $\underline{0}$, $\underline{1}$, $\underline{2}$, ..., **suc**, **add**, **cond**, **true**, ... are part of the language used to talk about the λ-calculus, i.e. they are part of the *metalanguage*. In a real functional programming language these things will be predefined variables; the definitions being done automatically for the user. One way to represent this is to imagine a big declaration D_{initial} which binds the representations of standard objects like numbers, truth values, etc. to their usual names. So D_{initial} might start out:

$$\text{let } 0 = \lambda f \ x. \ x;$$
$$\vdots$$
$$\text{let } n = \lambda f \ x. \ f^n \ x;$$
$$\vdots$$
$$\text{let true} = \lambda x \ y. \ x;$$
$$\vdots$$
$$\text{let hd} = \lambda l. \ (\text{null } l \to \bot \mid \text{fst(snd } l));$$
$$\vdots$$

Any expressions E will then be assumed to be in the scope of D_{initial}. (i.e. E will really mean D_{initial} in E).

6.4   A compiling algorithm

In this section the notations just described are gathered together into a language. The syntax of declarations is;

$$D ::= \text{let } B \mid \text{letrec } B \mid D_1 ; D_2 \mid D_1 \text{ ins } D_2$$
$$B ::= X = E \mid X_1 = E_1 \text{ and } \cdots \text{ and } X_n = E_n$$
$$X ::= V \mid (X_1, \ldots, X_n) \mid V \ F_1 \ldots F_n \mid V(F_1, \ldots, F_n)$$
$$F ::= V \mid (V_1, \ldots, V_n)$$

Here E, E_1, $\ldots$, E_n range over expressions; these are either ordinary λ-expressions, or things of the form D in E where D is a declaration. Thus:

$$E ::= V \mid (E_1 \ E_2) \mid \lambda V. \ E \mid D \text{ in } E$$

V ranges over variables. The Bs used in defining declarations are called *bindings*. The Xs are called *variable structures* and the Fs are called *parameter specifications*.

The language just described includes things that have not been discussed, for example:

$$\text{let } ((f \ x, \ y), \ (z_1, z_2)) = E \text{ in } E'$$

There follows a description of a 'compiler' from this language to simple λ-expressions as defined on page 60. For example, the expression above will compile to:

$$(\lambda(f, y, z_1, z_2). \ E') \ ((\lambda x. \ E \downarrow 1 \downarrow 1), \ E \downarrow 1 \downarrow 2, \ E \downarrow 2 \downarrow 1, \ E \downarrow 2 \downarrow 2))$$

This denotes a simple λ-expression via the definitions of $\lambda(x_1, \ldots, x_n)$. E and $\downarrow$.

The compilation alogorithm will be described via a sequence of transformations (passes). The notation '$X \rightsquigarrow Y$' will mean 'replace X by Y'.

Expressions of the form D in E are compiled by the following steps (which should be performed in the order given):

Step 1: Remove bindings of the form $(X_1, \ldots, X_n) = E$.

$$(X_1, \ldots, X_n) = E \quad \rightsquigarrow \quad X_1 = E_1 \overset{n}{\downarrow} 1 \text{ and } \cdots \text{ and } X_n = E_n \overset{n}{\downarrow} n$$

Example: Applying Step 1 to:

$$\text{let } ((f \ x, \ y), \ (z_1, z_2)) = E \text{ in } E'$$

yields:
$$\texttt{let } (f\ x,\ y) = E \downarrow 1 \texttt{ and } (z_1, z_2) = E \downarrow 2 \texttt{ in } E'$$
Applying Step 1 again yields:

$$
\begin{aligned}
\texttt{let } f\ x\ &= E \downarrow 1 \downarrow 1 \\
\texttt{and } y\ \ \ &= E \downarrow 1 \downarrow 2 \\
\texttt{and } z_1\ &= E \downarrow 2 \downarrow 1 \\
\texttt{and } z_2\ &= E \downarrow 2 \downarrow 2 \\
\texttt{in } E'
\end{aligned}
$$

□

Step 2: Put bindings in the form $V = E$.

$$V\ X_1 \ldots X_n = E \ \leadsto\ V = \lambda X_1 \ldots X_n.\ E$$

$$V(X_1, \ldots, X_n) = E \ \leadsto\ V = \lambda(X_1, \ldots, X_n).\ E$$

Example: Applying Step 2 to the result of the previous example yields:

$$
\begin{aligned}
\texttt{let } f\ \ &= \lambda x.\ E \downarrow 1 \downarrow 1 \\
\texttt{and } y\ \ &= E \downarrow 1 \downarrow 2 \\
\texttt{and } z_1\ &= E \downarrow 2 \downarrow 1 \\
\texttt{and } z_2\ &= E \downarrow 2 \downarrow 2 \\
\texttt{in } E'
\end{aligned}
$$

□

Step 3: Remove **ins**.

$$D \texttt{ ins let } V_1 = E_1 \texttt{ and } \cdots \texttt{ and } V_n = E_n$$
$$\leadsto\ \texttt{let } V_1 = (D \texttt{ in } E_1) \texttt{ and } \cdots \texttt{ and let } V_n = (D \texttt{ in } E_n)$$

Example:

$$\texttt{let } x = \underline{1} \texttt{ ins let } y = x + \underline{1} \ \leadsto\ \texttt{let } y = (\texttt{let } x = \underline{1} \texttt{ in } x + \underline{1})$$

□

Step 4: Remove **in**.

$$\texttt{let } V_1 = E_1 \texttt{ and } \cdots \texttt{ and } V_n = E_n \texttt{ in } E$$
$$\leadsto\ (\lambda(V_1, \ldots, V_n).\ E)(E_1, \ldots, E_n)$$

$$\texttt{letrec } V_1 = E_1 \texttt{ and } \cdots \texttt{ and } V_n = E_n \texttt{ in } E$$
$$\leadsto\ (\lambda(V_1, \ldots, V_n).E)(\mathbf{Y}(\lambda(V_1, \ldots, V_n)(E_1, \ldots, E_n)))$$

Example: Applying Step 4 to the result of Step 2 in the example before last yields:

$$(\lambda(f, y, z_1, z_2). \ E') \ ((\lambda x. \ E \downarrow 1 \downarrow 1), \ E \downarrow 1 \downarrow 2, \ E \downarrow 2 \downarrow 1, \ E \downarrow 2 \downarrow 2)$$

□

Exercise 76
Compile:

$$\textbf{letrec fact } n = (\textbf{iszero } n \rightarrow \underline{0} \mid \textbf{mult } n \ (\textbf{fact } (\textbf{pre } n)))$$
$$\textbf{in fact } 6$$

□

6.5   Example functional programs

A functional program consists of a sequence of function definitions followed by an expression (involving the functions) which evaluates to the result one is trying to compute.

For example, the functional program below computes the average of the squares of the numbers 64, 23, 104, 8, 72 and 20. It has the form

$$\textbf{letrec sumlist } l = \ \cdots \ \textbf{and}$$
$$\textbf{letrec length } l = \ \cdots \ \textbf{and}$$
$$\textbf{letrec map } f \ l = \ \cdots \ \textbf{ins}$$
$$\textbf{let avsq } l = \ \cdots$$
$$\textbf{in}$$
$$\textbf{avsq } [\underline{64}; \ \underline{23}; \ \underline{104}; \ \underline{8}; \ \underline{72}; \ \underline{20}]$$

where the three functions **sumlist**, **length** and **map** are local to the declaration of **avsq**, which is the function for computing the average of the sum of squares. The functions **sumlist** and **length** compute the sum of a list of numbers and its length, respectively. The higher-order function **map** takes as arguments a function f and a list $[E_1; \ \ldots \ ; E_n]$ and returns as result the list $[(f \ E_1); \ \ldots \ ; (f \ E_n)]$. For example,

$$\textbf{map } (\lambda n. \ \textbf{mult } n \ n) \ l$$

evaluates to the list obtained from l by squaring each element. Here is the complete program:

letrec sumlist l = (null l → $\underline{0}$ | add (hd l) (sumlist (tl l))) and
letrec length l = (null l → $\underline{0}$ | add $\underline{1}$ (length (tl l))) and
letrec map f l = (null l → [ ] | cons (f (hd l)) (map f (tl l))) ins
let avsq l = fst (div (sumlist (map (λn. mult n n) l)) (length l))
in
avsq [$\underline{64}$; $\underline{23}$; $\underline{104}$; $\underline{8}$; $\underline{72}$; $\underline{20}$]

Higher-order 'iteration functions' like **map** are very powerful and are used frequently in functional programming. Another example is **lit**[1]

$$\text{lit } f \; [x_1; x_2; \; \dots \; ; x_n] \; x = f \; x_1 \; (f \; x_2 \; \dots \; (f \; x_n \; x) \; \dots \;)$$

lit is a generalization of the standard mathematical notation for iterated sums and products:

$$\sum_{i=1}^{n} x_i = \text{lit add } [x_1; x_2; \; \dots \; ; x_n] \; \underline{0}$$

$$\prod_{i=1}^{n} x_i = \text{lit mult } [x_1; x_2; \; \dots \; ; x_n] \; \underline{1}$$

Thus **sumlist** l is just **lit add** l $\underline{0}$.

Many simple list processing functions can be defined using **lit** and no other recursion. For example:

$$\textbf{append } = \textbf{ lit cons}$$

This works because:

append [x_1; ... ; x_m] [y_1; ... ; y_n]
  = lit cons [x_1; ... ; x_m] [y_1; ... ; y_n]
  = cons x_1 (cons x_2 (... (cons x_m [y_1; ... ; y_n]) ...))
  = [x_1; ... ; x_m; y_1; ... ; y_n]

The list-reversing function **rev**, where:

$$\textbf{rev } [x_1; \; \dots \; ; x_m] \; = \; [x_m; \; \dots \; ; x_1]$$

can then be defined by:

$$\textbf{rev } l = \textbf{lit } (\lambda x \; l_1. \textbf{ append } l_1 \; [x]) \; l \; [\;]$$

Here are some more examples:

---

[1] The function **lit** is sometimes called **reduce** or **itlist**: it is similar to operators in the programming language APL. An early occurrence of it is in Barron and Strachey's article [5].

1. If **member** x l is **true** if x is a member of list l and **false** otherwise, then:

> **member** x l
> = **lit** $(\lambda x_1\ b.\ (\text{eq } b \text{ true} \rightarrow \text{true} \mid (\text{eq } x_1\ x \rightarrow \text{true} \mid \text{false})))$
> l
> **false**

For example, **member** $\underline{2}$ [$\underline{5}$; $\underline{2}$; $\underline{3}$; $\underline{4}$; $\underline{5}$; $\underline{6}$; $\underline{7}$] = **true** and **member** $\underline{8}$ [$\underline{1}$; $\underline{2}$; $\underline{3}$; $\underline{4}$; $\underline{5}$; $\underline{6}$; $\underline{7}$] = **false**.

2. If **union** l_1 l_2 is the set-theoretic union of l_1 and l_2 then:

> **union** l_1 l_2
> = **lit** $(\lambda x\ l_3.\ (\text{member } x\ l_2 \rightarrow l_3 \mid \text{cons } x\ l_3))\ l_1\ l_2$

For example, **union** [$\underline{1}$; $\underline{2}$; $\underline{3}$] [$\underline{2}$; $\underline{4}$; $\underline{5}$] = [$\underline{1}$; $\underline{3}$; $\underline{2}$; $\underline{4}$; $\underline{5}$].

3. If **intersection** l_1 l_2 is the set-theoretic union of l_1 and l_2 then:

> **intersection** l_1 l_2
> = **lit** $(\lambda x\ l_3.\ (\text{member } x\ l_2 \rightarrow \text{cons } x\ l_3 \mid l_3))\ l_1$ [ ]

For example, **intersection** [$\underline{1}$; $\underline{2}$; $\underline{3}$] [$\underline{2}$; $\underline{4}$; $\underline{5}$] = [$\underline{2}$].

These examples are from the paper 'On the power of list iteration' [21] where it is also shown that both the set of all sublists of a list and the cartesian product of a list of lists can be computed by expressions built up out of **lit**. It is also shown that any primitive recursive function can be computed in this way, but that the equality of lists cannot.

Exercise 77
Program the function **length** for computing the length of a list using **lit**.
□

An excellent book containing lots of examples of functional programs is *Recursive Programming Techniques* by W. Burge [9].

Chapter 7

Theorems about the λ-calculus

Several important theorems about the λ-calculus are stated without proof. These include the Church-Rosser theorem, the normalization theorem, and the undecidability of the halting problem. The significance of these is explained and various applications are described.

If $E_1 \longrightarrow E_2$ then E_2 can be thought of as having been got from E_1 by 'evaluation'. If there are no (β- or η-) redexes in E_2 then it can be thought of as 'fully evaluated'.

A λ-expression is said to be *in normal form* if it contains no β- or η-redexes (i.e. if the only conversion rule that can be applied is α-conversion). Thus a λ-expression in normal form is 'fully evaluated'.

Examples

(i) The representations of numbers are all in normal form.

(ii) $(\lambda x.\ x)\ \underline{0}$ is not in normal form.

$\square$

Suppose an expression E is 'evaluated' in two different ways by applying two different sequences of reductions until two normal forms E_1 and E_2 are obtained. The Church-Rosser theorem stated below shows that E_1 and E_2 will be the same except for having possibly different names of bound variables.

Because the results of reductions do not depend on the order in which they are done, separate redexes can be evaluated in parallel. Various research projects are currently trying to exploit this fact by designing multiprocessor architectures for evaluating λ-expressions. It is too early to tell how successful this work will be. There is a possibility that the communication overhead of distributing redexes to different processors and then

117

collecting together the results will cancel out the theoretical advantages of
the approach. Let us hope this pessimistic possibility can be avoided. It is
a remarkable fact that the Church-Rosser theorem, an obscure mathematical result dating from before computers were invented, may underpin the
design of the next generation of computing systems.

Here is the statement of the Church-Rosser theorem. It is an example
of something that is intuitively obvious, but very hard to prove. Many
properties of the λ-calculus share this property.

The Church-Rosser theorem

If $E_1 = E_2$ then there exists an E such that $E_1 \longrightarrow E$ and $E_2 \longrightarrow E$.

It is now possible to see why the Chuch-Rosser theorem shows that
λ-expressions can be evaluated in any order. Suppose an expression E
is 'evaluated' in two different ways by applying two different sequences
of reductions until two normal forms E_1 and E_2 are obtained. Since E_1
and E_2 are obtained from E by sequences of conversions, it follows by
the definition of $=$ that $E = E_1$ and $E = E_2$ and hence $E_1 = E_2$. By
the Church-Rosser theorem there exists an expression, E' say, such that
$E_1 \longrightarrow E'$ and $E_2 \longrightarrow E'$. Now if E_1 and E_2 are in normal form, then the
only redexes they can contain are α-redexes and so the only way that E_1
and E_2 can be reduced to E' is by changing the names of bound variables.
Thus E_1 and E_2 must be the same up to renaming of bound variables (i.e.
α-conversion).

Another application of the Church-Rosser theorem is to show that if
$m \neq n$ then the λ-expressions representing m and n are not equal, i.e.
$\underline{m} \neq \underline{n}$. Suppose $m \neq n$ but $\underline{m} = \underline{n}$; by the Church-Rosser theorem
$\underline{m} \longrightarrow E$ and $\underline{n} \longrightarrow E$ for some E. But it is obvious from the definitions
of $\underline{m}$ and $\underline{n}$, namely

$$\underline{m} = \lambda f\ x.\ f^m\ x$$
$$\underline{n} = \lambda f\ x.\ f^n\ x$$

that no such E can exist. The only conversions that are applicable to $\underline{m}$
and $\underline{n}$ are α-conversions and these cannot change the number of function
applications in an expression ($\underline{m}$ contains m applications and $\underline{n}$ contains n
applications).

A λ-expression E *has a normal form* if $E = E'$ for some E' in normal
form. The following corollary relates expressions *in* normal form to those
that *have* a normal form; it summarizes some of the statements made above.

> ### Corollary to the Church-Rosser theorem
>
> (i) If E has a normal form then $E \longrightarrow E'$ for some E' in normal form.
>
> (ii) If E has a normal form and $E = E'$ then E' has a normal form.
>
> (iii) If $E = E'$ and E and E' are both in normal form, then E and E' are identical up to α-conversion.

Proof

(i) If E has a normal form then $E = E'$ for some E' in normal form. By the Church-Rosser theorem there exists E'' such that $E \longrightarrow E'$ and $E \longrightarrow E''$. As E' is in normal form the only redexes it can have are α-redexes, so the reduction $E' \longrightarrow E''$ must consist of a sequence of α-conversions. Thus E'' must be identical to E' except for some renaming of bound variables; it must thus be in normal form as E' is.

(ii) Suppose E has a normal form and $E = E'$. As E has a normal form, $E = E''$ where E'' is in normal form. Hence $E' = E''$ by the transitivity of $=$ (see page 69) and so E' has a normal form.

(iii) This was proved above.

□

Exercise 78
For each of the following λ-expressions *either* find its normal form *or* show that it has no normal form:

(i) **add** $\underline{3}$

(ii) **add** $\underline{3}$ $\underline{5}$

(iii) $(\lambda x.\ x\ x)\ (\lambda x.\ x)$

(iv) $(\lambda x.\ x\ x)\ (\lambda x.\ x\ x)$

(v) **Y**

(vi) **Y** $(\lambda y.\ y)$

(vii) **Y** $(\lambda f\ x.\ (\text{iszero}\ x \to \underline{0}\ |\ f\ (\text{pre}\ x)))\ \underline{7}$

□

Notice that a λ-expression E might have a normal form even if there exists an infinite sequence $E \longrightarrow E_1 \longrightarrow E_2 \cdots$. For example $(\lambda x.\ \underline{1})\ (\mathbf{Y}\ f)$ has a normal form $\underline{1}$ even though:

$$(\lambda x.\ \underline{1})\ (\mathbf{Y}\ f) \longrightarrow (\lambda x.\ \underline{1})\ (f\ (\mathbf{Y}\ f)) \longrightarrow \cdots (\lambda x.\ \underline{1})\ (f^n\ (\mathbf{Y}\ f)) \longrightarrow \cdots$$

The normalization theorem stated below tells us that such blind alleys can always be avoided by reducing the *leftmost* β- or η-redex, where by 'leftmost' is meant the redex whose beginning λ is as far to the left as possible.

Another important point to note is that E_1 may not have a normal form even though $E_1\ E_2$ does have one. For example, $\mathbf{Y}$ has no normal form, but $\mathbf{Y}\ (\lambda x.\ \underline{1}) \longrightarrow \underline{1}$. It is a common mistake to think of λ-expressions without a normal form as denoting 'undefined' functions; $\mathbf{Y}$ has no normal form but it denotes a perfectly well defined function[1]. Analysis beyond the scope of this book (see Wadsworth's paper [71]) shows that a λ-expression denotes an undefined function if and only if it *cannot* be converted to an expression in *head normal form*, where E is in head normal form if it has the form

$$\lambda V_1 \cdots V_m.\ V\ E_1 \cdots E_n$$

where $V_1, \ldots, V_m$ and V are variables and $E_1, \ldots, E_n$ are λ-expressions (V can either be equal to V_i, for some i, or it can be distinct from all of them). It follows that the fixed-point operator $\mathbf{Y}$ is not undefined because it can be converted to

$$\lambda f.\ f\ ((\lambda x.\ f(x\ x))\ (\lambda x.\ f(x\ x)))$$

which is in head normal form.

It can be shown that an expression E has a head normal form if and only if there exist expressions $E_1, \ldots, E_n$ such that $E\ E_1 \ldots E_n$ has a normal form. This supports the interpretation of expressions without head normal forms as denoting undefined functions: E being undefined means that $E\ E_1 \ldots E_n$ never terminates for *any* $E_1, \ldots, E_n$. Full details on head normal forms and their relation to definedness can be found in Barendregt's book [4].

Exercise 79
In Section 5.7.3 a representation of a partial recursive function f was defined by a λ-expression $\underline{f}$. Is it the case that with this representation, if $f(x_1, \ldots, x_n) = y$ is undefined then $\underline{f}(\underline{x_1}, \ldots, \underline{x_n}) = \underline{y}$ does not have a head normal form? $\square$

---

[1] The mathematical characterization of the function denoted by $\mathbf{Y}$ can be found in Stoy's book [67].

The normalization theorem

If E has a normal form, then repeatedly reducing the leftmost β- or η-redex (possibly after an α-conversion to avoid invalid substitutions) will terminate with an expression in normal form.

The remark about α-conversion in the statement of the theorem is to cover cases like:

$$(\lambda x.\ (\lambda y.\ x\ y))\ y \longrightarrow \lambda y'.\ y\ y'$$

where $\lambda y.\ x\ y \longrightarrow \lambda y'.\ x\ y'$ has been α-converted so as to avoid the invalid substitution $(\lambda y.\ x\ y)[y/x] = \lambda y.\ y\ y$.

A sequence of reductions in which the leftmost redex is always reduced is called a *normal order reduction sequence*.

The normalization theorem says that if E has a normal form (i.e. for some E' in normal form $E = E'$) then it can be found by normal order reduction. This, however, is not usually the 'most efficient' way to find it. For example, normal order reduction requires

$$(\lambda x. \frown x \frown x \frown)\ E$$

to be reduced to

$$\frown E \frown E \frown$$

If E is not in normal form then it would be more efficient to first reduce E to E' say (where E' is in normal form) and then to reduce

$$(\lambda x. \frown x \frown x \frown)\ E'$$

to

$$\frown E' \frown E' \frown$$

thereby avoiding having to reduce E twice.

Note, however, that this 'call-by-value' scheme is disastrous in cases like

$$(\lambda x.\underline{1})\ ((\lambda x.\ x\ x)\ (\lambda x.\ x\ x))$$

It is a difficult problem to find an optimal algorithm for choosing the next redex to reduce. For recent work in this area see Levy's paper [43].

Because normal order reduction appears so inefficient, some programming languages based on the λ-calculus, e.g. LISP, have used call by value even though it doesn't always terminate. Actually, call by value has other advantages besides efficiency, especially when the language is 'impure', i.e. has constructs with side effects (e.g. assignments). On the other hand, recent research suggests that maybe normal order evaluation is not as inefficient as was originally thought if one uses cunning implementation tricks like graph reduction (see page 136). Whether functional programming languages should use normal order or call by value is still a controversial issue.

7.1   Some undecidability results

In Section 5.7 it was shown that the λ-calculus is a computing mechanism at least as powerful as the partial recursive functions. There follow some examples of things that cannot be computed.

Suppose a λ-expression **hasnf** (for 'has a normal form') could be devised with the property that for any E:

$$\textbf{hasnf } E = \begin{cases} \textbf{true} & \text{if } E \text{ has a normal form} \\ \textbf{false} & \text{if } E \text{ doesn't have a normal form} \end{cases}$$

Define another λ-expression **W** which satisfies the equation:

$$\textbf{W} = (\textbf{hasnf W} \rightarrow \bot \mid \underline{0})$$

(where $\bot$ is a λ-expression which doesn't have a normal form, e.g. the one defined on page 99). A suitable definition of **W** is:

$$\textbf{W} = \textbf{Y} \, (\lambda f. \, (\textbf{hasnf } f \rightarrow \bot \mid \underline{0}))$$

Does **W** have a normal form? There are two possible answers: 'yes' or 'no'.

(i) If 'yes' then **hasnf W** = **true** and then by the equation for **W** and properties of conditionals (see page 78) it follows that **W** = $\bot$. But $\bot$ doesn't have a normal form which contradicts (ii) of the corollary to the Church-Rosser theorem on page 118.

(ii) If 'no' then **hasnf W** = **false** and then by the equation for **W** and properties of conditionals (see page 78) it follows that **W** = $\underline{0}$. But $\underline{0}$ has a normal form (indeed, it is in normal form) which again contradicts (ii) of the corollary to the Church-Rosser theorem.

This shows that the assumption that **hasnf** exists leads to a contradiction in all cases and thus it cannot exist.

Exercise 80

Show that there cannot exist a λ-expression **equal** with the property that:

$$\textbf{equal } E_1 \ E_2 = \begin{cases} \textbf{true} & \text{if } E_1 = E_2 \\ \textbf{false} & \text{otherwise} \end{cases}$$

Hint: Choose **W** to satisfy $\textbf{W} = (\textbf{equal W } \underline{0} \rightarrow \underline{1} \mid \underline{0})$ and then consider whether $\textbf{W} = \underline{0}$. □

Exercise 81

Why doesn't non-existence of **equal** in the previous exercise contradict the existence of **eq** in Exercise 61 on page 88? □

The result on the non-existence of **hasnf** is not very strong because all that the evaluation of **hasnf** could do is apply expressions to E, and E to expressions. Maybe if **hasnf** were given some kind of representation of the syntax of E then it could use some algorithm to compute whether E terminates. To investigate this possibility, suppose that for each λ-expression E another λ-expression $\ulcorner E\urcorner$ has been defined such that $\ulcorner E_1\urcorner = \ulcorner E_2\urcorner$ if and only if E_1 is identical to E_2 (an outline of how to define $\ulcorner E\urcorner$ is given below). One can think of $\ulcorner E\urcorner$ as the parse tree of E represented as a λ-expression. Note that one cannot just take $\ulcorner E\urcorner$ to be E because then, for example, it would follow that $\ulcorner(\lambda x.\ x)\ \underline{1}\urcorner = \ulcorner\underline{1}\urcorner$, but $(\lambda x.\ x)\ \underline{1}$ is not identical to $\underline{1}$.

It will be shown that there is *no* λ-expression, **halts** say, such that for all E:

$$\textbf{halts}\ulcorner E\urcorner = \begin{cases} \textbf{true} & \text{if } E \text{ has a normal form} \\ \textbf{false} & \text{if } E \text{ doesn't have a normal form} \end{cases}$$

The argument is similar to the one above for **hasnf**, but slighly more cunning. It makes use of the second fixed-point theorem stated below.

Defining $\ulcorner E\urcorner$ for arbitary E is straightforward, but a bit tedious. First it is necessary to define a representation for character strings. If $c_1 c_2 \ldots c_n$ is a character string, define $"c_1 c_2 \ldots c_n"$ be the λ-expression $[a_1; a_2; \cdots; a_n]$ where a_i is the ASCII code for c_i (*e.g.* $"\texttt{fred}"$ is $[\underline{102}; \underline{114}; \underline{101}; \underline{100}]$).

Exercise 82

Using the definitions on pages 82 and 99 write out the λ-expression denoted by $"\texttt{def}"$. □

Exercise 83

Define a λ-expression eqstr such that:

$$\text{eqstr}("c_1 \ldots c_n", "c'_1 \ldots c'_m") = \begin{cases} \text{true} & \text{if } n = m \text{ and} \\ & c_i = c'_i \ (1 \le i \le n) \\ \text{false} & \text{otherwise} \end{cases}$$

□

If E is a λ-expression we define $\ulcorner E \urcorner$ by cases as follows:

(i) If E is a variable I then: $\ulcorner E \urcorner = (\underline{0}, "I")$

(ii) If E is a combination $(E_1 \ E_2)$ then: $\ulcorner E \urcorner = (\underline{1}, \ulcorner E_1 \urcorner, \ulcorner E_2 \urcorner)$

(iii) If E is an abstraction $(\lambda V. \ E')$ then: $\ulcorner E \urcorner = (\underline{2}, "V", \ulcorner E' \urcorner)$

Think of $\ulcorner E \urcorner$ as an internal represention (i.e. parse tree) of E. The first component of the pair $\ulcorner E \urcorner$ indicates the sort of expression that E is.

Example

$$\begin{aligned}\ulcorner \lambda x. \ (\lambda y. \ x \ y) \urcorner &= (\underline{2}, "x", \ulcorner \lambda y. \ x \ y \urcorner) \\ &= (\underline{2}, "x", (\underline{2}, "y", \ulcorner x \ y \urcorner)) \\ &= (\underline{2}, "x", (\underline{2}, "y", (\underline{1}, \ulcorner x \urcorner, \ulcorner y \urcorner))) \\ &= (\underline{2}, "x", (\underline{2}, "y", (\underline{1}, (\underline{0}, "x"), (\underline{0}, "y")))) \\ &= (\underline{2}, [120], (\underline{2}, [121], (\underline{1}, (\underline{0}, [120]), (\underline{0}, [121])))) \end{aligned}$$

□

The following λ-expressions are defined to represent abstract syntax *constructors*, *selectors* and *tests*.

Constructors

$\qquad$ LET mkvar $= \lambda x. \ (\underline{0}, x)$

$\qquad$ LET mkcomb $= \lambda(x, y). \ (\underline{1}, x, y)$

$\qquad$ LET mkabs $= \lambda(x, y). \ (\underline{2}, x, y)$

Selectors

$\qquad$ LET name $=$ snd

$\qquad$ LET rator $= \lambda e. \ e \downarrow 2$

$\qquad$ LET rand $= \lambda e. \ e \downarrow 3$

$\qquad$ LET bv $= \lambda e. \ e \downarrow 2$

Tests

$$\text{LET body} = \lambda e.\ e \downarrow 3$$

$$\text{LET isvar} = \lambda e.\ \text{eq (fst } e)\ \underline{0}$$
$$\text{LET iscomb} = \lambda e.\ \text{eq (fst } e)\ \underline{1}$$
$$\text{LET isabs} = \lambda e.\ \text{eq (fst } e)\ \underline{2}$$

See Exercise 61 on page 88 for **eq**.

Exercise 84
Show

 (i) **name** $\ulcorner x \urcorner = $ "x"

 (ii) **bv** $\ulcorner \lambda x.\ E \urcorner = $ "x"

 (iii) **body** $\ulcorner \lambda x.\ E \urcorner = \ulcorner E \urcorner$

 (iv) **rator** $\ulcorner E_1\ E_2 \urcorner = \ulcorner E_1 \urcorner$

  (v) **rand** $\ulcorner E_1\ E_2 \urcorner = \ulcorner E_2 \urcorner$

 (vi) **mkvar** "x" $= \ulcorner x \urcorner$

 (vii) **mkcomb**$(\ulcorner E_1 \urcorner, \ulcorner E_2 \urcorner) = \ulcorner E_1\ E_2 \urcorner$

(viii) **mkabs**$("x", \ulcorner E \urcorner) = \ulcorner \lambda x.\ E \urcorner$

□

The second fixed-point theorem stated below should be compared with
the first fixed-point theorem of Section 5.4 (see page 87). It is useful for
showing the non-existence of **halts**.

The second fixed-point theorem

For any λ-expression E there exists a λ-expression E' such that:

$$E' = E \ulcorner E' \urcorner$$

Proof outline

Suppose there is a λ-expression **quote** such that for every E

$$\text{quote} \ulcorner E \urcorner = \ulcorner \ulcorner E \urcorner \urcorner$$

Then one can define $E' = \mathbf{F}\ \ulcorner\mathbf{F}\urcorner$ where:

$$\mathbf{F} = \lambda x.\ E\ (\mathbf{mkcomb}\ (x, \mathbf{quote}\ x))$$

This works because

$$
\begin{aligned}
E' &= \mathbf{F}\ \ulcorner\mathbf{F}\urcorner \\
&= E\ (\mathbf{mkcomb}\ (\ulcorner\mathbf{F}\urcorner, \mathbf{quote}\ \ulcorner\mathbf{F}\urcorner)) \\
&= E\ (\mathbf{mkcomb}\ (\ulcorner\mathbf{F}\urcorner, \ulcorner\ulcorner\mathbf{F}\urcorner\urcorner)) \\
&= E\ (\ulcorner\mathbf{F}\ \ulcorner\mathbf{F}\urcorner\urcorner) \\
&= E\ \ulcorner E'\urcorner
\end{aligned}
$$

The definition of **quote** is straightforward; one just considers the various forms $\ulcorner E\urcorner$ can take as described on page 124. $\square$

Exercise 85
This exercise outlines the details of the definition of **quote**.

(i) Define a λ-expression **quotenum** such that for all n:

$$\mathbf{quotenum}\ \underline{n} = \ulcorner\underline{n}\urcorner$$

(ii) Define a λ-expression **quotestring** such that for all strings $"x_1 \ldots x_n"$

$$\mathbf{quotestring}\ "x_1 \ldots x_n" = \ulcorner"x_1 \ldots x_n"\urcorner$$

(iii) Define a λ-expression **quote** such that for all E

$$\mathbf{quote}\ \ulcorner E\urcorner = \ulcorner\ulcorner E\urcorner\urcorner$$

$\square$

7.2 The halting problem

Suppose one could devise a λ-expression **halts** with the property that:

$$
\mathbf{halts}\ \ulcorner E\urcorner = \begin{cases} \mathbf{true} & \text{if } E \text{ has a normal form} \\ \mathbf{false} & \text{if } E \text{ doesn't have a normal form.} \end{cases}
$$

Define **foo** by

$$\mathbf{foo} = \lambda x.\ (\mathbf{halts}\ x \rightarrow \bot\ |\ \underline{0})$$

By the second fixed-point theorem there is a λ-expression, $\mathbf{W}$ say, such that:
$$\mathbf{W} = \mathbf{foo} \ulcorner \mathbf{W} \urcorner = (\mathbf{halts} \ulcorner \mathbf{W} \urcorner \rightarrow \bot \mid \underline{0})$$
It can be seen that, in fact, such a $\mathbf{W}$ cannot exists by asking whether it has a normal form.

(i) If $\mathbf{W}$ has a normal form then $\mathbf{halts} \ulcorner \mathbf{W} \urcorner = \mathbf{true}$, so by the definition of $\mathbf{foo}$: $\mathbf{W} = \bot$. But this is impossible because if $\mathbf{W} = \bot$ then by the corollary to the Church-Rosser theorem (see page 118) $\bot$ would have to have a normal form also.

(ii) If $\mathbf{W}$ does not have a normal form then $\mathbf{halt} \ulcorner \mathbf{W} \urcorner = \mathbf{false}$, so $\mathbf{W} = \underline{0}$. But this is also impossible as $\underline{0}$ is in normal form.

This contradiction was derived by assuming that $\mathbf{halts}$ exists, hence $\mathbf{halts}$ does not exist.

Exercise 86
Show that there cannot exist a λ-expression $\mathbf{equiv}$ such that
$$\mathbf{equiv}(\ulcorner E_1 \urcorner, \ulcorner E_2 \urcorner) = \begin{cases} \mathbf{true} & \text{if } E_1 = E_2 \\ \mathbf{false} & \text{if } E_1 \neq E_2 \end{cases}$$

Hint: Replace $\mathbf{halts}$ by $\lambda x.\ \mathbf{equiv}\ (\ulcorner E_1 \urcorner, x)$ in the argument above. $\square$

Exercise 87
Suppose lists are represented as in Section 5.8 on page 98. Show that there cannot exist a λ-expression $\mathbf{null}$ such that:
$$\mathbf{null}\ E = \begin{cases} \mathbf{true} & \text{if } E = [\ ] \\ \mathbf{false} & \text{otherwise} \end{cases}$$

Does this result hold if $[\ ]$ is replaced by an arbitrary λ-expression E? $\square$

Chapter 8

Combinators

Combinators are motivated and described, and their relationship to the λ-calculus is discussed. Various algorithms for compiling λ-expressions into combinators are explained. A brief introduction to the combinator machines is given.

Combinators provide an alternative theory of functions to the λ-calculus. They were originally introduced by logicians as a way of studying the process of substitution. More recently, Turner has argued that combinators provide a good 'machine code' into which functional programs can be compiled [68]. Several experimental computers have been built based on Turner's ideas (see e.g. [12]) and the results are promising. How these machines work is explained in Section 8.3. Combinators also provide a good intermediate code for conventional machines; several of the best compilers for functional languages are based on them (e.g. [17,2]).

There are two equivalent ways of formulating the theory of combinators:

(i) within the λ-calculus, or

(ii) as a completely separate theory.

The approach here is to adopt (i) here as it is slightly simpler, but (ii) was how it was done originally[1]. It will be shown that *any* λ-expression is equal to an expression built from variables and two particular expressions, **K** and **S**, using only function application. This is done by mimicking λ-abstractions using combinations of **K** and **S**. It will be demonstrated how β-reductions can be simulated by simpler operations involving **K** and **S**. It is these simpler operations that combinator machines implement directly in hardware. The definitions of **K** and **S** are

---

[1] The two-volume treatise *Combinatory Logic* [14,15] is the definitive reference, but the more recent textbooks [31,4] are better places to start.

129

LET $K = \lambda x\ y.\ x$

LET $S = \lambda f\ g\ x.\ (f\ x)\ (g\ x)$

From these definitions it is clear by β-reduction that for all E_1, E_2 and E_3:

$$K\ E_1\ E_2 = E_1$$

$$S\ E_1\ E_2\ E_3 = (E_1\ E_3)\ (E_2\ E_3)$$

Any expression built by application (i.e. combination) from K and S is called a *combinator*; K and S are the *primitive combinators*.

In BNF, combinators have the following syntax:

<*combinator*> ::= K | S | (<*combinator*> <*combinator*>)

A *combinatory expression* is an expression built from K, S and zero or more variables. Thus a combinator is a combinatory expression not containing variables. In BNF, the syntax of combinatory expressions is:

<*combinatory expression*>
   ::= K | S
    | <*variable*>
    | (<*combinatory expression*> <*combinatory expression*>)

Exercise 88
Define I by:

$$\text{LET } I = \lambda x.\ x$$

Show that $I = S\ K\ K$. □

The identity function I defined in the last exercise is often taken as a primitive combinator, but as the exercise shows this is not necessary as it can be defined from K and S.

8.1   Combinator reduction

If E and E' are combinatory expressions then the notation $E \xrightarrow{c} E'$ is used if $E = E'$ or if E' can be got from E by a sequence of rewritings of the form:

(i) $K\ E_1\ E_2 \xrightarrow{c} E_1$

(ii) $\mathbf{S}\ E_1\ E_2\ E_3 \xrightarrow[c]{} (E_1\ E_3)\ (E_2\ E_3)$

(iii) $\mathbf{I}\ E \xrightarrow[c]{} E$

Note that the reduction $\mathbf{I}\ E \xrightarrow[c]{} E$ is derivable from (i) and (ii).

Example

$$\mathbf{S\ K\ K}\ x \xrightarrow[c]{} \mathbf{K}\ x\ (\mathbf{K}\ x) \qquad\qquad \text{by (ii)}$$

$$\xrightarrow[c]{} x \qquad\qquad \text{by (i)}$$

□

This example shows that for any E: $\mathbf{I}\ E \xrightarrow[c]{} E$.

Any sequence of combinatory reductions, i.e. reductions via $\xrightarrow[c]{}$, can be expanded into a sequence of β-conversions. This is clear because $\mathbf{K}\ E_1\ E_2$ and $\mathbf{S}\ E_1\ E_2\ E_3$ reduce to E_1 and $(E_1\ E_3)\ (E_2\ E_3)$, respectively, by sequences of β-conversions.

8.2   Functional completeness

A surprising fact is that any λ-expression can be translated to an equivalent combinatory expression. This result is called the functional completeness of combinators and is the basis for compilers for functional languages to the machine code of combinator machines.

The first step is to define, for an arbitrary variable V and combinatory expression E, another combinatory expression $\lambda^*V.\ E$ that simulates $\lambda V.\ E$ in the sense that $\lambda^*V.\ E = \lambda V.\ E$. This provides a way of using $\mathbf{K}$ and $\mathbf{S}$ to simulate adding 'λV' to an expression.

If V is a variable and E is a combinatory expression, then the combinatory expression $\lambda^*V.\ E$ is defined inductively on the structure of E as follows:

(i) $\lambda^*V.\ V = \mathbf{I}$

(ii) $\lambda^*V.\ V' = \mathbf{K}\ V'$ (if $V \neq V'$)

(iii) $\lambda^*V.\ C = \mathbf{K}\ C$ (if C is a combinator)

(iv) $\lambda^*V.\ (E_1\ E_2) = \mathbf{S}\ (\lambda^*V.\ E_1)\ (\lambda^*V.\ E_2)$

Note that $\lambda^*V.\ E$ is a combinatory expression not containing V.

Example: If f and x are variables and $f \neq x$, then:

$$\lambda^*x.\ f\ x = \mathbf{S}\ (\lambda^*x.\ f)\ (\lambda^*x.\ x)$$
$$= \mathbf{S}\ (\mathbf{K}\ f)\ \mathbf{I}$$

□

The following theorem shows that $\lambda^*V.\ E$ simulates λ-abstraction.

Theorem $(\lambda^*V.\ E) = \lambda V.\ E$

Proof We show that $(\lambda^*V.\ E)\ V = E$. It then follows immediately that $\lambda V.\ (\lambda^*V.\ E)\ V = \lambda V.E$ and hence by η-reduction that $\lambda^*V.\ E = \lambda V.\ E$.

The proof that $(\lambda^*V.\ E)\ V = E$ is by mathematical induction on the 'size' of E. The argument goes as follows:

(i) If $E = V$ then:

$$(\lambda^*V.\ E)\ V\ =\ \mathbf{I}\ V\ =\ (\lambda x.\ x)\ V\ =\ V\ =\ E$$

(ii) If $E = V'$ where $V' \neq V$ then:

$$(\lambda^*V.\ E)\ V\ =\ \mathbf{K}\ V'\ V\ =\ (\lambda x\ y.\ x)\ V'\ V\ =\ V'\ =\ E$$

(iii) If $E = C$ where C is a combinator, then:

$$(\lambda^*V.\ E)\ V\ =\ \mathbf{K}\ C\ =\ (\lambda x\ y.\ x)\ C\ V\ =\ C\ =\ E$$

(iv) If $E = (E_1\ E_2)$ then we can assume by induction that:

$$(\lambda^*V.\ E_1)\ V = E_1$$
$$(\lambda^*V.\ E_2)\ V = E_2$$

and hence

$$\begin{aligned}
(\lambda^*V.\ E)\ V &= (\lambda^*V.\ (E_1\ E_2))\ V \\
&= (\mathbf{S}\ (\lambda^*V.\ E_1)\ (\lambda^*V.\ E_2))\ V \\
&= (\lambda f\ g\ x.\ f\ x\ (g\ x))\ (\lambda^*V.\ E_1)\ (\lambda^*V.\ E_2)\ V \\
&= (\lambda^*V.\ E_1)\ V\ ((\lambda^*V.\ E_2)\ V) \\
&= E_1\ E_2 \qquad\qquad \text{(by induction assumption)} \\
&= E
\end{aligned}$$

□

The notation

$$\lambda^* V_1 \ V_2 \ \cdots \ V_n. \ E$$

is used to mean

$$\lambda^* V_1. \ \lambda^* V_2. \ \cdots \ \lambda^* V_n. \ E$$

Now define the translation of an arbitrary λ-expression E to a combinatory expression $(E)_C$:

(i) $(V)_C = x$

(ii) $(E_1 \ E_2)_C = (E_1)_C \ (E_2)_C$

(iii) $(\lambda V. \ E)_C = \lambda^* V. \ (E)_C$

Theorem For every λ-expression E we have: $E = (E)_C$

Proof
The proof is by induction on the size of E.

(i) If $E = V$ then $(E)_C = (V)_C = V$

(ii) If $E = (E_1 \ E_2)$ we can assume by induction that

$$E_1 = (E_1)_C$$
$$E_2 = (E_2)_C$$

hence

$$(E)_C \ = \ (E_1 \ E_2)_C \ = \ (E_1)_C \ (E_2)_C \ = \ E_1 \ E_2 \ = \ E$$

(iii) If $E = \lambda V. \ E'$ then we can assume by induction that

$$(E')_C = E'$$

hence

$$
\begin{aligned}
(E)_C \ &= (\lambda V. \ E')_C \\
&= \lambda^* V. \ (E')_C && \text{(by translation rules)} \\
&= \lambda^* V. \ E' && \text{(by induction assumption)} \\
&= \lambda V. \ E' && \text{(by previous theorem)} \\
&= E
\end{aligned}
$$

$\square$

This theorem shows that any λ-expression is equal to a λ-expression built up from $\mathbf{K}$ and $\mathbf{S}$ and variables by application, i.e. the class of λ-expressions E defined by the BNF:

$$E ::= V \mid \mathbf{K} \mid \mathbf{S} \mid E_1\, E_2$$

is equivalent to the full λ-calculus.

A collection of n combinators $C_1, \ldots, C_n$ is called an n-element *basis* (Barendregt [4], Chapter 8) if every λ-expression E is equal to an expression built from C_is and variables by function applications. The theorem above shows that $\mathbf{K}$ and $\mathbf{S}$ form a 2-element basis. The exercise below (from Section 8.1.5. of Barendregt) shows that there exists a 1-element basis.

Exercise 89
Find a combinator, $\mathbf{X}$ say, such that any λ-expression is equal to an expression built from $\mathbf{X}$ and variables by application. *Hint*: Consider $(\mathbf{K}, \mathbf{S}, \mathbf{K})\,(\mathbf{K}, \mathbf{S}, \mathbf{K})\,(\mathbf{K}, \mathbf{S}, \mathbf{K})$ and $(\mathbf{K}, \mathbf{S}, \mathbf{K})\,((\mathbf{K}, \mathbf{S}, \mathbf{K})\,(\mathbf{K}, \mathbf{S}, \mathbf{K}))$ □

Examples

$$
\begin{aligned}
\lambda^* f.\ \lambda^* x.\ f\ (x\ x) &= \lambda^* f.\ (\lambda^* x.\ f\ (x\ x)) \\
&= \lambda^* f.\ (\mathbf{S}\ (\lambda^* x.\ f)\ (\lambda^* x.\ x\ x)) \\
&= \lambda^* f.\ (\mathbf{S}\ (\mathbf{K}f)\ (\mathbf{S}(\lambda^* x.\ x)\ (\lambda^* x.\ x))) \\
&= \lambda^* f.\ (\mathbf{S}\ (\mathbf{K}f)\ (\mathbf{S}\ \mathbf{I}\ \mathbf{I})) \\
&= \mathbf{S}\ (\lambda^* f.\ \mathbf{S}\ (\mathbf{K}f))\ (\lambda^* f.\ \mathbf{S}\ \mathbf{I}\ \mathbf{I}) \\
&= \mathbf{S}\ (\mathbf{S}\ (\lambda^* f.\ \mathbf{S})\ (\lambda^* f.\ \mathbf{K}\ f))\ (\mathbf{K}\ (\mathbf{S}\ \mathbf{I}\ \mathbf{I})) \\
&= \mathbf{S}\ (\mathbf{S}\ (\mathbf{K}\ \mathbf{S})\ (\mathbf{S}\ (\lambda^* f.\ \mathbf{K})\ (\ \lambda^* f.\ f)))\ (\mathbf{K}\ (\mathbf{S}\ \mathbf{I}\ \mathbf{I})) \\
&= \mathbf{S}\ (\mathbf{S}\ (\mathbf{K}\ \mathbf{S})\ (\mathbf{S}\ (\mathbf{K}\ \mathbf{K})\ \mathbf{I}))\ (\mathbf{K}\ (\mathbf{S}\ \mathbf{I}\ \mathbf{I}))
\end{aligned}
$$

$$
\begin{aligned}
(\mathbf{Y})_{\mathbf{C}} &= (\lambda f.\ (\lambda x.\ f(x\ x)\ (\lambda x.\ f(x\ x)))_{\mathbf{C}} \\
&= \lambda^* f.\ ((\lambda x.\ f(x\ x))\ (\lambda x.\ f(x\ x)))_{\mathbf{C}} \\
&= \lambda^* f.\ ((\lambda x.\ f(x\ x))_{\mathbf{C}}\ (\lambda x.\ f(x\ x))_{\mathbf{C}}) \\
&= \lambda^* f.\ (\lambda^* x.\ (f(x\ x))_{\mathbf{C}})\ (\lambda^* x.\ (f(x\ x))_{\mathbf{C}}) \\
&= \lambda^* f.\ (\lambda^* x.\ f(x\ x))\ (\lambda^* x.\ f(x\ x)) \\
&= \mathbf{S}\ (\lambda^* f.\ \lambda^* x.\ f(x\ x))\ (\lambda^* f.\ \lambda^* x.\ f(x\ x)) \\
&= \mathbf{S}(\mathbf{S}(\mathbf{S}(\mathbf{KS})(\mathbf{S}(\mathbf{KK})\mathbf{I}))(\mathbf{K}(\mathbf{SII})))(\mathbf{S}(\mathbf{S}(\mathbf{KS})(\mathbf{S}(\mathbf{KK})\mathbf{I}))(\mathbf{K}(\mathbf{SII})))
\end{aligned}
$$

□

8.3   Reduction machines

Until Dave Turner published his paper [68], combinators were regarded as a mathematical curiosity. In his paper Turner argued that translating functional languages, i.e. languages based on the λ-calculus, to combinators and then reducing the resulting expressions using the rewrites given on page 130 is a *practical* way of implementing these languages.

Turner's idea is to represent combinatory expressions by trees. For example, S $(f\ x)\ (K\ y)\ z$ would be represented by:

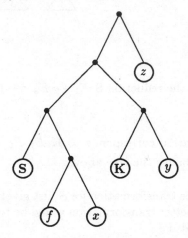

Such trees are represented as pointer structures in memory. Special hardware or firmware can then be implemented to transform such trees according to the rules of combinator reduction defining $\xrightarrow[c]{}$.

For example, the tree above could be transformed to:

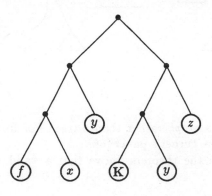

using the transformation

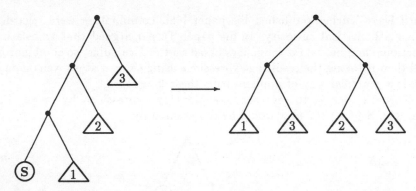

which corresponds to the reduction $S\ E_1\ E_2\ E_3 \xrightarrow{c} (E_1\ E_2)\ (E_2\ E_3)$.

Exercise 90
What tree transformation corresponds to $K\ E_1\ E_2 \xrightarrow{c} E_1$? How would
this transformation change the tree above? □

Notice that the tree transformation for S just given duplicates a subtree.
This wastes space; a better transformation would be to generate one subtree
with two pointers to it, i.e.

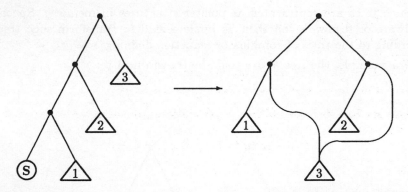

This generates a *graph* rather than a tree. For further details of such
graph reductions see Turner's paper [68].
It is clear from the theorem above that a valid way of reducing λ-
expressions is:

(i) Translating to combinators (i.e. $E \mapsto (E)_C$).

(ii) Applying the rewrites

$$\mathbf{K}\ E_1\ E_2 \xrightarrow[c]{} E_1$$
$$\mathbf{S}\ E_1\ E_2\ E_3 \xrightarrow[c]{} (E_1\ E_3)\ (E_2\ E_3)$$

until no more rewriting is possible.

An interesting question is whether this process will 'fully evaluate' expressions. If some expression E is translated to combinators, then reduced using $\xrightarrow{c}$, is the resulting expression as 'fully evaluated' as the result of λ-reducing E directly, or is it only partially evaluated? Surprisingly, there doesn't seem to be anything in the literature on this important question[2]. However, combinator machines have been built and they appear to work [12]!

It is well known that if $E_1 \longrightarrow E_2$ in the λ-calculus, then it is *not* necessarily the case that $(E_1)_{\mathbf{C}} \xrightarrow{c} (E_2)_{\mathbf{C}}$. For example, take

$$E_1 = \lambda y.\ (\lambda z.\ y)\ (x\ y)$$
$$E_2 = \lambda y.\ y$$

Exercise 91
With E_1 and E_2 as above show that $E_1 \longrightarrow E_2$ in the λ-calculus, but it is not the case that $(E_1)_{\mathbf{C}} \xrightarrow{c} (E_2)_{\mathbf{C}}$. $\square$

A combinatory expression is defined to be in *combinatory normal form* if it contains no subexpressions of the form $\mathbf{K}\ E_1\ E_2$ or $\mathbf{S}\ E_1\ E_2\ E_3$. Then the normalization theorem holds for combinatory expressions, i.e. always reducing the leftmost combinatory redex will find a combinatory normal form if it exists.

Note that if E is in combinatory normal form, then it does not necessarily follow that it is a λ-expression in normal form.

Example: $\mathbf{S}\ \mathbf{K}$ is in combinatory normal form, but it contains a β-redex, namely:

$$(\lambda f.\ (\lambda g\ x.\ (f\ x\ (g\ x))))\ (\lambda x\ y.\ x)$$

$\square$

Exercise 92
Construct a combinatory expression E which is in combinatory normal form, but has no normal form. $\square$

---

[2] The most relevant paper I could find is one by Hindley [30]. This compares λ-reduction with combinatory reduction, but not in a way that is prima facie relevant to the termination of combinator machines.

8.4   Improved translation to combinators

The examples on page 134 show that simple λ-expressions can translate to quite complex combinatory expressions via the rules on page 133.

To make the 'code' executed by reduction machines more compact, various optimizations have been devised.

Examples

(i) Let E be a combinatory expression and x a variable not occurring in E. Then:

$$\textbf{S }(\textbf{K } E)\textbf{ I } x \xrightarrow[c]{} (\textbf{K } E\ x)\ (\textbf{I } x) \xrightarrow[c]{} E\ x$$

hence $\textbf{S }(\textbf{K}E)\textbf{ I } x = E\ x$ (because $E_1 \xrightarrow[c]{} E_2$ implies $E_1 \longrightarrow E_2$), so by extensionality (Section 4.7, see on page 71):

$$\textbf{S }(\textbf{K } E)\textbf{ I} = E$$

(ii) Let E_1, E_2 be combinatory expressions and x a variable not occurring in either of them. Then:

$$\textbf{S }(\textbf{K } E_1)\ (\textbf{K } E_2)\ x \xrightarrow[c]{} \textbf{K } E_1\ x\ (\textbf{K } E_2)\ x \xrightarrow[c]{} E_1\ E_2$$

Thus
$$\textbf{S }(\textbf{K } E_1)\ (\textbf{K } E_2)\ x\ =\ E_1\ E_2$$

Now
$$\textbf{K }(E_1\ E_2)\ x \xrightarrow[c]{} E_1\ E_2$$

hence $\textbf{K }(E_1\ E_2)\ x = E_1\ E_2$. Thus

$$\textbf{S }(\textbf{K } E_1)\ (\textbf{K } E_2)\ x\ =\ E_1\ E_2\ =\ \textbf{K }(E_1\ E_2)\ x$$

It follows by extensionality that:

$$\textbf{S }(\textbf{K } E_1)\ (\textbf{K } E_2)\ =\ \textbf{K }(E_1\ E_2)$$

□

Since $\textbf{S }(\textbf{K } E)\textbf{ I} = E$ for any E, whenever a combinatory expression of the form $\textbf{S }(\textbf{K } E)\textbf{ I}$ is generated, it can be 'peephole optimized' to just E. Similarly, whenever an expression of the form $\textbf{S }(\textbf{K } E_1)\ (\textbf{K } E_2)$ is generated, it can be optimized to $\textbf{K }(E_1\ E_2)$.

Example: On page 134 it was shown that:

$$\lambda^* f. \ \lambda^* x. \ f(x \ x) = S \ (S \ (K \ S) \ (S \ (K \ K) \ I)) \ (K \ (S \ I \ I))$$

Using the optimization $S \ (K \ E) \ I = E$ this simplifies to:

$$\lambda^* f. \ \lambda^* x. \ f(x \ x) = S \ (S \ (K \ S) \ K) \ (K \ (S \ I \ I))$$

☐

8.5 More combinators

It is easier to recognize the applicability of the optimization $S \ (K \ E) \ I = E$ if I has not been expanded to $S \ K \ K$, i.e. if I is taken as a primitive combinator. Various other combinators are also useful in the same way; for example, B and C defined by:

LET $B = \lambda f \ g \ x. \ f \ (g \ x)$

LET $C = \lambda f \ g \ x. \ f \ x \ g$

These have the following reduction rules:

$$B \ E_1 \ E_2 \ E_3 \ \xrightarrow{c} \ E_1 \ (E_2 \ E_3)$$
$$C \ E_1 \ E_2 \ E_3 \ \xrightarrow{c} \ E_1 \ E_3 \ E_2$$

Exercise 93
Show that with B, C defined as above:

$$S \ (K \ E_1) \ E_2 = B \ E_1 \ E_2$$
$$S \ E_1 \ (K \ E_2) = C \ E_1 \ E_2$$

(where E_1, E_2 are any two combinatory expressions). ☐

Using B and C, one can further optimize the translation of λ-expressions to combinators by replacing expressions of the form $S \ (K \ E_1) \ E_2$ and $S \ E_1 \ (K \ E_2)$ by $B \ E_1 \ E_2$ and $C \ E_1 \ E_2$.

8.6   Curry's algorithm

Combining the various optimizations described in the previous section leads
to *Curry's algorithm* for translating λ-expressions to combinatory expressions. This algorithm consists in using the definition of $(E)_C$ given on page
133, but whenever an expression of the form $S\ E_1\ E_2$ is generated one tries
to apply the following rewrite rules:

1. $S\ (K\ E_1)\ (K\ E_2) \longrightarrow (K\ E_1\ E_2)$

2. $S\ (K\ E)\ I \longrightarrow E$

3. $S\ (K\ E_1)\ E_2 \longrightarrow B\ E_1\ E_2$

4. $S E_1 (K E_2) \longrightarrow C E_1 E_2$

If more than one rule is applicable, the *earlier* one is used. For example,
$S\ (K\ E_1)\ (K\ E_2)$ is translated to $K\ (E_1\ E_2)$, not to $B\ E_1\ (K\ E_2)$.

Exercise 94
Show that using Curry's algorithm, Y is translated to the combinator:

$$S\ (C\ B\ (S\ I\ I))\ (C\ B\ (S\ I\ I))$$

□

Exercise 95
Show that:

$$S\ (S\ (K\ S)\ (S\ (K\ K)\ I))\ (K\ (S\ I\ I)) = C\ B\ (S\ I\ I)$$

□

8.7   Turner's algorithm

In a second paper, Turner proposed that Curry's algorithm be extended to
use another new primitive combinator called S' [69]. This is defined by:

$$\text{LET } S' = \lambda c\ f\ g\ x.\ c\ (f\ x)\ (g\ x)$$

---

and has the reduction rule:

$$\mathbf{S}' \ C \ E_1 \ E_2 \ E_3 \xrightarrow[\text{c}]{} C \ (E_1 \ E_3) \ (E_2 \ E_3)$$

where C, E_1, E_2, E_3 are arbitrary combinatory expressions. The reason why 'C' is used is that $\mathbf{S}'$ has the property that *if C is a combinator* (i.e. contains no variables), then for any E_1 and E_2:

$$\lambda^* x. \ C \ E_1 \ E_2 = \mathbf{S}' \ C \ (\lambda^* x. \ E_1) \ (\lambda^* x. \ E_2)$$

This can be shown using extensionality. Clearly x is a variable not occurring in $\lambda^* x. \ C \ E_1 \ E_2$ or $\mathbf{S}' \ C \ (\lambda^* x. \ E_1) \ (\lambda^* x. \ E_2)$ (exercise: why?), so it is sufficient to show:

$$(\lambda^* x. \ C \ E_1 \ E_2) \ x = (\mathbf{S}' \ C \ (\lambda^* x. \ E_1) \ (\lambda^* x. \ E_2)) \ x$$

From the definition of $\lambda^* x$ it easily follows that:

$$\lambda^* x. \ C \ E_1 \ E_2 = \mathbf{S} \ (\mathbf{S} \ (\mathbf{K} \ C) \ (\lambda^* x. \ E_1)) \ (\lambda^* x. \ E_2)$$

hence

$$
\begin{aligned}
(\lambda^* x. \ C \ E_1 \ E_2) \ x &= (\mathbf{S} \ (\mathbf{S} \ (\mathbf{K} \ C) \ (\lambda^* x. \ E_1)) \ (\lambda^* x. \ E_2)) \ x \\
&= \mathbf{S} \ (\mathbf{K} \ C) \ (\lambda^* x. \ E_1) \ x \ ((\lambda^* x. \ E_2)) \ x) \\
&= \mathbf{K} \ C \ x \ ((\lambda^* x. \ E_1) \ x) \ ((\lambda^* x. \ E_2)) \ x) \\
&= C \ ((\lambda^* x. \ E_1) \ x) \ ((\lambda^* x. \ E_2)) \ x)
\end{aligned}
$$

But $(\mathbf{S}' \ C \ (\lambda^* x. \ E_1) \ (\lambda^* x. \ E_2)) \ x = C \ ((\lambda^* x. \ E_1) \ x) \ ((\lambda^* x. \ E_2)) \ x)$ also, and so:

$$(\lambda^* x. \ C \ E_1 \ E_2) \ x = (\mathbf{S}' \ C \ (\lambda^* x. \ E_1) \ (\lambda^* x. \ E_2)) \ x$$

Exercise 96
Where in the argument above did we use the assumption that C is a combinator? ☐

Turner's combinator $\mathbf{S}'$ is useful when translating λ-expressions of the form $\lambda V_n \ \cdots \ V_2 \ V_1. \ E_1 \ E_2$ (it will be seen shortly why it is convenient to number the bound variables in descending order). To see this, following Turner [69], temporarily define

E'	to mean	$\lambda^* V_1. \ E$
E''	to mean	$\lambda^* V_2. \ (\lambda^* V_1. \ E)$
E'''	to mean	$\lambda^* V_3. \ (\lambda^* V_2. \ (\lambda^* V_1. \ E))$

$\vdots$

Recall that:

$$(\lambda V_n \; \cdots \; V_2 \; V_1 .\; E_1 \; E_2)_{\mathbf{C}} = \lambda^* V_n .\; (\; \cdots \; (\lambda^* V_2 .\; (\lambda^* V_1 .\; (E_1 \; E_2)_{\mathbf{C}}))) \; \cdots \;)$$

The next exercise shows that:

$$\lambda^* V_n . \; \ldots \lambda^* V_2 . \; \lambda^* V_1 . \; (E_1 \; E_2)$$

gets very complicated as n increases.

Exercise 97
Show that:

(i) $\lambda^* x_1 . \; E_1 \; E_2 = \mathbf{S} \; E_1' \; E_2'$

(ii) $\lambda^* x_2 . \; (\lambda^* x_1 . \; E_1 \; E_2) = \mathbf{S} \; (\mathbf{B} \; \mathbf{S} \; E_1'') \; E_2''$

(iii) $\lambda^* x_3 . \; (\lambda^* x_2 . \; (\lambda^* x_1 . \; E_1 \; E_2)) = \mathbf{S} \; (\mathbf{B} \; \mathbf{S} \; (\mathbf{B} \; (\mathbf{B} \; \mathbf{S}) \; E_1''')) \; E_2'''$

(iv) $\lambda^* x_4 . \; (\lambda^* x_3 . \; (\lambda^* x_2 . \; (\lambda^* x_1 . \; E_1 \; E_2))) =$
      $\mathbf{S} \; (\mathbf{B} \; \mathbf{S} \; (\mathbf{B} \; (\mathbf{B} \; \mathbf{S}) \; (\mathbf{B} \; (\mathbf{B} \; (\mathbf{B} \; \mathbf{S}))) \; E_1'''')) \; E_2''''$

□

The size of $\lambda^* V_n . \; \ldots \lambda^* V_2 . \; \lambda^* V_1 . \; (E_1 \; E_2)$ is proportional to the *square* of n. Using $\mathbf{S}'$, the size can be made to grow *linearly* with n:

$$
\begin{aligned}
\lambda^* x_2 . \; (\lambda^* x_1 . \; E_1 \; E_2) \quad &= \lambda^* x_2 . \; \mathbf{S} \; E_1' \; E_2' \\
&= \mathbf{S}' \; \mathbf{S} \; (\lambda^* x_2 . \; E_1') \; (\lambda^* x_2 . \; E_2') \\
&= \mathbf{S}' \; \mathbf{S} \; E_1'' \; E_2''
\end{aligned}
$$

$$
\begin{aligned}
\lambda^* x_3 . \; (\lambda^* x_2 . \; (\lambda^* x_1 . \; E_1 \; E_2)) \quad &= \lambda^* x_3 . \; \mathbf{S}' \; \mathbf{S} \; E_1'' \; E_2'' \\
&= \mathbf{S}' \; (\mathbf{S}' \; \mathbf{S}) \; (\lambda^* x_3 . \; E_1'') \; (\lambda^* x_3 . \; E_2'') \\
&= \mathbf{S}' \; (\mathbf{S}' \; \mathbf{S}) \; E_1''' \; E_2'''
\end{aligned}
$$

$$
\begin{aligned}
\lambda^* x_4 . \; \lambda^* x_3 . \; (\lambda^* x_2 . \; (\lambda^* x_1 . \; E_1 \; E_2))) \quad &= \lambda^* x_4 . \; \mathbf{S}' \; (\mathbf{S}' \; \mathbf{S}) \; E_1''' \; E_2''' \\
&= \mathbf{S}' \; (\mathbf{S}' \; (\mathbf{S}' \; \mathbf{S})) \; (\lambda^* x_4 . \; E_1''') \; (\lambda^* x_4 . \; E_2''') \\
&= \mathbf{S}' \; (\mathbf{S}' \; (\mathbf{S}' \; \mathbf{S})) \; E_1'''' \; E_2''''
\end{aligned}
$$

Just as $\mathbf{B}$ and $\mathbf{C}$ were introduced to simplify combinatory expressions of the form $\mathbf{S} \; (\mathbf{K} \; E_1) \; E_2$ and $\mathbf{S} \; E_1 \; (\mathbf{K} \; E_2)$ respectively, Turner also devised $\mathbf{B}'$ and $\mathbf{C}'$ with an analogous role for $\mathbf{S}'$. The properties required are:

$$\mathbf{S}' \; C \; (\mathbf{K} \; E_1) \; E_2 = \mathbf{B}' \; C \; E_1 \; E_2$$
$$\mathbf{S}' \; C \; E_1 \; (\mathbf{K} \; E_2) = \mathbf{C}' \; C \; E_1 \; E_2$$

(where C is any combinator, and E_1, E_2 are arbitrary combinatory expressions). This is achieved if $\mathbf{B}'$ and $\mathbf{C}'$ are defined by:

LET $\mathbf{B}' = \lambda c\ f\ g\ x.\ c\ f\ (g\ x)$

LET $\mathbf{C}' = \lambda c\ f\ g\ x.\ c\ (f\ x)\ g$

Clearly $\mathbf{B}'$ and $\mathbf{C}'$ will have the property that for arbitrary λ-expressions C, E_1, E_2 and E_3:

$$\mathbf{B}'\ C\ E_1\ E_2\ E_3 \xrightarrow{c} C\ E_1\ (E_2\ E_3)$$

$$\mathbf{C}'\ C\ E_1\ E_2\ E_3 \xrightarrow{c} C\ (E_1\ E_3)\ E_2$$

Exercise 98
Show that for arbitrary λ-expressions C, E_1, E_2 and E_3:

(i) $\mathbf{S}'\ C\ (\mathbf{K}\ E_1)\ E_2 = \mathbf{B}'\ C\ E_1\ E_2$

(ii) $\mathbf{S}'\ C\ E_1\ (\mathbf{K}\ E_2) = \mathbf{C}'\ C\ E_1\ E_2$

(iii) $\mathbf{S}\ (\mathbf{B}\ \mathbf{K}\ E_1)\ E_2 = \mathbf{S}'\ \mathbf{K}\ E_1\ E_2$

(iv) $\mathbf{B}\ (\mathbf{K}\ E_1)\ E_2 = \mathbf{B}'\ \mathbf{K}\ E_1\ E_2$

(v) $\mathbf{C}\ (\mathbf{B}\ \mathbf{K}\ E_1)\ E_2 = \mathbf{C}'\ \mathbf{K}\ E_1\ E_2$

□

Turner's algorithm for translating λ-expressions to combinatory expressions is described by him [69] as follows:

Use the algorithm of Curry but whenever a term beginning in $\mathbf{S}$, $\mathbf{B}$ or $\mathbf{C}$ is formed use one of the following transformations if it is possible to do so

$$\mathbf{S}\ (\mathbf{B}\ K\ A)\ B \longrightarrow \mathbf{S}'\ K\ A\ B,$$

$$\mathbf{B}\ (K\ A)\ B \longrightarrow \mathbf{B}'\ K\ A\ B,$$

$$\mathbf{C}\ (\mathbf{B}\ K\ A)\ B \longrightarrow \mathbf{C}'\ K\ A\ B.$$

Here A and B stand for arbitrary terms as usual and K is any term composed entirely of constants. The correctness of the new algorithm can be inferred from the correctness of the Curry algorithm by demonstrating that in each of the above transformations the left- and right-hand sides are extensionally equal. In each case this follows directly from the definitions of the combinators involved.

Since Turner's pioneering papers appeared, many people have worked on improving the basic idea. For example, John Hughes has devised a scheme for dynamically generating an 'optimal' set of primitive combinators (called *supercombinators*) for each program [36]. The idea is that the compiler will generate combinatory expressions built out of the supercombinators for the program being compiled. It will also dynamically produce 'microcode' to implement the reduction rules for these supercombinators. The result is that each program runs on a reduction machine tailored specially for it. Most current high-performance implementations of functional languages use supercombinators [2,17]. Another avenue of research is to use combinators based on the De Bruijn notation briefly described on page 74. The 'Categorical Abstract Machine' [51] uses this approach.

Part III

Implementing the Theories

Chapter 9

A Quick Introduction to LISP

The LISP programming language is introduced. Enough detail is given to enable the reader to understand all the programs making up the theorem prover in Chapter 10, the verifier in Chapter 11 and the λ-calculus toolkit in Chapter 12.

In Part III of this book the ideas in the preceding two parts are illustrated by describing some LISP programs which embody the theories described there. These programs are small enough so that it is feasible to type them into a file and play with them; they are, however, often rather inefficient. The code has been written to be short and easy to follow; this has sometimes been at the expense of efficiency. The goal is that the programs be efficient enough for *simple* experiments; it is not expected that they will have anything more than educational value. Readers interested in implementing more efficient versions can use the prototypes provided here as a starting point and, with suitable intrumentation, can do experiments to determine those things that need optimizing. The purpose of this chapter is to provide a sufficient introduction to LISP so that the programs that follow will be comprehensible to readers who have not met the language before. For a more comprehensive introduction Wilensky's book *LISPcraft* [73] is recommended. From now on this will be referred to as 'Wilensky'.

LISP is probably the second oldest programming language in widespread use (FORTRAN is the oldest). It is the first functional language to have been developed and its design was strongly based on the λ-calculus. Unfortunately, LISP functions differ in subtle and confusing ways from ordinary mathematical functions (and hence from the λ-calculus). This is partly for efficiency reasons and partly due to errors in the original design. For example, McCarthy, the inventor of the language, says in his paper on the history of LISP [52] that the dynamic binding of free variables (see Section 9.7) used by LISP's λ-expressions was a mistake.

It is possible to do imperative programming in LISP (see the description of the prog feature on page 159) and the resulting potential for side effects also complicates the relation between mathematical functions and LISP functions, so much so that some authors regard LISP as a bad influence. Here, for example, is a quotation by David Turner [70] from the discussion after his paper in the book *Mathematical Logic and Programming Languages* [35]:

> It needs to be said very firmly that LISP, at least as represented by the dialects in common use, is not a functional language at all. LISP does have a functional subset, but that is a rather inconvenient programming language and there exists no significant body of programs written in it. Almost all serious programming in LISP makes heavy use of side effects and other referentially opaque features.

> I think that the historical importance of LISP is that it was the first language to provide 'garbage-collected' heap storage. This was a very important step forward. For the development of functional programming, however, I feel that the contribution of LISP has been a negative one. My suspicion is that the success of LISP set back the development of a properly functional style of programming by at least ten years.

I have some sympathy for this view, but unfortunately there are no robust and efficient functional language implementations that I felt could reasonably be used instead of LISP. The best that are available are probably Standard ML [55] and Miranda [70]. Although current ML implementations[1] rival or exceed LISP in robustness and efficiency, they have not yet become widely distributed. Furthermore, ML, like LISP, has imperative features that complicate its semantics; however, unlike LISP, pure ML functions (i.e. ones without side effects) do correspond to mathematical functions. The Miranda system is very elegant, but it is currently not efficient enough for the kind of applications given here. Furthermore, Miranda is not available free and the expense of buying a system may unfortunately slow down its distribution.

If a suitable functional programming language becomes widely distributed, then it would probably be used in future editions of this book. To the extent that is practical, only the functional subset of LISP will be used here.

---

[1] Implementations of ML are available from Edinburgh University, Bell Laboratories, Imperial Software Technology and as part of Sussex University's Poplog system.

9.1   Features of LISP

According to John McCarthy, LISP is characterized by the ideas listed below (see his history of the language [52] and Mason's book [50]):

- Computing with symbolic expressions rather than numbers.

- Representation of symbolic expressions and other information by list structure in the memory of a computer.

- A small set of selector and constructor operations expressed as functions.

- Composition of functions as a tool for forming more complex functions.

- The use of conditional expressions for getting branching into function definitions.

- The recursive use of conditional expressions as a sufficient tool for building computable functions.

- The use of λ-expressions for naming functions.

- The representation of LISP programs as LISP data that can be manipulated by other programs.

- The conditional expression interpretation of Boolean connectives.

- The LISP function `eval` that serves both as a formal definition of the language and as an interpreter.

- Garbage collection.

- LISP statements as a command language for an interactive environment.

Some of these ideas were taken from other languages, but most were new (and due to McCarthy).

There are many versions of LISP in current use, for example:

- Maclisp. An influential LISP system produced at MIT.

- Zetalisp. An enhancement of Maclisp that runs on Symbolics LISP Machines.

- Franz LISP. A version of Maclisp that runs on Vaxes and Sun workstations.

- Interlisp. A sophisticated LISP programming environment developed at BBN and Xerox PARC. It runs on the Xerox workstations.

- Standard LISP. An early attempt to produce a standard lead by a group from the University of Utah.

- Cambridge LISP. This this was originally developed for IBM mainframes, but versions are now available for BBC microcomputers and Commodore Amigas. Cambridge LISP is quite similar to Standard LISP.

- Common LISP. A recent, fairly successful, attempt to produce a standard. Many people are now converting to Common LISP. Some of the horrors in the treatment of functions in other LISPs are corrected in Standard LISP.

In this book, the intention is to stay within a subset that is common to most LISPs. Where arbitrary notational choices are made, Franz LISP is used. This is the version of LISP used in Wilensky and public domain implementations are available for Vax and Sun computers running Unix. If no suitable purely functional languages become available, future editions of this book will probably use Common LISP because of its superior treatment of functions (lexical scoping is the default, see Section 9.7).

9.2   Some history

The earliest versions of LISP used a notation called M-expressions (described in [53]) that was 'intended to resemble FORTRAN as much as possible' [52]. The data manipulated by these M-expressions were things called S-expressions. The 'M' and 'S' in 'M-expression' and 'S-expression' abbreviate 'meta' and 'symbolic'.

To explain the semantics of LISP, McCarthy wrote an interpreter for LISP in LISP. This interpreter, called eval, used an encoding of M-expressions as S-expressions, so that programs (i.e. M-expressions) could be manipulated as data (i.e. S-expressions). This encoding provided an alternative syntax for LISP which rapidly replaced the M-expression syntax. Now only the S-expression notation is used and M-expressions are a historical relic. This little bit of history is worth knowing because it explains various features of the language. For example, McCarthy says [52]

> The unexpected appearance of an interpreter tended to freeze the form of the language, and some of the decisions made rather lightheartedly ... later proved unfortunate. These included the

COND notation for conditional expressions which leads to unnecessary depth of parentheses.

Later, McCarthy adds:

> Another reason for the initial acceptance of awkwardnesses in the internal form of LISP is that we still expected to switch to writing programs as M-expressions. The project of defining M-expressions precisely and compiling them or at least translating them into S-expressions was neither finalized nor explicitly abandoned. It just receded into the indefinite future, and a new generation of programmers appeared who preferred internal notation to any FORTRAN-like or ALGOL-like notation that could be devised.

9.3   S-expressions

LISP programs consist of functions for manipulating S-expressions. The functions themselves are also represented by S-expressions. The process of running a program consists in *evaluating* an S-expression representing the application of a function to some arguments.

An S-expression is either an atom or a *dotted-pair* $(S_1 \, . \, S_2)$ where S_1 and S_2 are S-expressions. Dotted pairs are sometimes called lists, but this term is used here in a different way (see Section 9.3.1 below). Small italics will be used for arbitrary S-expressions (e.g. S, S_1, S_2 etc.) and small typewriter font for particular S-expressions (e.g. foo, (foo . FOO)).

Atoms are sequences of characters, for example:

x, y, foo, 22, +, -, *, =, <, >, >=, <=

The exact syntax of atoms is implementation dependent. Most of the atoms to be used will be the names of variables or functions. Such names will consist of sequences of letters or numbers starting with a letter. Other atoms represent numbers and mathematical operations. Some characters have a special meaning to the LISP reader. To include such characters in an atom, the atom name must be input with vertical bars (i.e. |'s) surrounding it. For example, |'''| is an atom whose name consists of three quote characters; note that the vertical bars are not part of the atom.

The atoms t and nil have a special role in LISP; as will be seen in Section 9.5.2 they represent 'true' and 'false' respectively. Some LISPs (e.g. Common LISP) do not distinguish upper and lower case; however Franz LISP does distinguish them: for example, for us (but not for some systems) the atoms FOO and foo are different.

Examples of S-expressions are:

    nil, FOO, (FOO . foo), ((A . nil) . ((B . nil) . nil))

Strings are a special kind of atom. They are input as a sequence of characters surrounded by quotes ("). For example,

    "string1", "**?!", "This is a long string containing spaces."

Strings evaluate to themselves; they are useful for error messages and are more efficiently implemented then arbitrary atoms.

9.3.1   Lists

A *list* is the atom nil or a dotted-pair $(S_1 . S_2)$. Note that nil is the only S-expression that is both an atom and a list. It is called the *empty list*. Lists of the form:

$$(S_1 . (S_2 . (S_3 \cdots (S_n . nil) \cdots)))$$

are called *linear lists* and are written as:

$$(S_1 \ S_2 \ S_3 \cdots S_n)$$

The notation () denotes the atom nil.

Warnings:

  (i) Sometimes the term 'list' is used for what we call 'linear list'.

 (ii) In some LISPs (e.g. Franz LISP) the expression (A.B) (where A and B are atoms) will be interpreted as the S-expression (A.B . nil), where A.B is a single atom. This is because some LISP readers do not recognize dotted pairs unless there are spaces around the dot. In such LISPs, (A.B) would be different from (A . B). A further complication is that in Franz LISP (1.2) is the linear list containing the floating point number 1.2; this atom is different from the atom |1.2| (see the descriptions of the predicates symbolp and numberp in Section 9.12).

Each S-expression has a *value* which is obtained by evaluating it. The atoms t and nil evaluate to themselves, as do strings " ... " and the numbers 0, 1, 2 etc.

9.4 Variables and the environment

LISP atoms can be *bound* to S-expressions in the *environment*. Such atoms are called *variables* and when they are evaluated the result is the corresponding S-expression. Variables can either be part of the top-level interaction with LISP (*global* variables) or they can be local to the application of a function.

A variable x can be set to the value of an S-expression S by evaluating the S-expression (setq x S). For example, evaluating (setq one 1) sets the value of one to 1.

If S is an S-expression then (quote S) is an S-expression that evaluates to S. For example, (setq mike (quote (1 2 3))) binds the variable mike to (1 2 3). Note that evaluating (setq mike (1 2 3)) would result in an error, because setq would try to evaluate (1 2 3), but 1 is not a function; this is explained further in the next section.

The S-expression (quote S) can be abbreviated by 'S. Thus evaluating (setq mike '(1 2 3)) binds mike to (1 2 3).

9.5 Functions

If S is an S-expression representing a LISP function (see below) then

$$(S \ S_1 \ ... \ S_n)$$

is normally evaluated by

(i) first evaluating $S_1, \ ... \ , S_n$ (in that order)

(ii) and then *applying* (see below) S to the resulting values.

For example, (add 2 3) evaluates to 5. If S is not an S-expression representing a function, then an error results. Thus, since 1 is not a function, evaluating (1 2 3) will cause an error. We will generally use f, g, h etc. to range over S-expressions representing functions.

Certains names are bound to special functions that do not evaluate their arguments. For example, setq does not evaluate its first argument. There is a function set that does evaluate its first argument: (setq x S) is equivalent to (set (quote x) S). Both setq and set have a side effect of binding a variable to a value. They also have a value, which is the value of their second argument. For example, (setq x 1) evaluates to 1.

Exercise 99
What are the values and side effects of:

  (i) (add 1 (setq x 2))

 (ii) (add (setq x 1) (setq x (add x 2)))

(iii) (setq x (add (setq x 1) x)) ?

□

   Functions that do not evaluate their arguments are normally built-in
system functions (like setq). In most LISPs (but not Common LISP) one
can define a kind of function called an *fexpr* which does not evaluate its
arguments, however the use of fexprs is nowadays considered poor practice; see Chapter 12 of Wilensky for details. A facility that is very useful,
however, is the definition of *macros*; these provide a way of preprocessing S-
expressions before they are evaluated. By defining macros that insert quotes
around arguments, it is possible to control the evaluation of arguments in
a clean and efficient way. This is described in detail in Section 9.10.
   It is also possible to have functions that appear to take a variable number
of arguments (e.g. cond, casesq, and and or in Section 9.5.2). Most such
functions are built-in macros or fexprs.
   User defined LISP functions are represented by S-expressions of
the form (lambda $(x_1 \ldots x_n)$ S). Such functions are applied to arguments $S_1, \ldots , S_n$ by binding them to $x_1, \ldots , x_n$ respectively
and then evaluating S in the resulting environment. For example,
((lambda x y z) (add (add x y) z)) 1 2 3) evaluates to 6. The binding
of the arguments to the function variables $x_1, \ldots , x_n$ is local to the evaluation of S.
   A lambda-expression (lambda $(x_1 \ldots x_n)$ S) can be given a name f in
the environment by evaluating:

   (def f (lambda $(x_1 \ldots x_n)$ S))

Applying the name of a function is equivalent to applying the corresponding
lambda-expression. Instead of defining functions with def as above, it is
usual to use the equivalent simpler form:

   (defun f $(x_1 \ldots x_n)$ S)

defun is actually a macro; for its definition see page 171.
   One of the awkward aspects of LISP is that function definitions are not
held in the same environment in which variables are bound. Thus:

   (setq f (quote (lambda $(x_1 \ldots x_n)$ S)))

has a different effect from:

   (def f (lambda $(x_1 \ldots x_n)$ S))

It is possible to apply functions that have been bound in the environment with setq. If f is such a function, then evaluating:

    (funcall f S_1 ... S_n)

will apply the lambda-expression bound to f to the values of S_1, ... , S_n. Most LISPs (including Franz LISP) provide a special quoting mechanism for functions called function. Instead of

    (setq f (quote (lambda (x_1 ... x_n) S)))

it is better style to write

    (setq f (function (lambda (x_1 ... x_n) S)))

Although there is little semantic difference between quote and function in Franz LISP, other systems, especially Common LISP, try and make lambdas quoted with function behave more like true λ-expressions. There is more on the semantics of LISP lambda-expressions in Section 9.7.

9.5.1   Primitive list-processing functions

The names car, cdr, cons, atom and eq are bound to primitive functions with the following semantics.

1. (car S) evaluates S and if the resulting value is a list $(v_1 \ . \ v_2)$ then v_1 is returned.

2. (cdr S) evaluates S and if the resulting value is a list $(v_1 \ . \ v_2)$ then v_2 is returned.

3. (cons S_1 S_2) evaluates S_1 to get a value v_1 and then S_2 to get a value v_2 and then returns the list $(v_1 \ . \ v_2)$ as result.

4. (atom S) evaluates to t if the value of S is an atom, otherwise it evaluates to nil.

5. (eq S_1 S_2) evaluates to t if

    (a) S_1 and S_2 evaluate to the same atom, or

    (b) S_1 and S_2 evaluate to pointers to the same list cell (this is explained in Section 9.8)

otherwise (eq S_1 S_2) evaluates to nil. The exact semantics of eq is quite subtle and messy as it depends on the representation of lists as pointer structures in memory (see Section 9.8).

The names car and cdr are a historical curiosity; apparently they abbreviate 'contents of address register' and 'contents of data register'. This reflects how the first LISP systems at M.I.T. were implemented.

9.5.2 Flow of control functions

The flow of control in LISP programs is specified using various functions that do not evaluate all their arguments. The most basic such function is cond; all the other ones can be defined in terms of it.

The conditional function cond

An S-expression:

$$(\text{cond}\quad (S_{11}\ S_{12}\ S_{13}\ \ldots\ S_{1n_1})$$
$$(S_{21}\ S_{22}\ S_{23}\ \ldots\ S_{2n_2})$$
$$\vdots$$
$$(S_{m1}\ S_{m2}\ S_{m3}\ \ldots\ S_{mn_m}))$$

should be read as:

if S_{11} then S_{12} followed by S_{13} ... followed by S_{1n_1} else
if S_{21} then S_{22} followed by S_{23} ... followed by S_{2n_2} else
$\vdots$
if S_{m1} then S_{m2} followed by S_{m3} ... followed by S_{mn_m} else nil

The exact semantics is as follows: S_{11} is evaluated and if its value is not nil then $S_{12}, S_{13}, \ldots, S_{1n_1}$ are evaluated in that order and the value of S_{1n_1} is returned. If the value of S_{11} is nil then S_{21} is evaluated and if its value is not nil then $S_{22}, S_{23}, \ldots, S_{2n_2}$ are evaluated in that order and the value of S_{2n_2} is returned. If the value of S_{21} is nil then this process continues until the first S_{i1} is found that has a non-nil value and then $S_{i2}, S_{i3}, \ldots, S_{in_i}$ are then evaluated in that order and the value of S_{in_i} is returned. If all of $S_{21}, \ldots, S_{m1}$ evaluate to nil then the value of the cond-expression is nil.

Notice that nil represents 'false' and *any* S-expression not equal to nil represents 'true'.

The conditional function if

The S-expression

$$(\text{if}\ S\ S_1\ S_2)$$

should be read as 'if S then S_1 else S_2' and is an abbreviation for

$$(\text{cond}\ (S\ S_1)\ (\text{t}\ S_2))$$

The sequential conjunction and

The S-expression

(and S_1 S_2 ... S_n)

is evaluated by evaluating S_1, S_2 , ... in that order until the first S_i is found with value nil. The value of the and-expression is then nil. If all the S-expressions S_1, ... , S_n have non-nil values then the value of the and-expression is the value of S_n. The value of (and) is t.

Exercise 100
Show how to represent (and S_1 S_2 ... S_n) using cond. □

As the name suggests, and can be used to compute the logical conjunction (i.e. ∧) of a number of expressions. A common application is to do a sequence of tests like:

(and x (cdr x) (cdr(cdr x)))

which tests whether x has at least two elements. Evaluating the S-expression (cdr(cdr x)) would cause an error if x were an atom or one-element list (e.g. 1 or (1)); using (and x (cdr x) ...) prevents this.

The sequential disjunction or

The S-expression

(or S_1 S_2 ... S_n)

is evaluated by evaluating S_1, S_2 , ... in that order until the first S_i is found whose value is not equal to nil. The value of the or-expression is then the value of S_i. If all of S_1, ... , S_n have nil values then the value of the or-expression is nil. The value of (or) is nil.

Exercise 101
Show how to represent (or S_1 S_2 ... S_n) using cond. □

As the name suggests, or can be used to compute the logical disjunction (i.e. ∨) of a number of expressions.

An example of the use of and and or is the definition of the list reversing function **reverse** given on page 159.

The cases function casesq

A cases expression has the form:

```
(casesq  S
          (A₁  S₁₁ S₁₂  ...  S₁ₙ₁)
          (A₂  S₂₁ S₂₂  ...  S₂ₙ₂)
              ⋮
          (Aₘ  Sₘ₁ Sₘ₂  ...  Sₘₙₘ))
```

A casesq-expression assumes that the value of S is an atom, A say. This value is compared with $A_1, \ldots, A_n$ (in that order). If

(i) A_i is t, or

(ii) A_i is equal to A, or

(iii) A_i is a list containing A,

then $(S_{i1}\ S_{i2}\ \ldots\ S_{in_i}$ are evaluated in that order and the value of S_{in_i} is returned. If A is not equal to any A_i then nil is returned. Note that the $A_1, \ldots, A_n$ are *not* evaluated.

A casesq-expression is roughly equivalent to (but more efficient than)

```
(cond
  ((or (eq S t) (eq S 'A₁) (memq S 'A₁)) S₁₁ ... S₁ₙ₁)
  ((or (eq S t) (eq S 'A₂) (memq S 'A₂)) S₂₁ ... S₂ₙ₂)
      ⋮
  (or (eq S t) (eq S 'Aₘ) (memq S 'Aₘ)) (Sₘ₁ ... Sₘₙₘ))
```

The membership testing function memq is described on page 176.

Exercise 102

Why is the cond-expression above not exactly equivalent to a casesq-expression? *Hint:* Consider what happens if S is (setq x (add x 1)). □

The local declaration function let

The expression:

```
(let ((x₁ S₁) ... (xₙ Sₙ))  S)
```

is evaluated as follows:

(i) $S_1, \ldots, S_n$ are evaluated in that order and their values bound to the variables $x_1, \ldots, x_n$ respectively;

(ii) S is evaluated in the resulting environment.

A let-expression is equivalent to:

$$((\text{lambda } (x_1 \ \ldots \ x_n) \ S) \ S_1 \ \ldots \ S_n)$$

The program function prog

FORTRAN-like imperative programming can be done in LISP using the function prog. We only use this once, to format the output produced by our program verifier.

A prog-expression has the form shown below where each l_i is an atom acting as a label for the expression S_i. If a label for S_i is not needed then l_i can be omitted.

$$
\begin{aligned}
&(\text{prog} \quad (x_1 \ \ldots \ x_n) \\
&\quad l_1 \quad S_1 \\
&\quad l_2 \quad S_2 \\
&\qquad \vdots \\
&\quad l_n \quad S_n)
\end{aligned}
$$

A prog-expression is evaluated by evaluating the S-expressions $S_1, \ldots, S_n$ in turn. The variables $x_1, \ldots, x_n$ are local, so that a setq to them in an S_i will not be felt outside the prog-expression. They are initialized to nil on entry to the prog-expression. If an expression (return S) is evaluated inside an S_i, then the evaluation of the whole prog-expression is terminated and the value of S is returned. If an expression (go l_i) is evaluated then, control transfers to the corresponding expression S_i.

Here, for example, is the definition of a function reverse that reverses a list, i.e. (reverse '$(S_1 \ \ldots \ S_n)$) evaluates to $(S_n \ \ldots \ S_1)$.

```
(defun reverse (x)
  (prog (temp result)
        (setq temp x)
        (setq result nil)
   loop (cond ((eq temp nil) (return result)))
        (setq result (cons (car temp) result))
        (setq temp (cdr temp))
        (go loop)))
```

In Franz LISP, the local variable temp would not be needed because the function parameter x could be used instead. On exit from reverse, the value of x on entry is restored. Also, since local variables of prog-expressions are initialized to nil, the explicit initialization (setq result nil) is not needed. Thus a simpler definition of reverse would be:

```
(defun reverse (x)
 (prog (result)
   loop (cond ((eq x nil) (return result)))
        (setq result (cons (car x) result))
        (setq x (cdr x))
        (go loop)))
```

This simpler definition of reverse is not really good style as it exploits specific features of Franz LISP and thus makes the definition less portable. It is good practice to always explicitly initialize local variables as this helps document the algorithm being implemented.

The functions catch and throw

Evaluating (catch S) causes S to be evaluated. If during this evaluation (throw S₁) is evaluated, then the evaluation of S is terminated and the value of S₁ returned as the value of (catch S). If a call to throw is not encountered, then the value of (catch S) is the value of S. Thus, to quote Wilensky, 'throw throws the value of its argument through any number of levels of intermediate function calls directly to the most recent catch'. The functions catch and throw are used in the pattern matcher described in Section 10.1.

9.5.3   Recursive functions

The description of function application given on page 154 was incomplete. If function f has been defined by

$$\text{(defun } f \ (x_1 \ \ldots \ x_n) \ S)$$

then when an S-expression $(f \ S_1 \ \ldots \ S_n)$ is evaluated, S is evaluated in an environment in which:

(i) the values of $S_1, \ldots, S_n$ are bound to $x_1, \ldots, x_n$ respectively, and

(ii) the function name f is bound to (lambda $(x_1 \ \ldots \ x_n) \ S$).

Thus if f is applied within S, then this application will be interpreted as a recursive call because at the point of call f will be bound to (lambda $(x_1 \ \ldots \ x_n) \ S$).

Example: The following recursive definition defines append to be the function that concatenates two lists:

```
(defun append (x y)
 (if (atom x) y (cons (car x) (append (cdr x) y))))
```

Evaluating

> (append '(X_1 ... X_n) '(Y_1 ... Y_n))

results in

> (X_1 ... X_n Y_1 ... Y_n)

□

9.6   The LISP top-level

LISP is interactive. The user inputs S-expressions and the LISP system
evaluates them and prints out the result. Franz LISP prompts for input
using ->. Here is a little session on the author's Sun workstation. The
machine is called **gwyndir** and the Unix prompt is **gwyndir%**. The session
starts with Franz LISP being run, then the values of the variables **x** and
y are set to be 1 and 2, then the S-expression (add x y) is evaluated and
finally the LISP session is terminated.

```
gwyndir% lisp
Franz Lisp, Opus 38.69
-> (setq x 1)
1
-> (setq y 2)
2
-> (add x y)
3
-> (exit)
gwyndir%
```

Functions are defined interactively too, for example:

```
-> (defun add3 (x y z) (add x (add y z)))
add3
-> (add3 1 2 3)
6
-> (add3 (add3 1 2 3) (add3 4 5 6) (add3 7 8 9))
45
->
```

During interactive sessions, LISP prints out values using the function
print (see page 176). The printing of linear lists is as expected, but the
printing of dotted pairs can look a bit funny. For example:

```
-> '(1 2 3)
(1 2 3)
-> '(1 . (2 . 3))
(1 2 . 3)
```

A sequence of S-expressions can be typed into a file called `file` and then read in as though they had been input interactively. This is done by evaluating:

```
(read 'file)
```

The function `include` is like `read`, but it doesn't evaluate its argument (see also Section 9.11.5).

9.7   Dynamic binding

In all common LISPs except Common LISP, free variables in functions are interpreted *dynamically*. This means that the value of the free variable is looked up in whatever environment happens to be in force when the variable is evaluated. Consider, for example, the following session with LISP:

```
-> (setq z 1)
1
-> (defun addz (x) (add x z))
addz
-> (setq z 2)
2
-> (addz 0)
2
-> ((lambda (z) (addz 0)) 3)
3
-> z
2
->
```

The first time (addz 0) is evaluated the value of z is 2 and thus the result of the evaluation is 2. Note, however, that when addz was defined the value of z was 1. The second time (addz 0) is evaluated it is inside (lambda (z) (addz 0)). By the time it is evaluated, z will have been locally bound to 3 by the enclosing ((lambda (z) ⋯) 3); the result is thus 3. Notice that the binding of z to 3 inside the lambda-expression is local. Thus when the evaluation is finished, z reverts to being bound to its previous value, namely 2.

Unfortunately, dynamic binding makes LISP `lambda`-expressions behave differently from λ-calculus λ-expressions. For example, the λ-expression

$$(\lambda x.\ ((\lambda f.\ (\lambda x.\ (f\ 0))\ 1)\ (\lambda y.\ x))\ 2$$

reduces to **2**, whereas the LISP S-expression

```
((lambda (x)
  ((lambda (f)
    ((lambda (x) (funcall f 0)) 1))
   (quote(lambda (y) x))))
 2)
```

evaluates to 1.

Exercise 103
Verify the above assertion. □

The differences between LISP functions and conventional mathematical functions means that much of the theory developed for the λ-calculus does not apply to LISP. This is one of the reasons for the low opinion of LISP held by some functional programming enthusiasts (e.g. see the quote by Turner on page 148). According to McCarthy [52], dynamic binding was a bug in the first LISP implementation, but it soon became a feature.

There is a class of particularly horrible bugs, called context bugs, that result from LISP functions not behaving like mathematical functions. These can be very frustrating if one attempts to do any significant higher-order programming. Fortunately, Common LISP uses a binding scheme (called *static binding* or *lexical scoping*) that corresponds to the λ-calculus and thus, as people switch to Common LISP, context bugs may become a thing of the past. However, if one really wants to make serious use of higher-order functions, it would be much better to use a proper functional language like ML or Miranda. Even Common LISP is pretty awkward to use for higher-order programming.

Exercise 104
Reduce the following λ-expression to normal form:

$$\mathbf{Y}\ (\lambda f\ x.\ (y \rightarrow \mathbf{true}\ |\ (x \rightarrow \mathbf{false}\ |\ ((\lambda y.\ f\ y)\ \mathbf{true}))))$$

Compare your reduction to the evaluation of the S-expression

```
((lambda (y) (tricky nil)) nil)
```

where the function `tricky` is defined by:

```
(defun tricky (x)
 (cond (y t)
       (x nil)
       (t ((lambda (y) (tricky y)) t))))
```

□

Over the years there has been quite a bit of debate on the advantages and disadvantages of dynamic binding. The advantages are:

(i) It is easy to implement as there is no need to remember old environments. Nothing special is needed to get recursion to work properly (for example, see the mutually recursive definitions of three functions making up the unparser on page 222).

(ii) Functions can be invoked without all the functions they use being defined. This makes it easy to do a 'top-down' development of a program.

(iii) Functions can be defined in any order; for example, in the programs in the next three chapters, it often happens that f_1 calls f_2, but it is convenient for f_1 to be defined before f_2 in the source file.

(iv) If a function is changed then this change will be instantly felt by all functions that call it. This is useful for debugging: functions can be modified to print out information when they are entered and exited and no recompilation of programs that call such traced functions is needed. Powerful debugging packages based on this idea are provided by most LISP systems.

The disadvantages are:

(i) It makes the semantics more complex and precludes the use of standard theories like the λ-calculus. Formal theories of LISP do exist (e.g. see my own paper on the semantics of dynamic binding [22], or the specialized logics in Mason's book [50] and Manna and Waldinger's paper [48]); however, these theories are still rather experimental.

(ii) It makes higher-order programming fraught with danger due to the possibility of subtle 'context bugs'.

(iii) Existing programs can stop working if a function is changed. This makes large continuously evolving programs hard to maintain (modern LISP systems usually provide mechanisms to help alleviate this problem).

The LISP community seems to have at last decided that the disadvantages outweigh the advantages. This has always been the view of the funtional programming community.

9.8   List equality and identity

When an S-expression is read in, the LISP reader builds a structure in the computer's memory to represent it[2]. The thing that is actually returned as a result of the read is the address of this structure. Atoms with the same name are always represented by the same structure. The first time an atom with a given name is encountered during a session, the system builds a structure to represent it. If the atom is typed in again, then the system will return the address of the structure that it has already built. When a dotted pair is read in, LISP always builds a new structure to represent it. Thus if two identical dotted pairs are input they will result in different addresses being returned. The primitive function eq works by testing the equality of addresses. Thus if the same atom is read in twice the resulting values will be eq, but if the same dotted pair is read in twice the resulting values will not be eq. Here is a session to illustrate this:

```
-> (setq x 'foo)
foo
-> (setq y 'foo)
foo
-> (eq x y)
t
-> (setq x '(1 2 3))
(1 2 3)
-> (setq y '(1 2 3))
(1 2 3)
-> (eq x y)
nil
->
```

Exercise 105
What are the values of the following two S-expressions?

(i) (eq 'mike 'mike)

---

[2]The details in this section are somewhat simplified (e.g. we omit discussion of the representation of numbers and strings). The description given is, however, adequate for understanding the programs in this book.

(ii) `(eq '(mike) '(mike))`

□

If a variable x is bound to an S-expression S in the environment, then x will actually be associated with the machine address of the memory structure representing S. If `(setq y x)` is subsequently evaluated then y will also be associated with this address and thus x and y will be `eq`.

```
-> (setq x '(1 2 3))
(1 2 3)
-> (setq y x)
(1 2 3)
-> (eq x y)
t
->
```

The standard function `equal` tests the equality of S-expressions. If it was not already provided it could be defined recursively by the following definition (which is deliberately written in a rather obscure style to illustrate the sequential use of and and or).

```
(defun equal (x y)
  (or (eq x y)
      (and (not(atom x))
           (not(atom y))
           (equal (car x) (car y))
           (equal (cdr x) (cdr y)))))
```

9.9   Property lists

When the LISP reader inputs an atom, it builds a memory structure holding the characters making up the atom's name. It also builds a list called the *property list* of the atom. This list is initially `nil`. It is used to hold various S-expressions that are associated with the atom. In early LISP implementations, the values of variables and the definitions of functions were held on the property list of the corresponding name. In more recent implementations, like Franz LISP, property lists are no longer used for this purpose, but they are still very useful as a way of 'tagging' atoms with information. For example, the pattern matcher described in Section 10.1 looks at the property lists of atoms occuring in patterns to see if they represent constants or variables. In Chapter 7 of Wilensky there is an example of a library database system in which data about books (title, author, publisher etc.) are held on property lists.

The property list of an atom has the form

$$(property_1 \ value_1 \ property_2 \ value_2 \ \ldots \ property_n \ value_n)$$

where $property_1, \ldots, property_n$ are S-expressions (normally atoms) naming 'properties' and $value_1, \ldots, value_n$ are the corresponding 'property values'. Arbitrary properties can be associated with arbitrary values using the following functions:

1. (putprop *atom value property*) modifies the property list of *atom* by associating *value* with the property *property*. If *atom* already has a property called *property*, then its value is modified; if not, (*property value*) is added to the front of the property list of *atom*. The value returned by (putprop *atom value property*) is the value of *value*; putprop evaluates all its arguments.

2. The function defprop is like putprop except that is does not evaluate any of its arguments.

3. (get *atom property*) returns the S-expression associated with the property *property* on the property list of *atom*. If there is no such property, nil is returned; get evaluates its arguments.

4. (plist *atom*) returns the property list of *atom*; put evaluates its argument.

These functions are illustrated below:

```
-> (plist 'mike)
nil
-> (putprop 'mike t 'nice)
t
-> (plist 'mike)
(nice t)
-> (defprop mike nil lazy)
nil
-> (plist 'mike)
(lazy nil nice t)
-> (get 'mike 'nice)
t
-> (get 'mike 'hungry)
nil
->
```

Warning: The functions `putprop`, `defprop` and `get` use `eq` not `equal` to compare properties. For example:

```
-> (defprop sid t (likes gas))
t
-> (plist 'sid)
((likes gas) t)
-> (setq prop '(likes gas))
(likes gas)
-> (putprop 'sid 'maybe prop)
maybe
-> (plist 'sid)
((likes gas) maybe (likes gas) t)
-> (putprop 'sid 'yes prop)
yes
-> (plist 'sid)
((likes gas) yes (likes gas) t)
->
```

The association between atoms and their property lists is global; there is no notion of local properties analogous to local variables.

Warning: Strings cannot have properties. For example:

```
-> (plist "mike")
Error: Only Atoms and disembodied property lists allowed for
        plist
<1>: (reset)

[Return to top level]
-> (putprop "mike" t 'nice)
Error: putprop: Bad first argument:  mike
<1>:
```

The function `reset` resets LISP to top level from the error state (being in an error state is indicated by a prompt of the form `<n>:`). See Wilensky for details of Franz LISP's error handling features.

9.10   Macros

Macros provide a way of preprocessing S-expressions before they are evaluated. A typical macro definition looks like:

(defmacro M (x_1 ... x_n) S)

If M is so defined then an S-expression (M S_1 ... S_n) is evaluated as follows:

(i) First S is evaluated in an environment in which S_1, ... , S_n are bound *unevaluated* to x_1, ... , x_n respectively. This is called the *macro expansion phase*.

(ii) Second, the value resulting from evaluating S during the expansion phase is evaluated. This is called the *evaluation phase*.

Thus, evaluating (M S_1 ... S_n) results in two evaluations.

Example: The following macro definition makes hd an abbreviation for car.

(defmacro hd (x) (list 'car x))

This works as follows:

(i) If (hd S) is evaluated, then during the expansion phase (list 'car x) is evaluated in an environment in which x is bound to S. This results in (car S).

(ii) The S-expression (car S) is then evaluated and this returns the car of the value of S.

□

An important fact about macros is that the expansion phase is done at compile time (see Section 9.11 below). Thus, with compiled programs, there is no run-time overhead in using a macro. If hd had been defined as a function, then every time an expression of the form (hd S) is evaluated there would be an extra function call; thus using hd instead of car would reduce efficiency.

Example: Suppose only set had been defined, but not setq; then setq could be defined as a macro by:

(defmacro setq (x y)
   (list 'set (list 'quote x) y))

During the expansion phase of evaluating (setq x S) the S-expression (list 'set (list 'quote x) y) is evaluated in an environment in which x is bound to x and y is bound to S. This results in (set (quote x) S). This is then evaluated to bind x to the value of S. □

Notice that since setq does not evaluate its first argument there is no way it could have been defined as a function using defun.

9.10.1   The backquote macro

A very useful built-in macro is the backquote macro. A backquoted expression `S is like a quoted expression 'S except that any S-expressions in S that is preceded by a comma is evaluated. Here is a LISP session illustrating the difference between ' and `:

```
-> (setq y '(1 2 3))
(1 2 3)
-> '(x y z)
(x y z)
-> `(x ,y z)
(x (1 2 3) z)
-> `(x ,(car y) z)
(x 1 z)
-> `(x (car ,y) z)
(x (car (1 2 3)) z)
->
```

Inside a backquote, an expression can also be preceded by ,@ (comma followed by an 'at' sign); the expression is then evaluated and the result 'spliced in', i.e. inserted without its outermost brackets. This is best illustrated with an example. Continuing the session above:

```
-> `(x ,@y z)
(x 1 2 3 z)
-> `(a b c ,(list 1 2 3) d e f)
(a b c (1 2 3) d e f)
-> `(a b c ,@(list 1 2 3) d e f)
(a b c 1 2 3 d e f)
->
```

Wilensky describes the semantics of backquote rather nicely as follows:

> The idea of the backquote macro is the following. Usually, in LISP, we evaluate expressions, and prevent evaluation by preceding an expression by quote. However, an expression that is backquoted works just the opposite way: all its elements are not evaluated *unless* they are preceeded by something that explicitly indicates evaluation.

Backquote is an example of a *read-macro*. These are single characters that have macros associated with them and are invoked whenever this character is encountered by the reader (with the following complete

S-expression as argument). When `(x ,y z) is read in, it is converted to
(cons 'a (cons y '(z))) and when `(x ,@y z) is read in, it is converted to
(append 'a (append y '(z))). We will not describe how read-macros are
defined in Franz LISP; Chapter 14 of Wilensky is devoted to this. Another
read-macro is the ordinary quote character '. When 'S is read in it is
converted to (quote S).

Example: The macros hd and setq could be defined more lucidly using
backquote as follows.

```
(defmacro hd (x) `(car ,x))

(defmacro setq (x y) `(set (quote ,x) ,y))
```

□

Example: Suppose only def had been defined, but not defun; then defun
could be defined as a macro by:

```
(defmacro defun (name args body)
  `(def ,name (lambda ,args ,body)))
```

□

A useful collection of macros are first, second, third, ... , ninth, which
get the first, second, third, ... , ninth elements of lists. These are just
sequences of cars and cdrs and can be defined using the built-in LISP functions with names of the form c···d, where '···' is any sequence of a's or d's.
The idea of these functions is best conveyed by a few examples: (cadr S)
abbreviates (car(cdr S)), (cadar S) abbreviates (car(cdr(car S))) and
(cddaar S) abbreviates (cdr(cdr(car(car S)))). In general, the sequence
of a's and d's determines the corresponding sequence of car's and cdr's.
Using these functions one can define the much more mnemonically named
first, second etc. by:

```
(defmacro first   (x) `(car ,x))
(defmacro second  (x) `(cadr ,x))
(defmacro third   (x) `(caddr ,x))
(defmacro fourth  (x) `(cadddr ,x))
(defmacro fifth   (x) `(caddddr ,x))
(defmacro sixth   (x) `(cadddddr ,x))
(defmacro seventh(x) `(caddddddr ,x))
(defmacro eighth  (x) `(cadddddddr ,x))
(defmacro ninth   (x) `(caddddddddr ,x))
(defmacro tenth   (x) `(cadddddddddr ,x))
```

Also cdr is given a more mnemonic name:

```
(defmacro rest (x) '(cdr ,x))
```

Exercise 106
Define a macro backquote such that (backquote S) is like (quote S) except
that any expression inside S of the form (comma S_1) is replaced by the value
of S_1, and any expression inside S of the form (comma@ S_1) results in the
value of S_1 being spliced into S.

Thus backquote is a macro analogous to the read-macro ' with comma
and comma@ being analogous to , and ,@ respectively. □

When debugging macros it is useful to be able to see the result of expansion. Evaluating (macroexpand S) returns the result of macro expanding
any macros occurring in the value of S. For example, suppose hd, setq and
defun are defined to be macros as above, then:

```
-> (macroexpand '(hd '(1 2 3)))
(car '(1 2 3))
-> (macroexpand '(setq x (hd '(1 2 3))))
(set 'x (car '(1 2 3)))
-> (macroexpand '(defun foo (x y z) (list x y z)))
(def foo (lambda (x y z) (list x y z)))
```

9.11   Compilation

The LISP *compiler* is a program that translates function definitions into
machine code. Compiling a function usually makes it execute several times
faster. In many LISP systems there is a system function compile which
when applied to function names has the side effect of replacing their S-
expression definitions by equivalent machine code. Unfortunately, the Franz
LISP compiler does not work this way. Instead, the functions to be compiled
must be put into a file and then the compiler, called liszt, must be invoked
on this file from outside LISP. For example, suppose the file rev.l contains
the definition of reverse.

```
gwyndir% cat rev.l

(defun reverse (x)
  (prog (temp result)
        (setq temp x)
        (setq result nil)
```

```
       loop (cond ((eq temp nil) (return result)))
            (setq result (cons (car temp) result))
            (setq temp (cdr temp))
            (go loop)))

    gwyndir%
```

Then all the functions in the file rev.l (actually there is only one, reverse)
can be compiled by executing liszt rev as shown below.

```
    gwyndir% ls rev.*
    rev.l
    gwyndir% liszt rev
    Compilation begins with Liszt 68000 version 8.36
    source: rev.l, result: rev.o
    reverse
    %Note: rev.l: Compilation complete
    %Note: rev.l: Time: Real: 0:1,CPU: 0:0.13,GC: 0:0.00 for 0 gcs
    %Note: rev.l: Assembly begins
    %Note: rev.l: Assembly completed successfully
    gwyndir% ls rev.*
    rev.l   rev.o
    gwyndir%
```

The compiler has produced a new file rev.o, called the *object file*, which
contains the compiled code. To use the compiled reverse the file rev.o
must be loaded into LISP.

```
    gwyndir% lisp
    Franz Lisp, Opus 38.69
    -> (load 'rev)
    [fasl rev.o]
    t
    -> (reverse '(1 2 3 4 5 6 7 8 9))
    (9 8 7 6 5 4 3 2 1)
    ->
```

The message [fasl rev.o] from LISP indicates that the object file is being
loaded (fasl is a function, 'fast load', for loading files produced by liszt).
Both the Unix command liszt and the LISP function load do not require
the file extension '.l'; they will look for a file called file.l if they cannot
find file. In addition, as illustrated above, load will look first for a file
with extension '.o' and load that if it finds it; the source file file.l will
only be loaded if there is no object file file.o.

9.11.1   Special variables

To work properly, the compiler needs to be told the names of *special* variables. These are variables that occur free in a function, i.e. occur in a function but are not local to it. For example, z is free in the function addz defined by

```
(defun addz (x) (add x z))
```

and so z must be declared special. This is done by placing

```
(declare (special z))
```

before the definition of addz. The compiler liszt will often automatically declare a variable to be special, but there are cases when it doesn't and this can lead to very obscure bugs. It is good practice to explicitly declare all special variables.

9.11.2   Compiling macros

The Franz LISP compiler liszt will expand any macro definitions that are in force when it compiles a function. This means that the compiled code has no reference to the macros and so their definitions are not needed at run time. The object file produced by liszt thus does not contain the macro definitions. Sometimes it is useful to keep the macros around at run time. This would be the case if it was planned to input new S-expressions containing the macro after the file containing the macro definitions was loaded. The compiler can be instructed to include in the object file all macro definitions in the source file with the declaration

```
(declare (macros t))
```

9.11.3   Local functions

Functions f_1, f_2, ... , f_n, can be declared local to a file by executing

```
(declare (localf f₁ ... fₙ))
```

Declaring functions to be local has two advantages:

(i) The compiler liszt can produce much faster code for local functions.

(ii) Local functions are only known to the other functions in the file in which they are declared local. This provides a way of using the same name in two files without them getting confused. This is useful when several people are writing programs; it goes some way to overcome disadvantage (iii) of dynamic binding (see page 164).

9.11.4   Transfer tables

Evaluating the S-expression (sstatus translink on) will result in subsequently loaded compiled code running much faster. It also makes certain debugging tools (like baktrace) useless. For an explanation of what this magic actually does see Wilensky, Section 20.6, together with the documentation on the particular version of Franz LISP that you use. This arcane feature is mentioned here as it is useful for speeding up the painfully slow λ-calculus reducer described in Chapter 12.

Warning: After executing (sstatus translink on) you may find that loading redefinitions of previously loaded functions has no effect. To prevent this you should execute (sstatus translink nil) before doing the redefinition. When you have got them working, do (sstatus translink on) again.

9.11.5   Including files

If (include *file*) occurs at top level in a file, then the compiler will treat the contents of *file* (or *file*.1) as though they were textually inserted in place of the S-expression (include *file*). This enables the compiler to generate an object file in which there are fast links between functions in *file* and functions in the file in which *file* is included. Furthermore, any local functions in *file* will be available in both files.

9.12   Some standard functions and macros

Many of the functions and macros listed in this section can be defined in terms of the primitive functions, but they are provided for convenience. LISP systems differ in the predefined functions that they provide. For the examples in this book only a minute subset of the functions available in Franz LISP are used. The functions listed below are in alphabetical order; they all evaluate all their arguments.

1. (add S_1 S_2) evaluates to the sum of the values of S_1 and S_2. An error results if either of these values is not a number.

2. (add1 S) is equivalent to (add S 1).

3. (append S_1 S_2) appends the values of S_1 and S_2 (see the example in Section 9.5.3 on page 161).

4. (assoc S '((S_{11} . S_{12}) ... (S_{n1} . S_{n2}))) returns (S_{i1} . S_{i2}) where S_{i1} is the first value in the sequence S_{11}, S_{21} etc. that is equal to the value of S; assq is like assoc but uses eq instead of equal.

5. (concat A_1 A_2) concatenates atoms and/or strings; A_1 and A_2 can evaluate to either atoms or strings, but the result is always an atom.

6. (equal S_1 S_2) evaluates to t if the values of S_1 and S_2 are equal, otherwise it returns nil. Note that (eq '(1 2) '(1 2)) evaluates to to nil, but (equal '(1 2) '(1 2)) evaluates to t. There is a definition of equal on page 166.

7. (list S_1 S_2 ... S_n) evaluates to a list of the values of S_1, S_2, ... , S_n; it is equivalent to

    (cons S_1 (cons S_2 (... (cons S_n nil) ...)))

8. (listp S) evaluates to t if the value of S is a list (i.e. nil or a dotted pair) and to nil otherwise.

9. (mapcar f '(S_1 ... S_n)) applies f successively to the S-expressions S_1, ... , S_n and returns a list of the resulting values. For example, (mapcar (function add1) '(1 2 3)) evaluates to (2 3 4).

10. (member S '(S_1 ... S_n)) evaluates to t if the value of S is equal to one of S_1, ... , S_n; it evaluates to nil otherwise.

11. (memq S '(S_1 ... S_n)) evaluates to t if the value of S is eq to one of S_1, ... , S_n; it evaluates to nil otherwise. The functions member and memq differ in that they test for membership using equal and eq, respectively.

12. (not S) evaluates to t if S evaluates to nil, otherwise it evaluates to nil.

13. (null S) is equivalent to (eq S nil).

14. (numberp S) evaluates to t if the value of S is a number and to nil otherwise (see the description of symbolp below).

15. (pp-form S) pretty-prints the value of S, i.e. prints S in a nicely indented format with line-breaks at sensible places. The value of S is returned.

16. (princ S) prints the value of S and then returns t. If the value of S contains atoms or strings then no quotes (") or vertical bars (|) are printed.

17. (print S) prints the value of S followed by a carriage return and then returns nil. Atoms and strings are printed with vertical bars (if necessary) and quotes surrounding them.

18. (prog1 S_1 ... S_n) evaluates S_1, ... , S_n in that order and then returns the value of S_1 as result.

19. (prog2 S_1 ... S_n) evaluates S_1, ... , S_n in that order and then returns the value of S_2 as result.

20. (progn S_1 ... S_n) evaluates S_1, ... , S_n in that order and then returns the value of S_n as result.

21. (reset) resets LISP back to the top-level. It is the thing to do after detecting an error.

22. (sublis '((S_{11} . S_{12}) ... (S_{n1} . S_{n2})) S) returns the result of substituting S_{i2} for S_{i1} (for all i such that $1 \leq i \leq n$) in the value of S.

23. (subst S_1 S_2 S_3) substitutes the value of S_1 for all occurrences of the value of S_2 in the value of S_3.

24. (symbolp S) evaluates to t if the value of S is a symbol and to nil otherwise (e.g. if the value is a number). What this means is described in Chapter 18 of Wilensky; for our puposes it is sufficient to think of symbols as names (i.e. sequences of letters and numbers starting with a letter), the only other data type we use is numbers (see the description of numberp above).

25. (terpri) outputs a carriage return.

Chapter 10

A Simple Theorem Prover

A simple theorem prover is described. It is based on higher-order rewriting operators and is implemented in LISP.

In this chapter, a very simple theorem proving program is described. The aim is to provide an example system that can automatically prove many of the verification conditions arising from the examples in Chapter 3. The reader should be aware that there are two respects in which the techniques described here are inadequate:

(i) The proof strategy used is very ad hoc and is not representative of the current state of research. An example of a powerful general-purpose theorem prover is the Boyer-Moore system [7].

(ii) The programming style used is insecure and not suitable for building theorem provers for safety-critical applications. This is discussed further in Section 10.3.

Readers interested in learning more about automatic theorem proving should consult the texts *Symbolic Logic and Mechanical Theorem Proving* by Chang and Lee [10], *Logical Foundations of Artificial Intelligence* by Genesereth and Nilsson [19] and *Automated Reasoning: Introduction and Applications* by Wos et al. [74].

The theorem prover described below is based on rewriting: a statement is proved by repeatedly replacing (i.e. rewriting) subexpressions by equivalent subexpressions until truth, represented by the atom T, is obtained, or the prover gets stuck. The prover rewrites E_1 to E_2 if:

1. $(E_1 = E_2)$ is an *instance* of an equation provided to the system, or

2. E_1 represents $S_1 \Rightarrow S_2$ and E_2 represents $S_1 \Rightarrow (S_2 [\text{T}/S_1])$, or

3. E_1 represents $(x = E) \Rightarrow S$ and E_2 represents $(x = E) \Rightarrow (S[E/x])$

179

where, as usual, $S[S_1/S_2]$ denotes the result of substituting S_1 for all occurrences of S_2 in S.

Exercise 107
Show that

(i) $\vdash S_1 \Rightarrow S_2$ if and only if $\vdash S_1 \Rightarrow (S_2[\mathtt{T}/S_1])$.

(ii) $\vdash (x = E) \Rightarrow S$ if and only if $\vdash (x = E) \Rightarrow (S[E/x])$.

□

Part of the theorem prover is a fairly general rewriting engine. This will also be used to implement a (very inefficient) combinator reducer in Chapter 12. The rewriter takes a list of equations $((E_{11}{=}E_{12}) \ldots (E_{n1}{=}E_{n2}))$ and an expression E to be rewritten, and then repeatedly replaces instances of E_{1i} by the corresponding instances of E_{2i} until no more changes occur.

To avoid having to write a parser, a LISP-like syntax for terms and statements will be used. This is illustrated in the table below:

Mathematical notation	Representation in LISP
$(X \times Y) + Z$	`((X * Y) + Z)`
$(-X) - Y$	`((- X) - Y)`
$\sin(X) + \cos(Y)$	`((sin X) + (cos Y))`
$P(E_1, \ldots, E_n)$	`(P E_1 ... E_n)`
$S_1 \wedge S_2$	`(S_1 and S_2)`
$S_1 \vee S_2$	`(S_1 or S_2)`
$\neg S$	`(not S)`
$S_1 \Rightarrow S_2$	`(S_1 implies S_2)`

To implement the rewriting engine two main programs are needed:

(i) A pattern matcher: this determines if the left-hand side of a supplied equation matches an expression.

(ii) A scanner: this repeatedly goes through expressions matching left-hand sides of equations with subexpressions and replacing them with the corresponding instances of the right-hand side, if a match is found.

Here a straightforward recursive pattern matcher is used. The approach to scanning is based on ideas from a paper by Paulson [59].

The code for our theorem prover is presented in a sequence of boxes. To experiment with this code, you should create a file called prover.l which contains the S-expressions in these boxes in the order in which they occur in this chapter. At the beginning of this file are some declarations of special variables (see Section 9.11.1), an instruction to the compiler to include macros in the object file (see Section 9.11.2) and the magic transfer table trick to speed up compiled code (see Section 9.11.4).

```
(declare (special rewrite-flag culprit eqns facts))
(declare (macros t))
(sstatus translink on)
```

The macros first, second, third etc. and rest are also defined. They are described on page 171.

```
(defmacro first  (x) '(car ,x))
(defmacro second (x) '(cadr ,x))
(defmacro third  (x) '(caddr ,x))
(defmacro fourth (x) '(cadddr ,x))
(defmacro fifth  (x) '(caddddr ,x))
(defmacro sixth  (x) '(caddddddr ,x))

(defmacro rest   (x) '(cdr ,x))
```

10.1   A pattern matcher

A function match will be defined such that evaluating (match *pat exp*):

(i) returns an S-expression $((X_1 . E_1) ... (X_n . E_n))$ such that (sublis '((X_1 . E_1) ... (X_n . E_n)) *pat*)

evaluates to *exp* where X_1, ... , X_n are variables (see below) occurring in *pat*; and

(ii) returns the atom `fail` if no such substitution exists.

A variable in a pattern is any atom that is not a number and that does not have a property with name `constant` and value `t`. Thus a constant is explicitly marked on its property list and any other atom (that isn't a number) is a variable. The non-number constants to be used are:

+, -, <, <=, >, >=, *, =, T, F, DIV, not, and, or, implies

To set their `constant` property to t simply evaluate:

```
(mapcar
 (function (lambda (x) (putprop x t 'constant)))
 '(+ - < <= > >= * = T F DIV not and or implies ))
```

To test whether something is a variable define the macro

```
(defmacro is-variable (x)
 '(not (or (null ,x) (numberp ,x) (get ,x 'constant))))
```

Now define a function `matchfn` that matches a pattern against an expression in the context of a substitution. Suppose *sub* is a substitution

((X_1 . E_1) ... (X_n . E_n))

then (`matchfn` *pat exp sub*) matches *pat* against *exp*, but treats any occurrence of a variable X_i (where $1 \leq i \leq n$) in *pat* as though it were an occurrence of the constant E_i. Here are some examples to illustrate what `matchfn` does:

```
-> (matchfn '(x 2 z) '(1 2 3) nil)
((z . 3) (x . 1))
-> (matchfn '(x 2 z) '(1 2 3) '((x . 1)))
((z . 3) (x . 1))
-> (matchfn
     '((x + y) * (z * y)) '((3 + 1) * (3 * 1)) '((z . 3)))
((y . 1) (x . 3) (z . 3))
-> (matchfn
     '((x + y) * (z * y)) '((x + 1) * (x * 1)) '((z . x)))
((y . 1) (x . x) (z . x))
```

If *pat* does not match *exp* then matchfn exits by doing (throw 'fail); this will be caught by the function match that calls matchfn. Here is the definition of matchfn:

```
(defun matchfn (pat exp sub)
 (if (atom pat)
     (if (is-variable pat)
         (if (assoc pat sub)
             (if (equal (cdr(assoc pat sub)) exp)
                 sub
                 (throw 'fail))
             (cons (cons pat exp) sub))
         (if (eq pat exp) sub (throw 'fail)))
     (if (atom exp)
         (throw 'fail)
         (matchfn
          (rest pat)
          (rest exp)
          (matchfn (first pat) (first exp) sub)))))
```

Now match can simply be defined to call matchfn with an empty initial substitution; it must also catch any throws from matchfn:

```
(defun match (pat exp) (catch (matchfn pat exp nil)))
```

Here are some examples of match in use:

```
-> (match '(x + y) '(1 + 2))
((y . 2) (x . 1))
-> (match '(x + x) '(1 + 2))
fail
->
```

10.2 Some rewriting tools

Evaluating (rewrite1 '(E_1 = E_2) E), where the function rewrite1 is defined below, treats E_1 as a pattern and matches it against the value of E. If the match succeeds then the corresponding instance of E_2 is returned, otherwise E is returned unchanged. For example:

```
-> (rewrite1 '((x + 0) = x) '((1 * 2) + 0))
(1 * 2)
-> (rewrite1 '((x + 0) = x) '((1 * 2) * 0))
((1 * 2) * 0)
->
```

The obvious definition of rewrite1, but not the one we will use, is:

```
(defun rewrite1 (eqn exp)
  (let ((l (first eqn)) (r (third eqn)))
    (let ((sub (match l exp)))
      (if (eq sub 'fail) exp (sublis sub r)))))
```

This is not used because it is convenient to provide a facility for tracing those rewrites that are done. A global variable rewrite-flag is used to control tracing: if it has value t then tracing is activated, otherwise it isn't. The default is no tracing (i.e. rewrite-flag set to nil). To implement tracing the definition of rewrite1 above is modified so that if rewrite-flag is t, then it prints out the instance of any equation that it succeeds in rewriting with. Thus the definition of rewrite1 is:

```
(setq rewrite-flag nil)

(defun rewrite1 (eqn exp)
  (let ((l (first eqn)) (r (third eqn)))
    (let ((sub (match l exp)))
      (if (eq sub 'fail)
          exp
          (prog2
           (cond (rewrite-flag
                  (pp-form (sublis sub eqn))
                  (terpri)))
           (sublis sub r))))))
```

Here is the new rewrite1 in action:

```
-> (setq rewrite-flag t)
t
-> (rewrite1 '((x + 0) = x) '((1 * 2) + 0))

(((1 * 2) + 0) = (1 * 2))
(1 * 2)
->
```

Next define a function `rewrite` that takes a list of equations rather than
a single one and rewrites with each equation in turn:

```
(defun rewrite (eqns exp)
 (if (null eqns)
     exp
     (rewrite (rest eqns) (rewrite1 (first eqns) exp))))
```

Note that `rewrite` rewrites using the equations in the order they are
given. When designing rewrite lists one has to take this order into account.

```
-> (setq rewrite-flag nil)
nil
-> (rewrite '(((x + 0) = x) ((x * 1) = x)) '((X * 1) + 0))
X
-> (rewrite '(((x * 1) = x) ((x + 0) = x)) '((X * 1) + 0))
(X * 1)
->
```

Shortly it will be shown how to repeatedly apply `rewrite` to all subexpressions of an expression, but first the two special rewrites described at the
begining of the chapter (2 and 3 on page 179) must be implemented. Both
these rewrites transform expressions of the form (*P* implies *Q*). To simplify their definition, four macros are useful: the macro `is-imp` tests whether
its argument has the form (*P* implies *Q*); the macro `mk-imp` builds such
an implication given *P* and *Q*; the macro `antecedent` extracts *P* from such
an implication and the macro `consequent` extracts *Q*.

```
(defmacro is-imp (x)
 '(and (listp ,x)
       (eq (length ,x) 3)
       (eq (second ,x) 'implies)))

(defmacro mk-imp (p q) '(list ,p (quote implies) ,q))

(defmacro antecedent (x) '(first ,x))

(defmacro consequent (x) '(third ,x))
```

The function `imp-subst-simp` defined below transforms any S-expression
of the form

$(P$ implies $Q)$

to one of the form

$(P$ implies $Q[\text{T}/P])$.

```
(defun imp-subst-simp (exp)
 (if (is-imp exp)
     (let ((a (antecedent exp))
           (c (consequent exp)))
       (mk-imp a (subst 'T a c)))
     exp))
```

The function `imp-and-simp` defined below transforms any S-expression of the form

$((X = E)$ implies $Q)$

to one of the form

$((X = E)$ implies $Q[E/X])$

First define a macro `is-eqn` that tests whether its argument has the form $(E_1 = E_2)$:

```
(defmacro is-eqn (x)
 '(and (listp ,x) (eq (length ,x) 3) (eq (second ,x) '=)))
```

The function `imp-and-simp` is defined by:

```
(defun imp-and-simp (exp)
 (if (and (is-imp exp) (is-eqn (antecedent exp)))
     (let ((a (antecedent exp))
           (c (consequent exp)))
       (mk-imp a (subst (third a) (first a) c)))
     exp))
```

The function `imp-simp` first applies `imp-subst-simp` and then applies `imp-and-simp` to the result:

```
(defun imp-simp (exp) (imp-and-simp (imp-subst-simp exp)))
```

10.2.1   Higher-order rewriting functions

The higher-order functions `repeat`, `depth-conv`, `top-depth-conv` and `re-depth-conv` described in this section are based on rewriting operators from Paulson's elegant paper [59]. These operators specify the order in which subexpressions are rewritten.

Suppose f is a function that when applied to an expression will either change it or leave it alone, then (`repeat` f E) repeatedly applies f until no more change occurs.

```
(defun repeat (f exp)
 (let ((exp1 (funcall f exp)))
  (if (equal exp exp1)
      exp
      (repeat f exp1))))
```

The function `depth-conv` repeatedly applies a function f to all subexpressions of an expression exp in a 'bottom-up' order:

(i) if exp is an atom then f is repeatedly applied to exp;

(ii) if exp has the form $(E_1 \ . \ E_2)$ then

    (a) E_1 is recursively rewritten to $\hat{E}_1$,

    (b) E_2 is recursively rewritten to $\hat{E}_2$,

    (c) f is repeatedly applied to $(\hat{E}_1 \ . \ \hat{E}_2)$ and the result returned.

```
(defun depth-conv (f exp)
 (if (atom exp)
     (repeat f exp)
     (repeat
      f
      (cons (depth-conv f (first exp))
            (depth-conv f (rest exp))))))
```

Now use `depth-conv` to define a function `depth-imp-simp` that applies `imp-simp` to all subexpressions of an expression:

```
(defun depth-imp-simp (exp)
 (depth-conv
  (function (lambda (x) (imp-simp x)))
  exp))
```

Here is an example illustrating `depth-imp-simp` in action:

```
-> (depth-imp-simp '((x = 1) implies ((y = x) implies (y = z))))
((x = 1) implies ((y = 1) implies (1 = z)))
->
```

Next define a function called `top-depth-conv` that is like `depth-conv` except that it rewrites 'top-down' before rewriting 'bottom-up': if exp is a dotted pair $(E_1 \ . \ E_2)$, then `(top-depth-conv f exp)` repeatedly applies f to E_1 and E_2 before descending inside them.

```
(defun top-depth-conv (f exp)
  (let ((exp1 (repeat f exp)))
    (if (atom exp1)
        exp1
        (repeat
         f
         (cons (top-depth-conv f (first exp1))
               (top-depth-conv f (rest exp1)))))))
```

Using `top-depth-conv` define a function for repeatedly rewriting all subexpressions of an expression in top-down order using a supplied list of equations. The top-down order is important.

```
(defun top-depth-rewrite (eqns exp)
  (top-depth-conv
   (function (lambda (x) (rewrite eqns x)))
   exp))
```

Notice that the variable `eqns` is free in the `lambda`-expression in which it occurs and must thus be declared special (see Section 9.11.1). To see that the top-down order is important consider the following example:

```
-> (top-depth-rewrite
    '(((not(x >= y)) = (x < y))
      ((x >= y) = ((x = y) or (x > y))))
    '(not(1 >= 2)))
(1 < 2)
->
```

If a rewriter `depth-rewrite` is defined that uses `depth-conv` instead of `top-depth-conv`, i.e.

```
(defun depth-rewrite (eqns exp)
 (depth-conv
  (function (lambda (x) (rewrite eqns x)))
  exp))
```

then a different answer results:

```
-> (depth-rewrite
    '(((not(x >= y)) = (x < y))
      ((x >= y) = ((x = y) or (x > y))))
    '(not(1 >= 2)))
(not ((1 = 2) or (1 > 2)))
->
```

It is a difficult problem to decide which rewriting order to use: some problems might be solved with depth-rewrite but not solved with top-depth-rewrite. However, for simple 'brute force' rewriting, it seems that top-depth-rewrite is usually satisfactory. Interactive theorem provers like LCF [60] provide the user with control over the order of rewriting by letting him or her decide whether to use a top-down or bottom-up order, or maybe even some other order specially tailored to the problem at hand. This flexibility is the theme of Paulson's paper [59]; he provides a powerful kit for building both specialized and general purpose rewriting tools.

Yet another 'depth conversion' is re-depth-conv; this will be useful in Chapter 12 for rewriting combinatory expressions (see Section 12.3):

```
(defun re-depth-conv (f exp)
 (if (atom exp)
     (repeat f exp)
     (let ((exp1 (cons (re-depth-conv f (first exp))
                       (re-depth-conv f (rest exp)))))
       (let ((exp2 (funcall f exp1)))
         (if (equal exp1 exp2) exp1 (re-depth-conv f exp2)))))))
```

The corresponding rewriting function is:

```
(defun re-depth-rewrite (eqns exp)
 (re-depth-conv
  (function (lambda (x) (rewrite eqns x)))
  exp))
```

Exercise 108

What is the difference between the functions re-depth-conv, depth-conv and top-depth-conv? Think up a list of equations eqns and an expression exp such that (depth-rewrite eqns exp), (top-depth-rewrite eqns exp) and (re-depth-rewrite eqns exp) all give different answers. □

The simple theorem prover can now be assembled by defining a function prove that repeatedly applies depth-imp-simp followed by rewriting using top-depth-rewrite:

```
(defun prove (eqns exp)
 (repeat
  (function
   (lambda (x) (top-depth-rewrite eqns (depth-imp-simp x))))
  exp))
```

The equations used for rewriting will be structured into two lists:

(i) A list called logic containing various properties of implies and and.

(ii) A list called arithmetic containing various arithmetical facts.

The verifier in Chapter 11 uses prove with (append logic arithmetic) as its list of equations. Both logic and arithmetic have been somewhat 'tuned' (in their content and order) so that they solve many of the verification conditions for the examples discussed in Chapters 2 and 3. The need that the equations in the lists themselves be mechanically verified is discussed in Section 10.3. Here is the definition of logic:

```
(setq
 logic
 '(
   ((T implies X) = X)
   ((F implies X) = T)
   ((X implies T) = T)
   ((X implies X) = T)
   ((T and X) = X)
   ((X and T) = X)
   ((F and X) = F)
   ((X and F) = F)
   ((X = X) = T)
   (((X and Y) implies Z) = (X implies (Y implies Z)))
   ))
```

Here is the definition of `arithmetic`. The particular collection of arithmetical facts included in it is very ad hoc. They have been chosen just so that various examples go through. The order in which they are listed has also been carefully 'tuned'. An interesting exercise is to switch tracing on (by `(setq rewrite-flag t)`) and then experiment both with different collections of facts and also with the same facts but in a different order. This will give a good feel for how rewriting works.

```
(setq
 arithmetic
 '(
   ((X + 0) = X)
   ((0 + X) = X)
   ((X * 0) = 0)
   ((0 * X) = 0)
   ((X * 1) = X)
   ((1 * X) = X)
   ((not(X <= Y)) = (Y < X))
   ((not(X >= Y)) = (Y > X))
   ((not(X < Y)) = (X >= Y))
   (((- X) >= (- Y)) = (X <= Y))
   (((- X) >= Y) = (X <= (- Y)))
   ((- 0) = 0)
   (((X < Y) implies (X <= Y)) = T)
   ((X - X) = 0)
   (((X + Y) - Z) = (X + (Y - Z)))
   (((X - Y) * Z) = ((X * Z) - (Y * Z)))
   ((X * (Y + Z)) = ((X * Y) + (X * Z)))
   (((X + Y) * Z) = ((X * Z) + (Y * Z)))
   (((X >= Y) implies ((X < Y) implies Z)) = T)
   (((X <= Y) implies ((Y < X) implies Z)) = T)
   ((0 DIV X) = 0)
   (((X DIV Y) + Z) = ((X + (Y * Z)) DIV Y))
   (((X - Y) + Z) = (X + (Z - Y)))
   ((2 * X) = (X + X))
   ))
```

The list `facts` is then defined by:

```
(setq facts (append logic arithmetic))
```

An example of something that can be proved is:

```
-> (prove
     facts
     '(((X = (((N - 1) * N) DIV 2)) and ((1 <= N) and (N <= M)))
      implies
      ((X + N) = (((((N + 1) - 1) * (N + 1)) DIV 2))))
T
->
```

An example of something that cannot be proved with the theorem prover
is:

```
-> (prove
     facts
     '(((T and (X >= Y)) implies (X = (max X Y)))
      and
      ((T and (not (X >= Y))) implies (Y = (max X Y)))))
(((X >= Y) implies (X = (max X Y)))
 and
 ((Y > X) implies (Y = (max X Y))))
```

These could be proved by adding some arithmetical facts about max (see
page 216). Here is a trace of the instances of equations used during a proof,
obtained by setting rewrite-flag to t:

```
-> (setq rewrite-flag t)
t
-> (prove
     facts
     '(((R = X) and (Q = 0)) implies (X = (R + (Y * Q)))))

((((R = X) and (Q = 0)) implies (X = (R + (Y * Q))))
=
((R = X) implies ((Q = 0) implies (X = (R + (Y * Q))))))

((Y * 0) = 0)

((X + 0) = X)

((X = X) = T)

(((Q = 0) implies T) = T)

(((R = X) implies T) = T)
T
```

Exercise 109
Consider the following definition of prove1:

```
(defun prove1 (eqns exp)
(re-depth-conv
(function (lambda (x) (rewrite eqns (imp-simp x))))
exp))
```

(i) Is prove1 equivalent to prove?

(ii) If it is equivalent, is it more or less efficient? If it is not equivalent, devise an example to show the difference.

□

10.3   Validity of the theorem prover

How can one be sure that there are not bugs in our theorem prover which enable it to prove things that are not true? These bugs could be of two kinds:

(i) bugs in the underlying algorithm,

(ii) bugs in the equations in the list facts.

An example of (ii) would be:

$$(((X \text{ DIV } Z) + (Y \text{ DIV } Z)) = ((X + Y) \text{ DIV } Z))$$

which was originally included in the list arithmetic until it was noticed that it was not true (take X, Y and Z to be 3, 5 and 2, respectively). So this was replaced with

$$(((X \text{ DIV } Y) + Z) = ((X + (Y * Z)) \text{ DIV } Y))$$

However, how can one be sure this is true? A well known verifier developed by a U.S. company has a large number of rewrite rules in its knowledge base and every so often someone spots that one of them is wrong, usually as a result of a simple typing error when the equations were typed in.

Various methods have been developed to decrease the frequency of errors in mechanical theorem provers. One approach, invented by Robin Milner, is to employ a programming language type discipline to ensure that only 'safe' operations can be used to deduce new theorems. It is not possible to go into this here; interested readers are referred to the original LCF book [25], my tutorial paper on the use of ML [24] or Paulson's recent monograph on Cambridge LCF [60]. Another approach is to have the theorem prover generate a representation of a formal proof rather than just magically announce 'T'. This proof can then be separately checked by a special proof-checking program. Such a program can be quite simple, and can be subject to especially rigorous analysis so that it has a very low probability of being wrong. Thus the correctness of an arbitrary program can be reduced to the correctness of a single proof checking program. This idea was originally proposed by Malcolm Newey in the early 1970s. More recently it has been discussed by Bob Boyer and J Moore and also advocated, in the context of hardware verification, by Keith Hanna.

As far as I know no one has implemented such a system. One can never attain complete certainty of the correctness of a theorem prover, but by methods like the ones just discussed, one can gain a very high degree of confidence.

Chapter 11

A Simple Program Verifier

A simple program verifier implemented in LISP *is described. This consists of a verification condition generator and the theorem prover described in Chapter 10.*

The verifier described in this chapter is based on the principles explained in Chapter 3 and uses the theorem prover described in Chapter 10. It consists of two main LISP functions, vc-gen and prove, whose role is shown in the diagram below.

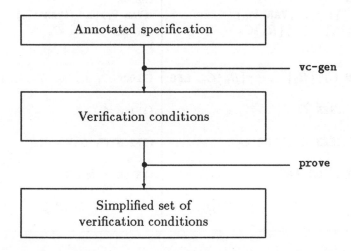

The input to the verifier is an annotated partial correctness specification. This is then checked to ensure that it is syntactically well formed and that annotations have been properly inserted according to the rules on page 44. The verification conditions are then generated and passed to the theorem prover. The final result is either an announcement 'all proved' indicating that the specification has been proved or a list of simplified verification conditions that the prover could not prove.

The bulk of the LISP code is in the well-formedness checker. The verification condition generator is a simple one-pass recursive function.

To avoid having to write a parser, a LISP-like syntax will be used for partial correctness specifications. The table below illustrates this.

Standard notation	Representation in LISP
$\{P\}\ C\ \{Q\}$	(SPEC P C Q)
$V\mathtt{:=}E$	(ASSIGN V E)
$C_1;\{R_2\}\ \dots\ ;\{R_n\}C_n$	(SEQ C_1 R_2 ... R_n C_n)
BEGIN VAR V_1; ... ;VAR V_m; $C_1;\{R_2\}\ \dots\ ;\{R_n\}C_n$ END	(BLOCK (VAR V_1) ... (VAR V_m) C_1 R_2 ... R_n C_n)
BEGIN $C_1;\{R_2\}\ \dots\ ;\{R_n\}C_n$ END	(BLOCK C_1 R_2 ... R_n C_n)
IF S THEN C	(IF1 S C)
IF S THEN C_1 ELSE C_2	(IF2 S C_1 C_2)
WHILE S DO $\{R\}$ C	(WHILE S R C)
FOR $V\mathtt{:=}E_1$ UNTIL E_2 DO $\{R\}$ C	(FOR V E_1 E_2 R C)

Terms and statements will be represented as illustrated in the table on page 180. Annotations are represented by (ASSERT S) where S is the representation of the annotating statement. For example:

```
{T}
 BEGIN
   R:=X;
   Q:=0;  {R=X ∧ Q=0}
   WHILE Y≤R DO {X = R+Y×Q}
      BEGIN R:=R-Y; Q:=Q+1 END
 END
 {X = R+Y×Q ∧ R<Y}
```

would be represented by:

```
(SPEC
 T
 (BLOCK
  (ASSIGN R X)
  (ASSIGN Q 0)
  (ASSERT ((R = X) and (Q = 0)))
  (WHILE
    (<= Y R)
    (ASSERT (X = (R + (Y * Q))))
    (BLOCK (ASSIGN R (R - Y)) (ASSIGN Q (Q + 1))))
  ((R < Y) and (X = (R + (Y * Q)))))))
```

As with the theorem prover in Chapter 10, the code for our program verifier is presented in a sequence of boxes. To experiment with the verifier, you should create a file called verifier.l containing the S-expressions in these boxes in the order in which they occur in this chapter. Since the verifier will use the theorem prover, the code for the prover is included with the LISP function include (see page 175). The effect of this is as though the file prover.l was textually inserted at the beginning of the file verifier.l; this enables the compiler to compile the prover and verifier into a single object file:

```
(include prover)
```

The implementation begins with some functions and macros for manipulating LISP representations of terms, statements, commands and specifications.

11.1   Selectors, constructors and predicates

The verifier uses many macros to make the code more readable. These can be grouped into various kinds.

(i) Selectors: these extract components of data structures. Their names correspond the type of component they are selecting. For example, the macro precondition selects the the precondition part P of a partial correctnes specification (SPEC P C Q).

(ii) Constructors: these construct a data-structure from its components. Their names have the form mk-*thing*, where *thing* is the kind of thing being constructed. For example, the macro mk-spec constructs a specification (SPEC P C Q) from the three components P, C and Q.

(iii) Predicates: these are predicates that test whether an S-expression is a representation of a particular kind of object. They return t if the test succeeds and nil otherwise. Their names have the form is-*thing*, where *thing* is the kind of thing being tested. For example, the macro is-assign tests whether an S-expression represents an assignment command, i.e. whether it has the form (ASSIGN S_1 S_2).

11.1.1   Selector macros

The following three macros extract the components of a specification (SPEC P C Q):

```
(defmacro precondition  (x) '(second ,x))
(defmacro command       (x) '(third ,x))
(defmacro postcondition (x) '(fourth ,x))
```

The macro command-type gets the constructor from a command; it is used in case-switches in the definition of chk-and-cmd (page 203), assigned-vars (page 205) and vc-gen (page 206):

```
(defmacro command-type (c) '(first ,c))
```

Next, two macros to get the left-hand side (lhs) and right-hand side (rhs) of an assignment command:

```
(defmacro lhs (c) '(second ,c))
(defmacro rhs (c) '(third ,c))
```

The next three macros get the list of commands in a sequence, the components (i.e. local variable declarations and commands) of a block and the name declared in a local variable declaration:

```
(defmacro seq-commands (c) '(rest ,c))
(defmacro block-body (c) '(rest ,c))
(defmacro var-name (v) '(second ,v))
```

The following three macros get the components of conditionals:

```
(defmacro if-test    (c) '(second ,c))
(defmacro then-part (c) '(third ,c))
(defmacro else-part (c) '(fourth ,c))
```

and the next three macros get the components of an annotated WHILE-commands:

```
(defmacro while-test       (c) '(second ,c))
(defmacro while-annotation (c) '(third ,c))
(defmacro while-body       (c) '(fourth ,c))
```

There are five macros to get the components of an annotated FOR-command:

```
(defmacro for-var        (c) '(second ,c))
(defmacro lower          (c) '(third ,c))
(defmacro upper          (c) '(fourth ,c))
(defmacro for-annotation (c) '(fifth ,c))
(defmacro for-body       (c) '(sixth ,c))
```

Finally, a macro to get the statement contained in an annotation (ASSERT *S*):

```
(defmacro statement (a) '(second ,a))
```

11.1.2   Constructor macros

Now define macros for constructing partial correctness specifications, negated statements, implications and conjunctions ($\wedge$s):

```
(defmacro mk-spec (p c q) '(list (quote SPEC) ,p ,c ,q))
(defmacro mk-not  (s)     '(list (quote not) ,s))
(defmacro mk-imp  (s1 s2) '(list ,s1 (quote implies) ,s2))
(defmacro mk-and  (s1 s2) '(list ,s1 (quote and) ,s2))
```

Three macros are defined to construct arithmetic expressions of the form
$m + n$, $m < n$ and $m \leq n$:

```
(defmacro mk-add      (m n) '(list ,m (quote +)  ,n))
(defmacro mk-less     (m n) '(list ,m (quote <)  ,n))
(defmacro mk-less-eq  (m n) '(list ,m (quote <=) ,n))
```

11.1.3   Test macros

Only two predicates are used; usually it is better to abort if a test fails,
rather than return nil. In such cases an error check (see Section 11.2 below)
is more appropriate.

The macro is-var is a predicate that tests whether something represents
a local variable declaration, i.e. has the form (VAR x), where x is a symbol:

```
(defmacro is-var (v)
 '(and ,v
       (eq (first ,v) 'VAR)
       (rest ,v)
       (symbolp (second ,v))))
```

The function is-assign is a predicate to test whether a command is an
assignment, i.e. has the form (ASSIGN S_1 S_2):

```
(defmacro is-assign (a)
 '(and ,a
       (eq (first ,a) 'ASSIGN)
       (rest ,a)
       (rest (rest ,a))))
```

11.2   Error checking functions and macros

To check that various things are well formed and that side conditions to
the block and FOR rules are met, a number of functions and macros are
defined that are like predicates, except that if the check fails, instead of
just returning nil they print out an error message and reset LISP back to
top-level. The names of such checks have the form chk-*thing*, where *thing* is
the kind of thing being checked. Sometimes a check has a second argument
which is the message to be printed if the test fails; for example, evaluating
(chk-assert S *message*) returns t if S has the form (ASSERT S_1), but if it

does not then *message* is printed out and LISP reset. Sometimes a check generates its own error message; for example (chk-ann-cmd S) checks whether the value of S is a well-formed command (with annotations correctly embedded within it); if not an appropriate error message (e.g. Bad lhs of ASSIGN) is generated.

Checks are implemented with the function error. This prints out an error message, puts the offending thing in the global variable culprit (so that the user can look at what caused the error, if the message isn't sufficient) and then resets LISP to top level:

```
(defun error (message thing)
 (progn (princ message)
        (terpri)
        (setq culprit thing)
        (reset)))
```

11.2.1   Checking wellformedness

The function chk-typ checks whether the first element of something has a given name; t is returned if it does, an error is generated if it doesn't:

```
(defun chk-typ (name thing msg)
 (if (or (null thing) (not (eq (first thing) name)))
     (error msg thing)
     t))
```

Evaluating (chk-parts (*constructor* x_1 ... x_m) n) checks that $m = n$ and if not raises the error "Parts of *constructor* missing" with culprit (*constructor* x_1 ... x_n):

```
(defun chk-parts (thing size)
 (or (eq (length thing) (add1 size))
     (error
       (get_pname (concat "Bad " (first thing)))
       thing)))
```

The macro chk-sym checks whether something is a LISP symbol:

```
(defmacro chk-sym (v msg) '(or (symbolp ,v) (error ,msg ,v)))
```

The function `chk-rev-ann-seq` checks whether a sequence is correctly annotated (see page 44). It is given its argument in reverse order by `chk-ann-cmd`; this makes the recursion easier. See also the discusion on page 208 preceding the definition of `rev-seq-vc-gen`.

```
(defun chk-rev-ann-seq (c-list)
 (cond ((null c-list) t)
       ((null(rest c-list)) (chk-ann-cmd (first c-list)))
       ((is-assign (first c-list))
        (chk-rev-ann-seq (rest c-list)))
       (t
        (chk-ann-cmd (first c-list))
        (chk-assert (second c-list) "Bad annotation in SEQ")
        (chk-rev-ann-seq (rest(rest c-list))))))
```

The function `chk-ann-block` checks whether the sequence of commands in a block is properly annotated. It uses the function `block-commands` that gets the sequence of commands in a block; it also uses `chk-rev-ann-seq`:

```
(defun chk-ann-block (c)
  (chk-rev-ann-seq (reverse (block-commands c))))

(defun block-commands (c)
 (strip-locals (block-body c)))

(defun strip-locals (c-list)
 (if (is-var (first c-list))
     (strip-locals (rest c-list))
     c-list))
```

The next two macros are intended to check whether statements and expressions (terms) are well-formed. These checks have not been implemented in this version of the verifier, so the macros just expand to `t`.

```
(defun chk-stat (s msg) t)
(defun chk-exp (e msg) t)
```

The function `chk-assert` checks whether something is an annotation and raises an error otherwise:

```
(defun chk-assert (s msg)
  (and (chk-typ 'ASSERT s msg)
       (chk-parts s 1)))
```

Here is the definition of the function chk-ann-cmd that checks whether a command is properly annotated. This function is just a cases-switch on the command type:

```
(defun chk-ann-cmd (c)
  (caseq (command-type c)
         (ASSIGN (and (chk-parts c 2)
                      (chk-sym (lhs c) "Bad lhs of ASSIGN")
                      (chk-exp (rhs c) "Bad rhs of ASSIGN")))
         (IF1    (and (chk-parts c 2)
                      (chk-stat (if-test c) "Bad test in IF1")
                      (chk-ann-cmd (then-part c))))
         (IF2    (and (chk-parts c 3)
                      (chk-stat (if-test c) "Bad test in IF2")
                      (chk-ann-cmd (then-part c))
                      (chk-ann-cmd (else-part c))))
         (WHILE  (and (chk-parts c 3)
                      (chk-stat
                       (while-test c)
                       "Bad test in WHILE")
                      (chk-assert
                       (while-annotation c)
                       "Bad annotation in WHILE")
                      (chk-ann-cmd (while-body c))))
         (FOR    (and (chk-parts c 5)
                      (chk-sym (for-var c) "Bad FOR variable")
                      (chk-exp (lower c) "Bad lower bound")
                      (chk-exp (upper c) "Bad upper bound")
                      (chk-assert
                       (for-annotation c)
                       "Bad annotation in FOR")
                      (chk-ann-cmd (for-body c))))
         (SEQ    (chk-rev-ann-seq (reverse (seq-commands c))))
         (BLOCK  (chk-ann-block c))
         (t      (error
                  "Unknown command type"
                  (command-type c)))))
```

The function `chk-ann-spec` checks whether something is a correctly annotated partial correctness specification and raises an error if it isn't:

```
(defun chk-ann-spec (a)
  (and (chk-typ 'SPEC a "Bad specification constructor")
       (chk-parts a 3)
       (chk-stat (precondition a) "Bad precondition")
       (chk-ann-cmd (command a))
       (chk-stat (postcondition a) "Bad postcondition")))
```

11.2.2   Checking side conditions

The functions `chk-block-side-condition` and `chk-for-side-condition`, which are defined at the end of this section, are used during verification condition generation to check that the syntactic side conditions for blocks and FOR-commands are met (see pages 48 and 50 respectively). First it is necessary to define some auxiliary functions.

Evaluating (`get-locals` ((VAR x_1) ... (VAR x_n) C_1 ... C_n)) returns (x_1 ... x_n):

```
(defun get-locals (c-list)
  (if (is-var (first c-list))
      (cons (var-name(first c-list))
            (get-locals(rest c-list)))
      nil))
```

The function `vars-in` computes the variables in a term; it is fairly crude in that it just 'flattens' the list:

```
(defun vars-in (e)
  (cond ((null e) nil)
        ((atom e) (list e))
        (t (append (vars-in (first e)) (vars-in (rest e))))))
```

The function `append-lists` appends together the members of a list of lists:

```
(defun append-lists (l)
  (if (null l)
      l
      (append (first l) (append-lists(rest l)))))
```

The function `assigned-vars` computes a list of the variables assigned to in a command. It is used by the function `chk-for-side-condition`:

```
(defun assigned-vars (c)
 (caseq (command-type c)
        (ASSIGN (list (lhs c)))
        (IF1 (assigned-vars(then-part c)))
        (IF2 (append (assigned-vars(then-part c))
                     (assigned-vars(else-part c))))
        (WHILE (assigned-vars(while-body c)))
        (FOR (assigned-vars(for-body c)))
        (SEQ
         (append-lists
          (mapcar (function assigned-vars)
                  (seq-commands c))))
        (BLOCK
         (append-lists
          (mapcar (function assigned-vars)
                  (block-commands c))))
        (t nil)))
```

The definition of the function `disjoint` below depends on the arguments of `and` and `or` being evaluated in left-to-right order:

```
(defun disjoint (x y)
 (or (null x)
     (and (not(member(first x) y))
          (disjoint (rest x) y))))
```

Evaluating (`chk-block-side-condition` P C Q) checks that if C represents a block, i.e. has the form

(BLOCK (VAR V_1) ... (VAR V_m) C_1 ... C_n)

then none of V_1, ... , V_m occur in P or Q. This check is done during verification condition generation by the function `vc-gen` of Section 11.3 below.

```
(defun chk-block-side-condition (p c q)
 (let ((p-vars (vars-in p))
       (c-vars (get-locals (block-body c)))
       (q-vars (vars-in q)))
   (or (disjoint c-vars (append p-vars q-vars))
       (error "Side condition of BLOCK violated" c-vars))))
```

Evaluating (chk-for-side-condition (FOR V E_1 E_2 R C)) checks that neither V, nor any variable occurring in E_1 or E_2 is assigned to inside C:

```
(defun chk-for-side-condition (c)
 (let ((v  (for-var c))
       (e1 (lower c))
       (e2 (upper c))
       (c1 (for-body c)))
   (or (disjoint
         (cons v (append (vars-in e1) (vars-in e2)))
         (assigned-vars c1))
       (error "Side condition in FOR violated" c1))))
```

11.3   The verification condition generator

Evaluating (vc-gen P C Q) returns the verification conditions from an annotated specification (SPEC P C Q). It calls the functions assign-vc-gen, if1-vc-gen, if2-vc-gen, while-vc-gen, for-vc-gen, seq-vc-gen and block-vc-gen, which are defined below.

```
(defun vc-gen (p c q)
 (caseq (command-type c)
        (ASSIGN (assign-vc-gen p c q))
        (IF1    (if1-vc-gen p c q))
        (IF2    (if2-vc-gen p c q))
        (WHILE  (while-vc-gen p c q))
        (FOR    (for-vc-gen p c q))
        (SEQ    (seq-vc-gen p c q))
        (BLOCK  (block-vc-gen p c q))))
```

The function assign-vc-gen generates a list of verification conditions according to the rule in the box on page 45:

```
(defun assign-vc-gen (p c q)
 (let ((v (lhs c))
       (e (rhs c)))
  (list (mk-imp p (subst e v q)))))
```

The function `if1-vc-gen` generates a list of verification conditions according to the rule in the box on page 45:

```
(defun if1-vc-gen (p c q)
 (let ((s  (if-test c))
       (c1 (then-part c)))
  (cons (mk-imp (mk-and p (mk-not s)) q)
        (vc-gen (mk-and p s) c1 q))))
```

The function `if2-vc-gen` generates a list of verification conditions according to the rule in the box on page 46:

```
(defun if2-vc-gen (p c q)
 (let ((s  (if-test c))
       (c1 (then-part c))
       (c2 (else-part c)))
  (append (vc-gen (mk-and p s) c1 q)
          (vc-gen (mk-and p (mk-not s)) c2 q))))
```

The function `while-vc-gen` generates a list of verification conditions according to the rule in the box on page 49:

```
(defun while-vc-gen (p c q)
 (let ((s  (while-test c))
       (r  (statement(while-annotation c)))
       (c1 (while-body c)))
  (cons
   (mk-imp p r)
   (cons (mk-imp (mk-and r (mk-not s)) q)
         (vc-gen (mk-and r s) c1 r)))))
```

The function `for-vc-gen` generates a list of verification conditions according to the rule in the box on page 50. The syntactic side condition is checked by `chk-for-side-condition` defined on page 206.

```
(defun for-vc-gen (p c q)
  (let ((v  (for-var c))
        (e1 (lower c))
        (e2 (upper c))
        (r  (statement(for-annotation c)))
        (c1 (for-body c)))
    (and (chk-for-side-condition c)
         (append
          (list
           (mk-imp p (subst e1 v r))
           (mk-imp (subst (mk-add e2 1) v r) q)
           (mk-imp (mk-and p (mk-less e2 e1)) q))
          (vc-gen
           (mk-and
            r
            (mk-and
             (mk-less-eq e1 v)
             (mk-less-eq v e2)))
           c1
           (subst (mk-add v 1) v r)))))))
```

The function seq-vc-gen generates a list of verification conditions according to the rule in the box on page 46. The process of generating these conditions is recursive, with the recursion being done at the end of the sequence. This is most simply implemented by having the recursion in a subsidiary function rev-seq-vc-gen which is passed the reversed list of commands by seq-vc-gen and can thus recurse on the cdr of its argument.

```
(defun seq-vc-gen (p c q)
  (rev-seq-vc-gen p (reverse (seq-commands c)) q))
```

The function rev-seq-vc-gen is a bit messy; this reflects the messiness of the algorithm for generating verification conditions from sequences. From the definition of seq-vc-gen, the verification conditions are generated from (SPEC P (SEQ C_1 ... C_n) Q) by evaluating

$$(\text{rev-seq-vc-gen } P \ (C_n \ ... \ C_1) \ Q)$$

There are two cases:

1. If C_n is an assignment (ASSIGN V E), then

$$(\text{rev-seq-vc-gen } P \ (C_{n-1} \ ... \ C_1) \ Q[E/V])$$

is evaluated. This corresponds to case 2 on page 46.

2. If C_n is not an assignment, then, by the rules of proper annotation
    (see page 44 and the definition of the function chk-rev-ann-seq on
    page 202), the penultimate element in the list $(C_1 \ldots C_n)$ passed
    to seq-vc-gen must represent an annotation, R say.   This will
    be the second element of the reversed list $(C_n \ldots C_1)$ passed to
    rev-seq-vc-gen.   Thus the verification conditions corresponding to
    case 1 on page 46 are computed by evaluating

$$(\text{rev-seq-vc-gen } P \ (C_{n-1} \ldots C_1) \ R)$$

and then appending to the result of this the verification conditions
generated from (SPEC R C_n Q).

The definition of rev-seq-vc-gen is thus:

```
(defun rev-seq-vc-gen (p c-list q)
 (cond ((null c-list)
        (error "Empty command list" (list p c-list q)))
       ((null (rest c-list)) (vc-gen p (first c-list) q))
       ((is-assign(first c-list))
        (let ((v (lhs (first c-list)))
              (e (rhs (first c-list))))
          (rev-seq-vc-gen p (rest c-list) (subst e v q))))
       (t
        (let ((cn (first c-list))
              (r  (statement(second c-list))))
          (append (rev-seq-vc-gen p (rest(rest c-list)) r)
                  (vc-gen r cn q)))))))
```

The function block-vc-gen generates a list of verification conditions according to the rule in the box on page 48. It needs to check the syntactic
side condition, using chk-block-side-condition defined on page 206; it then
generates the verification from the sequence of commands in its body. This
is done by directly applying rev-seq-vc-gen to the reversed sequence:

```
(defun block-vc-gen (p c q)
  (and (chk-block-side-condition p c q)
       (rev-seq-vc-gen p (reverse (block-commands c)) q)))
```

11.4   The complete verifier

Using the verification condition generator, vc-gen, and the theorem prover, prove, described in Chapter 10, the verification system can now be completed. The function verify takes an annotated specification and:

  (i) checks that it is annotatated correctly using chk-ann-spec;

 (ii) generates the verification conditions using vc-gen,

(iii) prints them out;

(iv) attempts to prove them with the theorem prover prove described in Chapter 10 (using the facts in the global variable facts);

 (v) prints out "all proved" if it succeeds in proving all the verification conditions, otherwise it prints out the things it cannot prove;

(vi) returns t if all the verifications are proved and nil otherwise.

Before defining verify a couple of auxiliary functions are needed. The first of these, print-list, prints out the elements of a list preceded by a blank line:

```
(defun print-list (list)
 (mapcar
  (function(lambda (x) (terpri) (pp-form x)))
  list))
```

The verifier prints (using print-list) the verification conditions that it cannot prove. This list is constructed by the function unproved-vcs, which removes occurrences of T (representing proved verification conditions) from the list returned by the theorem prover prove.

```
(defun unproved-vcs (l)
 (cond ((null l) nil)
       ((eq (first l) 'T) (unproved-vcs (rest l)))
       (t (cons (first l) (unproved-vcs (rest l))))))
```

Here, at last, is the definition of the verifier verify:

```
(defun verify (a)
 (prog (vcs vcs1)
       (terpri)
       (princ "Checking syntax of annotated program ... ")
       (chk-ann-spec a)
       (setq vcs (vc-gen (precondition a)
                         (command a)
                         (postcondition a)))
       (princ "OK.")
       (terpri)
       (princ "The verification conditions are:")
       (print-list vcs)
       (terpri) (terpri)
       (princ "Trying to prove verification conditions ...")
       (setq vcs1 (unproved-vcs (prove facts vcs)))
       (cond ((null vcs1)
                (princ " all proved."))
             (t (princ " can't prove:")
                (print-list vcs1)))
       (terpri) (terpri)
       (return (eq vcs1 nil))))
```

11.5   Examples using the verifier

Here are some examples showing the verifier in action. First, an example
where the verifier (correctly) fails:

```
-> (verify '(SPEC ((X = x) and (Y = y))
                  (SEQ (ASSIGN X Y) (ASSIGN Y X))
                  ((X = y) and (Y = x))))
```

```
Checking syntax of annotated program ... OK.
The verification conditions are:
```

```
(((X = x) and (Y = y)) implies ((Y = y) and (Y = x)))
```

```
Trying to prove verification conditions ... can't prove:
```

```
((X = x) implies ((Y = y) implies (y = x)))
```

```
nil
```

Here is the debugged program for swapping the values of two variables
(see page 47):

```
-> (verify '(SPEC
                 ((X = x) and (Y = y))
                 (SEQ (ASSIGN R X) (ASSIGN X Y) (ASSIGN Y R))
                 ((X = y) and (Y = x))))
```

Checking syntax of annotated program ... OK.
The verification conditions are:

```
(((X = x) and (Y = y)) implies ((Y = y) and (X = x)))
```

Trying to prove verification conditions ... all proved.

t

Here is the division program described on page 42:

```
-> (verify '(SPEC
                 T
                 (BLOCK
                   (ASSIGN R X)
                   (ASSIGN Q 0)
                   (ASSERT ((R = X) and (Q = 0)))
                   (WHILE (Y <= R)
                     (ASSERT (X = (R + (Y * Q))))
                     (BLOCK (ASSIGN R (R - Y))
                            (ASSIGN Q (Q + 1)))))
                 ((R < Y) and (X = (R + (Y * Q)))))))
```

Checking syntax of annotated program ... OK.
The verification conditions are:

```
(T implies ((X = X) and (0 = 0)))
```

```
(((R = X) and (Q = 0)) implies (X = (R + (Y * Q))))
```

```
(((X = (R + (Y * Q))) and (not (Y <= R)))
implies
((R < Y) and (X = (R + (Y * Q)))))
```

```
(((X = (R + (Y * Q))) and (Y <= R))
```

```
    implies
    (X = ((R - Y) + (Y * (Q + 1))))
```

Trying to prove verification conditions ... all proved.

t

The next example is from Exercise 15 on page 31:

```
-> (verify
    '(SPEC
      T
      (SEQ (ASSIGN X 0)
           (ASSERT (X = 0))
           (FOR N 1 M (ASSERT (X = (((N - 1) * N) DIV 2)))
                (ASSIGN X (X + N))))
      (X = ((M * (M + 1)) DIV 2))))
```

Checking syntax of annotated program ... OK.
The verification conditions are:

```
(T implies (0 = 0))

((X = 0) implies (X = (((1 - 1) * 1) DIV 2)))

((X = ((((M + 1) - 1) * (M + 1)) DIV 2))
 implies
 (X = ((M * (M + 1)) DIV 2)))

(((X = 0) and (M < 1)) implies (X = ((M * (M + 1)) DIV 2)))

(((X = (((N - 1) * N) DIV 2)) and ((1 <= N) and (N <= M)))
 implies
 ((X + N) = ((((N + 1) - 1) * (N + 1)) DIV 2)))
```

Trying to prove verification conditions ... can't prove:

```
((X = 0) implies ((M < 1) implies (0 = (((M * M) + M) DIV 2))))
```

nil

The unproved verification condition is not true unless M >= 1. This suggests changing the precondition from T to M >= 1:

```
-> (verify
   '(SPEC
     (M >= 1)
     (SEQ (ASSIGN X 0)
          (ASSERT (X = 0))
          (FOR N 1 M (ASSERT (X = (((N - 1) * N) DIV 2)))
          (ASSIGN X (X + N))))
     (X = ((M * (M + 1)) DIV 2))))
```

Checking syntax of annotated program ... OK.
The verification conditions are:

((M >= 1) implies (0 = 0))

((X = 0) implies (X = (((1 - 1) * 1) DIV 2)))

((X = ((((M + 1) - 1) * (M + 1)) DIV 2))
 implies
 (X = ((M * (M + 1)) DIV 2)))

(((X = 0) and (M < 1)) implies (X = ((M * (M + 1)) DIV 2)))

(((X = (((N - 1) * N) DIV 2)) and ((1 <= N) and (N <= M)))
implies
((X + N) = ((((N + 1) - 1) * (N + 1)) DIV 2)))

Trying to prove verification conditions ... can't prove:

((X = 0) implies ((M < 1) implies (0 = (((M * M) + M) DIV 2))))

nil

This did not quite work. It is necessary to add the annotation that M >= 1
just before the FOR-command. A smarter verifier could have done this
automatically by propagating annotations forwards if variables in them are
not assigned to.

Exercise 110
Implement an improved verification condition generator that will propagate
annotations in such a way that the example above is proved. □

The following program demonstrates that, with the extra annotation,
the example goes through:

```
-> (verify
   '(SPEC (M >= 1)
      (SEQ (ASSIGN X 0)
           (ASSERT ((X = 0) and (M >= 1)))
           (FOR N 1 M (ASSERT (X = (((N - 1) * N) DIV 2)))
           (ASSIGN X (X + N))))
      (X = ((M * (M + 1)) DIV 2))))
```

Checking syntax of annotated program ... OK.
The verification conditions are:

`((M >= 1) implies ((0 = 0) and (M >= 1)))`

`(((X = 0) and (M >= 1)) implies (X = (((1 - 1) * 1) DIV 2)))`

```
((X = (((((M + 1) - 1) * (M + 1)) DIV 2))
 implies
 (X = ((M * (M + 1)) DIV 2)))
```

```
((((X = 0) and (M >= 1)) and (M < 1))
 implies
 (X = ((M * (M + 1)) DIV 2)))
```

```
(((X = (((N - 1) * N) DIV 2)) and ((1 <= N) and (N <= M)))
 implies
 ((X + N) = ((((N + 1) - 1) * (N + 1)) DIV 2)))
```

Trying to prove verification conditions ... all proved.

t

Here is another example that fails:

```
-> (verify
   '(SPEC
     T
     (IF2 (X >= Y) (ASSIGN MAX X) (ASSIGN MAX Y))
     (MAX = (max X Y))))
```

Checking syntax of annotated program ... OK.
The verification conditions are:

`((T and (X >= Y)) implies (X = (max X Y)))`

```
((T and (not (X >= Y))) implies (Y = (max X Y)))
```

```
Trying to prove verification conditions ... can't prove:
```

```
((X >= Y) implies (X = (max X Y)))
```

```
((Y > X) implies (Y = (max X Y)))
```

```
nil
```

Some facts about `max` must be added to the knowledge base of the theorem prover:

```
-> (let ((facts (append
                   facts
                   '(((X >= Y) implies (X = (max X Y)))
                     ((Y > X) implies (Y = (max X Y)))))))
     (verify
      '(SPEC
        T
        (IF2 (X >= Y) (ASSIGN MAX X) (ASSIGN MAX Y))
        (MAX = (max X Y)))))
```

```
Checking syntax of annotated program ... OK.
The verification conditions are:
```

```
((T and (X >= Y)) implies (X = (max X Y)))
```

```
((T and (not (X >= Y))) implies (Y = (max X Y)))
```

```
Trying to prove verification conditions ... all proved.
```

```
t
```

A λ-calculus Toolkit

Programs for experimenting with the λ-calculus and combinators are described. These include a normal-order reduction engine, a program for compiling λ-expressions to combinators and a program for doing combinator reduction.

The programs described in this chapter provide tools, implemented in LISP, for:

(i) translating λ-expressions into and out of an internal representation, (Section 12.1);

(ii) reducing λ-expressions by β-conversion (Section 12.2);

(iii) translating λ-expressions to combinators (Section 12.3);

(iv) reducing combinatory expressions by combinator reduction (Section 12.4).

These tools provide a workbench for playing and experimenting with the theories described in Part II. In particular, they provide tools for exploring the inefficiencies of β-reduction and combinator reduction. Recent research has led to compiling techniques that yield implementations that are orders of magnitude faster than direct implementations of these reduction methods. These techniques are still very experimental; for an introduction to some of them see Peyton Jones's book [61].

12.1 Parsing and printing λ-expressions

To enable λ-expressions to be input and output in a readable form, a simple parser and pretty printer are provided for a 'user-friendly' external syntax. However, to make things simple this external syntax will still be LISP-like; it is designed to minimize brackets according to the conventions described in

217

Section 4.2. All the parser and printer really do is insert or remove brackets according to these conventions. The table below shows the external syntax and internal representation for λ-expressions. In this table, $\hat{E}$ denotes the internal representations of E.

λ-expression	External syntax	Internal representation
x	x	x
$\lambda x.\ E$	(L x E)	(L x $\hat{E}$)
$\lambda x_1\ x_2\ \ldots\ x_n.\ E$	(L x_1 x_2 $\ldots$ x_n E)	(L x_1 (L x_2 $\ldots$ (L x_n $\hat{E}$) $\ldots$))
$E_1\ E_2$	(E_1 E_2)	($\hat{E}_1$ $\hat{E}_2$)
$E_1\ E_2\ \ldots\ E_n$	(E_1 E_2 $\ldots$ E_n)	(($\ldots$ ($\hat{E}_1$ $\hat{E}_2$) $\ldots$) $\hat{E}_n$)

As in the previous two chapters, programs are presented in a sequence of boxes. To experiment with these, you should create a file called `lambda.l` containing the S-expressions in these boxes in the order in which they occur in this chapter. Since the programs for translating to combinators and reducing them will use the rewriting engine, the code for prover is included with the LISP function `include` (see page 175). The effect of this is as though the file `prover.l` was textually inserted at the beginning of the file `lambda.l`:

```
(include prover)
```

In the next section some macros are defined for constructing S-expressions that represent λ-expressions. These macros consist of selectors, constructors and tests, the general idea of which is described in Section 11.1.

12.1.1   Selectors, constructors and predicates

The following selector macros extract components of the representations of λ-expressions. The macros for names are redundant, but are defined for consistency and to make it easy to change representations later.

- **name** gets the name of a variable.

      (name 'x) = x

- **bv** and **body** get the bound variable and body of abstractions.

        (bv   '(L x E)) = x
        (body '(L x E)) = E

- **rator** and **rand** get the operator and operand of an application.

        (rator '(E_1 E_2)) = E_1
        (rand '(E_1 E_2)) = E_2

These macros are defined as follows:

```
(defmacro name (e) e)

(defmacro bv   (e) '(second ,e))
(defmacro body (e) '(third  ,e))

(defmacro rator (e) '(first ,e))
(defmacro rand  (e) '(second ,e))
```

The following constructor macros build internal representations of λ-expressions:

- **mk-var** builds the internal representation of a variable.

      (mk-var 'x) = x

- **mk-abs** builds the internal representation of a λ-abstraction.

      (mk-abs 'x 'E) = (L x E)

- **mk-comb** builds the internal representation of a combination.

      (mk-comb 'E_1 E_2) = (E_1 E_2)

Here are the definitions in LISP:

```
(defmacro mk-var  (x)    x)

(defmacro mk-abs  (x e)  '(list 'L ,x ,e))

(defmacro mk-comb (e1 e2) '(list ,e1 ,e2))
```

The macros defined below are predicates that test whether S-expressions represent variables, abstractions or combinations:

```
(defmacro is-var (e)
 '(and (symbolp ,e) (not (get ,e (quote DEFN)))))

(defmacro is-abs (e)
 '(and ,e (listp ,e) (eq (first ,e) 'L)))

(defmacro is-comb (e)
 '(and ,e (listp ,e) (not (eq (first ,e) 'L)) (rest ,e)))
```

12.1.2   Definitions

A λ-expression E can be given a name *name* by evaluating

   (LET *name* E)

The expression E is parsed (see Section 12.1.3) and then stored on the property list of *name* under the property DEFN. Names defined with LET can occur both in the external syntax and the internal representation of λ-expressions. The LISP definition of LET is given in Section 12.1.5.

The macro defn gets the expression associated with a name and the macro is-defn is a predicate that tests whether an atom is the name of an expression. When reading the definition of is-defn remember that any non-null S-expression counts as 'true' for and and that get returns nil if there is no appropriate property:

```
(defmacro defn (e) '(get ,e (quote DEFN)))

(defmacro is-defn (e)
 '(and (symbolp ,e) (get ,e (quote DEFN))))
```

To simplify the writing of functions that process expressions, we define selectors and tests that expand out names (if necessary). The names of these macros all end with *.

If the value of S is a name, then (defn* S) evaluates to the expression associated with the name; if S is not a name then (defn* S) evaluates to the value of S. It is possible that one name could be defined to be another, for example

```
(LET K (L x y x))

(LET TRUE K)
```

We want (defn* TRUE) to evaluate to (L x y x) and thus defn* may need
to be called recursively. This recursion is done by the auxiliary function
defn-fun below:

```
(defun defn-fun (e)
 (if (symbolp e) (defn-fun (defn e)) e))

(defmacro defn* (e)
 `(if (is-defn ,e) (defn-fun (defn ,e)) ,e))
```

The selectors and predicates defined below expand definitions using
defn*:

```
(defmacro name* (e) `(name (defn* ,e)))

(defmacro bv*    (e) `(bv    (defn* ,e)))
(defmacro body*  (e) `(body (defn* ,e)))

(defmacro rator* (e) `(rator (defn* ,e)))
(defmacro rand*  (e) `(rand  (defn* ,e)))

(defmacro is-var*  (e) `(is-var  (defn* ,e)))
(defmacro is-abs*  (e) `(is-abs  (defn* ,e)))
(defmacro is-comb* (e) `(is-comb (defn* ,e)))
```

12.1.3   A parser

The parser is now defined; this translates from external syntax to internal
representation. The function parse is a straightforward recursive function;
it calls an auxiliary function parse-seq to parse sequences:

$$(\text{parse-seq } E \ (E_1 \ E_2 \ \dots \ E_n)) \ = \ ((\ \dots \ ((E \ \hat{E}_1) \ \hat{E}_2) \ \dots \ ) \ \hat{E}_n)$$

where, as before, $\hat{E}_i$ is the result of parsing E_i.

```
(defun parse-seq (e l)
 (if (null l)
     e
     (parse-seq (mk-comb e (parse(first l)))
                (rest l))))
```

The main parsing function parse can then be defined by:

```
(defun parse (e)
 (cond ((atom e) (if (is-defn e) e (mk-var e)))
       ((eq (first e) 'L)
        (mk-abs
         (mk-var(second e))
         (if (null(cdddr e))
             (parse(third e))
             (parse (cons 'L (cddr e)))))))
       (t (parse-seq (parse(first e)) (rest e)))))
```

It is useful to define a macro parseq that is like parse, but quotes its argument:

```
(defmacro parseq (x) '(parse (quote ,x)))
```

Here is an example session with LISP illustrating the parser:

```
-> (parseq (L x y x))
(L x (L y x))
-> (parseq (L f ((L x (f x x))(L x (f x x)))))
(L f ((L x ((f x) x)) (L x ((f x) x))))
->
```

It is convenient to have an unparser to convert back to the external syntax.

12.1.4   An unparser

The function unparse converts the internal representation of a λ-expression to the external syntax. It is defined by mutual recursion with two other functions, unparse-abs and unparse-comb for unparsing abstractions and combinations. This sort of mutual recursion can be very convenient and illustrates one of the benefits of dynamic binding (see Section 9.7).

```
(unparse-abs '(L x₁ (L x₂ ... (L xₙ E) ... )))
  = (L x₁ x₂ ... xₙ E)
```

```
(unparse-comb '(( ... ((E E₁) E₂) ... ) Eₙ))
  = (E E₁ E₂ ... Eₙ)
```

```
(defun unparse (e)
 (cond ((is-var e)  (name e))
       ((is-abs e)  (unparse-abs e))
       ((is-comb e) (unparse-comb e))
       (t e)))
```

The definition of unparse-abs uses an auxiliary function strip-abs that
strips off the variables of an abstraction:

```
(strip-abs '(abs (var x₁) (abs (var x₂) ... (abs (var xₙ) E) ... )))
  = ((x₁ x₂ ... xₙ) . E)
```

```
(defun strip-abs (e)
 (let ((bv (name(bv e))) (body (body e)))
      (if (is-abs body)
          (let ((x (strip-abs body)))
               (let ((bvs (first x)) (body (rest x)))
                    (cons (cons bv bvs) body)))
          (cons (list bv) body))))

(defun unparse-abs (e)
 (let ((x (strip-abs e)))
      '(L ,@(first x) ,(unparse(rest x)))))
```

The definition of unparse-comb is just a simple recursion:

```
(defun unparse-comb (e)
 (if (is-comb (rator e))
     (append (unparse (rator e))
             (list (unparse (rand e))))
     (list (unparse (rator e)) (unparse (rand e)))))
```

The following session illustrates unparse:

```
-> (setq Y (parseq (L f ((L x (f x x))(L x (f x x)))))))
(L f ((L x ((f x) x)) (L x ((f x) x))))
-> (unparse Y)
(L f ((L x (f x x)) (L x (f x x))))
->
```

Exercise 111
Could the parser and unparser be implemented by rewriting? If so devise
a suitable set of equations. If not, why not? □

12.1.5   LET and LETREC

The following macro LET is used for making definitions. It first parses the
expression that is being given a name and then puts the result on the
property list of the name under the property DEFN. It also binds the name
to the expression using setq (this is just for the user's convenience).

```
(defmacro LET (x l)
  '(prog2 (putprop (quote ,x) (parseq ,l) (quote DEFN))
          (setq ,x (quote ,x))))
```

The table below shows how some of the definitions at the beginning of
Chapter 5 are represented using our S-expression syntax.

LET true $= \lambda x.\ \lambda y.\ x$	`(LET TRUE (L x y x))`
LET false $= \lambda x.\ \lambda y.\ y$	`(LET FALSE (L x y y))`
LET not $= \lambda t.\ t$ false true	`(LET NOT (L t (t FALSE TRUE)))`
LET $(E \rightarrow E_1 \mid E_2) = (E\ E_1\ E_2)$	`(LET IF (L t x y (t x y)))`
LET fst $= \lambda p.\ p$ true	`(LET FST (L p (p TRUE)))`
LET snd $= \lambda p.\ p$ false	`(LET SND (L p (p FALSE)))`
LET $(E_1, E_2) = \lambda f.\ f\ E_1\ E_2$	`(LET PAIR (L x y f (f x y)))`

The definition of the fixed-point operator Y is:

```
(LET Y (L f ((L x (f (x x))) (L x (f (x x)))))))
```

The macro LETREC provides a convenient way of defining functions recursively with Y. Evaluating

```
(LETREC f (x₁ ... xₙ) E)
```

is equivalent to

$$(\text{LET } f \ (Y \ (L \ f' \ x_1 \ \ldots \ x_n \ E[f'/f]))) $$

Note that this definition is not completely robust: it only works if f' does not occur in E. One could use f instead of f' since, logically, there should be no confusion between names of abbreviations and bound variables. Unfortunately such a confusion is possible with our simple implementation (see Exercise 112 below). To implement LETREC we need to define a macro that adds a prime to an atom:

```
(defmacro prime (x) '(concat ,x '|'|))
```

The macro prime is illustrated by:

```
-> (prime 'a)
|a'|
-> (prime (prime 'a))
|a''|
```

Here is the definition of LETREC:

```
(defmacro LETREC (name args body)
  (let ((g (prime name)))
    '(LET ,name (Y(L ,g ,@args ,(subst g name body))))))
```

Suppose ZERO, IS-ZERO, ADD and PRE have been defined (see page 232), then the multiplication function MULT can be defined by:

```
-> (LETREC MULT (m n)
            (IF (IS-ZERO m)
                ZERO
                (ADD n (MULT (PRE m) n))))
MULT
-> (unparse MULT)
MULT
-> (unparse (defn MULT))
(Y (L |MULT'| m n
    (IF (IS-ZERO m) ZERO (ADD n (|MULT'| (PRE m) n)))))
->
```

Exercise 112
Devise an example to show that the following definition of the macro LETREC
does not work.

```
(defmacro LETREC (name args body)
  '(LET ,name (Y(L ,name ,@args ,body))))
```

Modify the treatment of variables and/or definitions so that this will work.
□

12.2   A λ-calculus reducer

In this section some programs for doing normal order λ-reduction are described. The tricky part of this is making sure that the substitutions done
during β-reduction are valid. First a function frees is defined to compute the free variables in a λ-expression. This uses the function union for
computing the union of two lists; (union '(x_1 ... x_m) '(y_1 ... y_n)) evaluates to the result of adding to the front of (y_1 ... y_n) those members of
(x_1 ... x_m) that are not in it. For example:

$$(union \ '(1 \ 2 \ 3) \ '(2 \ 4 \ 6)) = (1 \ 3 \ 2 \ 4 \ 6)$$

```
(defun union (x y)
 (cond ((null x) y)
       ((member (first x) y) (union (rest x) y))
       (t (cons (first x) (union (rest x) y)))))
```

The definition of frees is now straightforward. First define an auxiliary
function frees-fun such that (frees-fun E $vars$) computes the free variables in E that are not in $vars$. The *-ed macros are used to ensure that
free variables in definitions are noticed.

```
(defun frees-fun (e vars)
 (cond ((and (symbolp e) (memq e vars))
        nil)
       ((is-var* e)
        (list (defn* e)))
       ((is-abs* e)
        (frees-fun (body* e) (cons (bv* e) vars)))
       ((is-comb* e)
        (union (frees-fun (rator* e) vars)
               (frees-fun (rand* e) vars)))))

(defun frees (e) (frees-fun e nil))
```

12.2.1   Substitution

The substitution algorithm of this section automatically renames variables
to avoid capture. To implement this a method of generating new names is
needed. Evaluating

$$(\text{variant } 'x \ '(x_1 \ \ldots \ x_n))$$

returns $x'^{\cdots'}$ which denotes x with sufficient primes added so that the resulting variable is different from x_i for $1 \leq i \leq n$.

```
(defun variant (v vlist)
 (cond ((and (not(member v vlist)) (not(is-defn v))) v)
       (t (let ((v1 (mk-var (prime (name* v)))))
            (variant v1 vlist)))))
```

This is illustrated by:

```
-> (variant 'a '(a |a'| |a''|))
|a'''|
->
```

The table below is based on the one on page 72, but with different
variable names and the rows reordered. With these changes it corresponds
to the definition of the function substitute below.

E	$E[E_1/x]$
x	E_1
y (where $x \neq y$)	y
$\lambda x.\ E_2$ (where $x = y$)	$\lambda x.\ E_2$
$\lambda y.\ E_2$ (where $x \neq y$ and y is not free in E_1)	$\lambda y.\ E_2[E_1/x]$
$\lambda y.\ E_2$ (where $x \neq y$ and y is free in E_1)	$\lambda y_1.\ E_2[y_1/y][E_1/x]$ where y_1 is a variable not free in E_1 or E_2
$E'\ E''$	$E'[E_1/x]\ E''[E_1/x]$

The LISP function substitute, defined below, implements this substitution algorithm. The idea is that:

$$(\text{substitute } E\ E_1\ x) = E[E_1/x]$$

Note that from the table it follows that:

(i) If x is not free in E then substitute just returns E.

(ii) If x is free in E, then substitute does a recursive descent through E according to the table above.

Although the definition of the LISP function substitute given below looks complicated, it is actually quite straightforward. The way to understand it is to compare it line by line with the table.

```
(defun substitute (e e1 x)
 (if (not (member x (frees e)))
     e
     (cond ((is-var* e)
            (if (eq (name* e) (name x)) e1 e))
           ((is-abs* e)
            (let ((y (bv* e))
                  (e2 (body* e)))
              (cond ((equal y x) e)
                    ((not(member y (frees e1)))
                     (mk-abs y (substitute e2 e1 x)))
                    (t
                     (let ((y1 (variant
                                    y
                                    (append
                                     (frees e1)
                                     (frees e2)))))
                       (mk-abs y1
                               (substitute
                                (substitute e2 y1 y)
                                e1
                                x)))))))
           ((is-comb* e)
            (mk-comb
             (substitute (rator* e) e1 x)
             (substitute (rand* e)  e1 x)))))))
```

The two sessions below illustrate substitute on examples (i) and (ii) in Exercise 50 on page 73:

```
-> (setq e (parseq (L y (x (L x x)))))
(L y (x (L x x)))
-> (setq e1 (parseq (L y (y x))))
(L y (y x))
-> (setq x (parseq x))
x
-> (setq e2 (substitute e e1 x))
(L y ((L y (y x)) (L x x)))
->

-> (setq e (parseq (y (L z (x z)))))
(y (L z (x z)))
```

```
-> (setq e1 (parseq (L y (z y))))
(L y (z y))
-> (substitute e e1 x)
(y (L |z'| ((L y (z y)) |z'|)))
->
```

12.2.2   β-reduction

The function **beta-conv**, defined below, reduces a β-redex; it returns **nil**
if applied to non-redexes. The global variable **beta-count** will be used to
hold a cumulative count of the number of β-reductions done. It is convenient to define a macro **inc** for incrementing variables: (**inc** x) expands to
(**setq** x (**add1** x)).

```
(setq beta-count 0)

(defmacro inc (x) '(setq ,x (add1 ,x)))

(defun beta-conv (e)
  (if (is-comb* e)
      (let ((e1 (rator* e)) (e2 (rand* e)))
        (cond ((is-abs* e1)
               (inc beta-count)
               (substitute (body* e1) e2 (bv* e1)))))))
```

The function **reduce1** finds the leftmost β-redex in an expression and
returns the expression that results when the redex is reduced; **beta-count** is
incremented. If the expression contains no β-redexes then **nil** is returned
(and **beta-count** is not incremented). The algorithm for finding the leftmost
redex in E is as follows:

1. If E is $\lambda x.\ E_1$ then **reduce1** is applied to E_1 to get E_{11}. If E_{11} in not
   nil (i.e. a redex was reduced) then $\lambda x.\ E_{11}$ is returned. If E_{11} is **nil**
   then there are no β-redexes in E and so **nil** is returned.

2. If E is $(E_1\ E_2)$ then if E is a β-redex it is reduced and the result
   returned, otherwise **reduce1** is applied to E_1 to get E_{11}. If this is not
   nil then $(E_{11}\ E_2)$ is returned. If E_{11} is **nil** then **reduce1** is applied
   to E_2 to get E_{22}. If this is not **nil** then $(E_1\ E_{22})$ is returned. If E_{22}
   is **nil** then there are no β-redexes in E and so **nil** is returned.

The definition of **reduce1** in LISP may be clearer than this explanation in
English:

```
(defun reduce1 (e)
 (cond ((is-abs* e)
        (let ((e1 (reduce1 (body* e))))
         (if e1 (mk-abs (bv* e) e1))))
       ((is-comb* e)
        (let ((e1 (beta-conv e)))
         (if e1
             e1
            (let ((e1 (rator* e)) (e2 (rand* e)))
             (let ((e11 (reduce1 e1)))
              (if e11
                  (mk-comb e11 e2)
                 (let ((e21 (reduce1 e2)))
                  (if e21 (mk-comb e1 e21) nil)))))))))))
```

The function reduce keeps reducing an expression until there is no more change. If the global flag reduce-flag is t then intermediate redexes are printed out:

```
(defun reduce (e)
 (let ((e1 (reduce1 e)))
  (if (and e1 reduce-flag)
      (progn (pp-form (unparse e1)) (terpri)))
  (if e1 (reduce e1) e)))
```

The macros trace-on and trace-off switch the printing of reductions on and off respectively:

```
(setq reduce-flag nil)

(defun trace-on  () (setq reduce-flag t))
(defun trace-off () (setq reduce-flag nil))
```

The macro REDUCE sets beta-count to 0 and then reduces the result of parsing its argument (which is not evaluated). It returns the unparse of the result of the reduction:

```
(defmacro REDUCE (e)
  '(prog2 (setq beta-count 0)
          (unparse (reduce (parseq ,e)))))
```

Here is an example illustrating the reducer:

```
-> (LET TRUE  (L x y x))
TRUE
-> (LET FALSE (L x y y))
FALSE
-> (LET IF (L t x y (t x y)))
IF
-> (REDUCE (IF TRUE E1 E2))
E1
-> (REDUCE (IF FALSE E1 E2))
E2
->
```

The reduction with tracing switched on is as follows:

```
-> (trace-on)
t
-> (REDUCE (IF TRUE E1 E2))

((L x y (TRUE x y)) E1 E2)

((L y (TRUE E1 y)) E2)

(TRUE E1 E2)

((L y E1) E2)

E1
E1
->
```

The reducer can be used to experiment with Church's representation of numbers. The definitions of ZERO, SUC and IS-ZERO are explained in Section 5.3.

```
-> (LET ZERO (L f x x))
ZERO
-> (LET SUC (L n f x (n f (f x))))
SUC
-> (LET IS-ZERO (L n (n (L x FALSE) TRUE)))
IS-ZERO
-> (trace-off)
```

```
nil
-> (REDUCE (IS-ZERO ZERO))
TRUE
-> (REDUCE (IS-ZERO (SUC ZERO)))
FALSE
-> (REDUCE (IS-ZERO (SUC X)))
(X (L x FALSE) FALSE)
```

Here is a session illustrating the addition function ADD:

```
-> (LET ADD (L m n f x (m f (n f x))))
ADD
-> (REDUCE (ADD (SUC ZERO) (SUC (SUC ZERO))))
(L f x (f (f (f x))))
```

The pairing functions FST, SND and PAIR are defined by:

```
-> (LET FST (L p (p TRUE)))
FST
-> (LET SND (L p (p FALSE)))
SND
-> (LET PAIR (L x y f (f x y)))
PAIR
-> (REDUCE (FST (PAIR E1 E2)))
E1
-> (REDUCE (SND (PAIR E1 E2)))
E2
->
```

The reducer can be used to check that the almost incomprehensible predecessor function described on page 84 works:

```
-> (LET
    PREFN
    (L f p (PAIR FALSE (IF (FST p) (SND p) (f (SND p))))))
PREFN
-> (LET PRE (L n f x (SND (n (PREFN f) (PAIR TRUE x)))))
PRE
-> (REDUCE (PRE (SUC (SUC ZERO))))
(L f x (f x))
-> beta-count
55
```

The multiplication function MULT was defined above to illustrate LETREC. Here is an example:

```
-> (LET Y (L f ((L x (f (x x))) (L x (f (x x)))))
Y
-> (LETREC MULT (m n)
     (IF (IS-ZERO m) ZERO (ADD n (MULT (PRE m) n))))
MULT
-> (REDUCE (MULT (SUC(SUC ZERO)) (SUC(SUC(SUC ZERO)))))
(L f x (f (f (f (f (f (f x)))))))
-> beta-count
213
```

The function `tricky` in Exercise 104 on page 163 is defined in the session below:

```
-> (defun tricky (x)
     (cond (y t)
           (x nil)
           (t ((lambda (y) (tricky y)) t))))
tricky
-> ((lambda (y) (tricky nil)) nil)
t
->
```

The corresponding definition in the λ-calculus is:

```
-> (LETREC TRICKY (x)
     (IF y TRUE (IF x FALSE ((L y (TRICKY y)) TRUE))))
TRICKY
-> (REDUCE ((L y (TRICKY FALSE)) FALSE))
FALSE
-> beta-count
29
```

Notice that the LISP `tricky` and the λ-calculus `TRICKY` give different results.

12.3   Translating to combinators

A modification of the rewriting engine of Chapter 10 can be used to translate λ-expressions to combinators. The idea (see page 131) is simply to rewrite using the equations

$$\lambda x.\, x \qquad = \mathbf{I}$$
$$\lambda x.\, y \qquad = \mathbf{K}\, y \quad (\text{if } x \neq y)$$
$$\lambda x.\, C \qquad = \mathbf{K}\, C \quad (\text{if } C \text{ is a combinator})$$
$$\lambda x.\, E_1\, E_2 \quad = \mathbf{S}\, (\lambda x.\, E_1)\, (\lambda x.\, E_2)$$

This suggests defining

```
(LET I (L x x))
(LET K (L x y x))
(LET S (L f g x ((f x) (g x))))
```

and then using the rewriter with the list of equations remove-lambdas defined below:

```
(setq
 remove-lambdas
 '(
   ((L v v) = I)
   ((L v v1) = (K v1))
   ((L v c) = (K c))
   ((L v (e1 e2)) = ((S (L v e1)) (L v e2)))
   ))
```

Unfortunately this won't work because, with the matcher defined in Chapter 10, there is no way of constraining v1 only to match variables and c only to match combinators. To enforce these necessary constraints the matcher must be modified. This is done by having it look at the property lists of variables occurring in patterns. If such a variable has a predicate P as its TYPE, then the variable will only match expressions E such that $(P\ E)$ evaluates to t. Here, for example, is a predicate is-combinator that only matches combinators:

```
(defun is-combinator (e) (null(frees(parse e))))
```

To declare that v, v1 and v2 only match variables and c, c1 and c2 only match combinators, the following function is used:

```
(defun map-putprop (list val prop)
  (mapcar (function (lambda (x) (putprop x val prop))) list))

(map-putprop '(v v1 v2) (function symbolp) 'TYPE)
(map-putprop '(c c1 c2) (function is-combinator) 'TYPE)
```

Here is the modified matcher; it should be compared with the one on page 183:

```
(defun matchfn (pat exp alist)
 (if (atom pat)
     (if (is-variable pat)
         (if (assoc pat alist)
             (if (equal (cdr(assoc pat alist)) exp)
                 alist
                 (throw 'fail))
             (if (get pat 'TYPE)
                 (if (funcall (get pat 'TYPE) exp)
                     (cons (cons pat exp) alist)
                     (throw 'fail))
                 (cons (cons pat exp) alist)))
         (if (eq pat exp) alist (throw 'fail)))
     (if (atom exp)
         (throw 'fail)
         (matchfn
          (rest pat)
          (rest exp)
          (matchfn (first pat) (first exp) alist)))))
```

Note that if this definition is loaded after the definition on page 183 then, by dynamic binding, it is the later definition that will be used. Thus, since the file prover.l has been included, the functions match, depth-conv etc. can be used and the new version of matchfn will be invoked by them.

It is necessary to make L into a constant for matching; later I, K, S, B, C, S1, B1 and C1 will also need to be constants.

```
(map-putprop '(L I K S B C S1 B1 C1) t 'constant)
```

To translate a λ-expression to a combinatory expression, the function re-depth-rewrite defined on page 189 can be used. A function trans is defined to take a list of equations and an expression and then to:

(i) parse the expression;

(ii) expand any names defined with LET to their definitions;

(iii) rewrite the result using re-depth-conv and the supplied list of equations; and

(iv) return the unparsed result of the rewriting.

For (ii) the function expand-defns is required that recursively goes through
an expression replacing names by their definitions:

```
(defun expand-defns (e)
 (cond ((is-var* e)
        (mk-var (name* e)))
       ((is-abs* e)
        (mk-abs (bv* e) (expand-defns (body* e))))
       ((is-comb* e)
        (mk-comb
         (expand-defns (rator* e))
         (expand-defns (rand* e))))
       (t (princ "Bad expression"))))
```

Here is an example illustrating expand-defns:

```
-> (expand-defns TRUE)
(L x (L y x))
-> (expand-defns IF)
(L t (L x (L y ((t x) y))))
-> (expand-defns (parseq (IF TRUE E1 E2)))
((((L t (L x (L y ((t x) y)))) (L x (L y x))) E1) E2)
```

The function trans is defined as follows:

```
(defun trans (eqns e)
 (unparse (re-depth-rewrite eqns (expand-defns (parse e)))))
```

Here are the translations of TRUE and FALSE using the equations in
remove-lambdas (we assume these have been defined using LET as above):

```
-> (trans remove-lambdas TRUE)
(S (K K) I)
-> (trans remove-lambdas FALSE)
(K I)
->
```

Here is the translation of Y (we assume it has been defined with LET as
above):

```
-> (trans remove-lambdas Y)
(S (S (S (K S) (S (K K) I)) (K (S I I)))
 (S (S (K S) (S (K K) I)) (K (S I I))))
```

To implement Curry's algorithm (Section 8.6) an appropriate set of equations called curry is defined:

```
(setq
 curry
 '(((L v v) = I)
   ((L v v1) = (K v1))
   ((L v c) = (K c))
   (((S (K e1)) (K e2)) = (K (e1 e2)))
   (((S (K e)) I) = e)
   (((S (K e1)) e2) = ((B e1) e2))
   (((S e1) (K e2)) = ((C e1) e2))
   ((L v (e1 e2)) = ((S (L v e1)) (L v e2)))
   ))
```

These equations can be used to give the translation of **Y** in Exercise 94 on page 140:

```
-> (trans curry Y)
(S (C B (S I I)) (C B (S I I)))
```

Exercise 113
Write a set of equations corresponding to Turner's algorithm (Section 8.7).
□

12.4   A combinator reducer

Combinators can be reduced using our rewriting engine. An appropriate list of equations for Curry's algorithm is:

```
(setq
 curry-reductions
 '(
   ((I x) = x)
   (((K x) y) = x)
   ((((S f) g) x) = ((f x) (g x)))
   ((((B x) y) z) = (x (y z)))
   (((((C x) y) z) = ((x z) y))
   ))
```

The function curry-reduce translates an expression to combinators and then reduces it:

```
(defun curry-reduce (e)
 (unparse
  (re-depth-rewrite
   curry-reductions
   (re-depth-rewrite curry (expand-defns(parse e))))))
```

This 'combinator machine' is incredibly slow, but you can use it for experiments. Here is an example:

```
-> (curry-reduce '(IF TRUE E1 E2))
E1
-> (curry-reduce '(IF FALSE E1 E2))
E2
-> (curry-reduce '(ADD (SUC ZERO) ZERO))
(S (B B (S (B B (K I)) I)) (K I))
-> (curry-reduce '(ADD (SUC ZERO) ZERO f x))
(f x)
-> (curry-reduce '(ADD (SUC ZERO) (SUC (SUC ZERO)) f x))
(f (f (f x)))
->
```

Exercise 114
Devise a set of equations corresponding to Turner's algorithm, as described by him in the quotation on page 143. □

Exercise 115
Implement as efficient a combinator reducer as you can. Compare its performance with the one described here. □

Bibliography

[1] Alagić, S. and Arbib, M.A., *The Design of Well-structured and Correct Programs*, Springer-Verlag, 1978.

[2] Augustsson, L., 'A compiler for lazy ML', in *Proceedings of the ACM Symposium on LISP and Functional Programming*, Austin, pp. 218-227, 1984.

[3] Backhouse, R.C., *Program Construction and Verification*, Prentice Hall, 1986.

[4] Barendregt, H.P., *The Lambda Calculus* (revised edition), Studies in Logic 103, North-Holland, Amsterdam, 1984.

[5] Barron, D.W. and Strachey, C. 'Programming', in Fox, L. (ed.), *Advances in Programming and Non-numerical Computation* (Chapter 3), Pergamon Press, 1966.

[6] Bird, R. and Wadler, P., *An Introduction to Functional Programming*, Prentice Hall, 1988.

[7] Boyer, R.S. and Moore, J S., *A Computational Logic*, Academic Press, 1979.

[8] De Bruijn, N.G., 'Lambda calculus notation with nameless dummies, a tool for automatic formula manipulation', *Indag. Math.*, **34**, pp. 381-392, 1972.

[9] Burge, W., *Recursive Programming Techniques*, Addison-Wesley, 1975.

[10] Chang, C. and Lee, R.C., *Symbolic Logic and Mechanical Theorem Proving*, Academic Press, 1973.

[11] Clarke, E.M. Jr., 'The characterization problem for Hoare logics', in Hoare, C.A.R. and Shepherdson, J.C. (eds), *Mathematical Logic and Programming Languages*, Prentice Hall, 1985.

[12] Clarke, T.J.W., et al., 'SKIM – the S, K, I Reduction Machine', in *Proceedings of the 1980 ACM LISP Conference*, pp. 128-135, 1980.

[13] Cohn, A.J., 'High level proof in LCF', in Joyner, W.H., Jr. (ed.), *Fourth Workshop on Automated Deduction*, pp. 73-80, 1979.

[14] Curry, H.B. and Feys, R., *Combinatory Logic, Vol. I*, North Holland, Amsterdam, 1958.

[15] Curry, H.B., Hindley, J.R. and Seldin, J.P. *Combinatory Logic, Vol. II*, Studies in Logic 65, North Holland, Amsterdam, 1972.

[16] Dijkstra, E.W., *A Discipline of Programming*, Prentice-Hall, 1976.

[17] Fairbairn, J. and Wray, S.C., 'Code generation techniques for functional languages', in *Proceedings of the 1986 ACM Conference on LISP and Functional Programming*, Cambridge, Mass., pp. 94-104, 1986.

[18] Floyd, R.W., 'Assigning meanings to programs', in Schwartz, J.T. (ed.), *Mathematical Aspects of Computer Science, Proceedings of Symposia in Applied Mathematics 19* (American Mathematical Society), Providence, pp. 19-32, 1967.

[19] Genesereth, M.R and Nilsson, N.J., *Logical Foundations of Artificial Intelligence*, Morgan Kaufman Publishers, Los Altos, 1987.

[20] Good, D.I., 'Mechanical proofs about computer programs', in Hoare, C.A.R. and Shepherdson, J.C. (eds), *Mathematical Logic and Programming Languages*, Prentice Hall, 1985.

[21] Gordon, M.J.C., 'On the power of list iteration', *The Computer Journal*, **22**, No. 4, 1979.

[22] Gordon, M.J.C., 'Operational reasoning and denotational semantics', in *Proceedings of the International Symposium on Proving and Improving Programs, Arc-et-Senans*, pp. 83-98, IRIA, Rocquencourt, France, 1975.

[23] Gordon, M.J.C.,*The Denotational Description of Programming Languages*, Springer-Verlag, 1979.

[24] Gordon, M.J.C., 'Representing a logic in the LCF metalanguage', in Néel, D. (ed.), *Tools and Notions for Program Construction*, Cambridge University Press, 1982.

[25] Gordon, M.J.C., Milner, A.J.R.G. and Wadsworth, C.P., *Edinburgh LCF: a mechanized logic of computation*, Springer Lecture Notes in Computer Science, Springer-Verlag, 1979.

[26] Gries, D., *The Science of Programming*, Springer-Verlag, 1981.

[27] Hehner, E.C.R., *The Logic of Programming*, Prentice Hall, 1984.

[28] Henderson, P., *Functional Programming, Application and Implementation*, Prentice Hall, 1980.

[29] Henderson, P. and Morris, J.M., 'A lazy evaluator', in *Proceedings of The Third Symposium on the Principles of Programming Languages, Atlanta, Georgia*, pp. 95-103, 1976.

[30] Hindley, J.R., 'Combinatory reductions and lambda-reductions compared', *Zeitschrift für Mathematische Logik und Grundlagen der Mathematik*, **23**, pp. 169-180, 1977.

[31] Hindley, J.R. and Seldin, J.P., *Introduction to Combinators and λ-Calculus*, London Mathematical Society Student Texts, 1, Cambridge University Press, 1986.

[32] Hoare, C.A.R., 'An axiomatic basis for computer programming', *Communications of the ACM*, **12**, pp. 576-583, October 1969.

[33] Hoare, C.A.R., 'A Note on the FOR Statement', BIT, **12**, pp. 334-341, 1972.

[34] Hoare, C.A.R., 'Programs are predicates', in Hoare, C.A.R. and Shepherdson, J.C. (eds), *Mathematical Logic and Programming Languages*, Prentice Hall, 1985.

[35] Hoare, C.A.R. and Shepherdson, J.C. (eds), *Mathematical Logic and Programming Languages*, Prentice Hall, 1985.

[36] Hughes, R.J.M., 'Super combinators: a new implementation method for applicative languages', in *Proceedings of the 1982 ACM Symposium on LISP and Functional Programming, Pittsburgh*, 1982.

[37] Jones, C.B., *Systematic Software Development Using VDM*, Prentice Hall, 1986.

[38] Joyce, E., 'Software bugs: a matter of life and liability', *Datamation*, **33**, No. 10, May 15, 1987.

[39] Kleene, S.C., 'λ-definability and recursiveness', *Duke Math. J.*, pp. 340-353, 1936.

[40] Krishnamurthy, E.V. and Vickers, B.P., 'Compact numeral representation with combinators', *The Journal of Symbolic Logic*, **52**, No. 2, pp. 519-525, June 1987.

[41] Lamport, L., LaTeX: *A Document Preparation System*, Addison-Wesley, 1986.

[42] Landin, P.J., 'The next 700 programming languages', *Comm. Assoc. Comput. Mach.*, **9**, pp. 157-164, 1966.

[43] Levy, J.-J., 'Optimal reductions in the lambda calculus', in Hindley, J.R. and Seldin, J.P. (eds), *To H.B. Curry: Essays on Combinatory Logic, Lambda-Calculus and Formalism*, Academic Press, New York and London, 1980.

[44] Ligler, G.T., 'A mathematical approach to language design', in *Proceedings of the Second ACM Symposium on Principles of Programming Languages*, pp. 41-53, 1985.

[45] Loeckx, J. and Sieber, K., *The Foundations of Program Verification*, John Wiley & Sons Ltd. and B.G. Teubner, Stuttgart, 1984.

[46] London, R.L., et al. 'Proof rules for the programming language Euclid', *Acta Informatica*, **10**, No. 1, 1978.

[47] Manna, Z., *Mathematical Theory of Computation*, McGraw-Hill, 1974.

[48] Manna, Z. and Waldinger, R., 'Problematic features of programming languages: a situational-logic approach', *Acta Informatica*, **16**, pp. 371-426, 1981.

[49] Manna, Z. and Waldinger, R., *The Logical Basis for Computer Programming*, Addison-Wesley, 1985.

[50] Mason, I.A., *The Semantics of Destructive LISP*, CSLI Lecture Notes 5, CSLI Publications, Ventura Hall, Stanford University, 1986.

[51] Mauny, M. and Suárez, A., 'Implementing functional languages in the categorical abstract machine', in *Proceedings of the 1986 ACM Conference on LISP and Functional Programming*, pp. 266-278, Cambridge, Mass., 1986.

[52] McCarthy, J., 'History of LISP', in *Proceedings of the ACM SIG-PLAN History of Programming Languages Conference*, published in *SIGPLAN Notices*, **13**, Number 8, August 1978.

[53] McCarthy, J. et al., *LISP 1.5 Manual*, The M.I.T. Press, 1965.

[54] Milne, R.E. and Strachey, C., *A Theory of Programming Language Semantics* (2 volumes; second one covers compiler correctness), Chapman and Hall, London (and Wiley, New York), 1975.

[55] Milner, A.J.R.G., 'A proposal for Standard ML', in *Proceedings of the ACM Symposium on LISP and Functional Programming, Austin*, 1984.

[56] Minsky, M., *Computation: Finite and Infinite Machines*, Prentice Hall, 1967.

[57] Morris, J.H., *Lambda Calculus Models of Programming Languages*, Ph.D. Dissertation, M.I.T., 1968.

[58] Nagel, E. and Newman, J.R., *Gödel's Proof*, Routledge & Kegan Paul, London, 1959.

[59] Paulson, L.C., 'A higher-order implementation of rewriting', *Science of Computer Programming*, **3**, pp 143-170, 1985.

[60] Paulson, L.C., *Logic and Computation: Interactive Proof with Cambridge LCF*, Cambridge University Press, 1987.

[61] Peyton Jones, S.L., *The Implementation of Functional Programming Languages*, Prentice Hall, 1987.

[62] Polak, W., *Compiler Specification and Verification*, Springer-Verlag Lecture Notes in Computer Science, No. 124, 1981.

[63] Reynolds, J.C., *The Craft of Programming*, Prentice Hall, London, 1981.

[64] Schoenfield, J.R., *Mathematical Logic*, Addison-Wesley, Reading, Mass., 1967.

[65] Schönfinkel, M., 'Über die Bausteine der mathematischen Logik', *Math. Annalen* **92**, pp. 305-316, 1924. Translation printed as 'On the building blocks of mathematical logic', in van Heijenoort, J. (ed.), *From Frege to Gödel*, Harvard University Press, 1967.

[66] Scott, D.S., 'Models for various type free calculi', in Suppes, P. et al. (eds), *Logic, Methodology and Philosophy of Science IV*, Studies in Logic 74, North-Holland, Amsterdam, 1973.

[67] Stoy, J.E., *Denotational Semantics: The Scott-Strachey Approach to Programming Language Theory*, M.I.T. Press, 1977.

[68] Turner, D.A., 'A new implementation technique for applicative languages', *Software Practice and Experience*, 9, pp. 31-49, 1979.

[69] Turner, D.A., 'Another algorithm for bracket abstraction', *The Journal of Symbolic Logic*, 44, No. 2, pp. 267-270, June 1979.

[70] Turner, D.A., 'Functional programs as executable specifications', in Hoare, C.A.R. and Shepherdson, J.C. (eds), *Mathematical Logic and Programming Languages*, Prentice Hall, 1985.

[71] Wadsworth, C.P., 'The relation between computational and denotational properties for Scott's D_∞-models of the lambda-calculus', *S.I.A.M. Journal of Computing*, 5, pp. 488-521, 1976.

[72] Wadsworth, C.P., 'Some unusual λ-calculus numeral systems', in Hindley, J.R. and Seldin, J.P. (eds), *To H.B. Curry: Essays on Combinatory Logic, Lambda-Calculus and Formalism*, Academic Press, New York and London, 1980.

[73] Wilensky, R., *LISPcraft*, W. W. Norton & Company, Inc., 1984.

[74] Wos, L. et al., *Automated Reasoning: Introduction and Applications*, Englewood Cliffs, NJ: Prentice Hall, 1984.

Index